Teachers and Philosophy

SUNY series, Horizons in the Philosophy of Education

David J. Blacker, editor

Teachers and Philosophy

Essays on the Contact Zone

Edited by

CARA E. FURMAN and
TOMAS DE REZENDE ROCHA

Published by State University of New York Press, Albany

© 2025 State University of New York

All rights reserved

No part of this book may be used or reproduced in any manner whatsoever without written permission. No part of this book may be stored in a retrieval system or transmitted in any form or by any means including electronic, electrostatic, magnetic tape, mechanical, photocopying, recording, or otherwise without the prior permission in writing of the publisher.

Links to third-party websites are provided as a convenience and for informational purposes only. They do not constitute an endorsement or an approval of any of the products, services, or opinions of the organization, companies, or individuals. SUNY Press bears no responsibility for the accuracy, legality, or content of a URL, the external website, or for that of subsequent websites.

For information, contact State University of New York Press, Albany, NY
www.sunypress.edu

Library of Congress Cataloging-in-Publication Data

Names: Furman, Cara E., editor. | Rocha, Tomas de Rezende, 1988– editor.
Title: Teachers and philosophy : essays on the contact zone / edited by
    Cara E. Furman and Tomas de Rezende Rocha.
Description: Albany : State University of New York Press, [2025] | Series:
    SUNY series, horizons in the philosophy of education | Includes
    bibliographical references.
Identifiers: LCCN 2024028656 | ISBN 9798855800982 (hardcover : alk. paper) |
    ISBN 9798855801002 (ebook)
Subjects: LCSH: Teaching—Philosophy. | Teaching—United States. | Democracy
    and education—United States.
Classification: LCC LB1025.3 .T3978 2025 | DDC 371.1020973—dc23/eng/20241105
LC record available at https://lccn.loc.gov/2024028656

Contents

Acknowledgments ix

Foreword xi
Mary Louise Pratt

Exactly What Is Needed: Editors' Introduction and
Chapter Descriptions 1
Cara E. Furman and Tomas de Rezende Rocha

Arts of the Contact Zone 19
Mary Louise Pratt

Chapter 1
Complicating Educators' Critical Consciousness:
Descriptive Inquiry as an Equitable Contact Zone 37
Rachel Seher and Alisa Algava

Chapter 2
Reimagining Contact as a Method: Portals and Portraits in
the Classroom 57
Vikramaditya (Vik) Joshi and Melissa Rosenthal

Chapter 3
Teaching Worms: Observation and Conversation 71
Cindy Ballenger

vi | Contents

Chapter 4
May We Be Angry? Teaching Responsively during Times of Crisis 85
   Stephanie A. Burdick-Shepherd and Michelle Johnson

Chapter 5
"No one wants to do that shit; no one wants to be in a
contact zone": On the Goals and Struggles of
"Contact Zone Pedagogy" 101
   Tomas de Rezende Rocha, Jamila H. Silver, and
   Emily S. L. Silver

Chapter 6
Learning Together to Stay with Trouble: Sustaining Educators
across Time and Space 119
   Cara E. Furman, Holly A. F. Lash, Hillary Post, and
   Lindsey Young

Chapter 7
Ignoring Difference: How an Antidivisive Concepts Law Changed
the Trajectory of an Antibias Curriculum Project 133
   Joy Dangora Erickson and Kyleigh P. Rousseau

Chapter 8
Finding a Place for Play in School: Risk, Ambiguity,
and Resistance 149
   Chris Moffett and Elisabeth Tam

Chapter 9
Katzi Txumu'n: Creating a Curriculum of Mesoamerican
Short Stories for Philosophical Conversations with Children
and Families 159
   Cristina Cammarano and Kimberly Arriaga-Gonzalez

Chapter 10
Taking Up Space or Opening It? Reconsidering Space in the
Social Foundations Course in Teacher Education 171
   Meghan A. Brindley

Contents | vii

Chapter 11
The Value of Therapized Education: Exploring the Story and
Theory of Reflexive Tension   183
  Steven Zhao and Jesse Haber

Chapter 12
Old Wisdom for Contemporary Problems: A Civic Republican
Approach to Dis/ability in Education   199
  Kevin Murray and Jessica D. Murray

Chapter 13
A Humanistic Baseline in the Rural School   215
  Sarah Freye and Dini Metro-Roland

Chapter 14
Alone in the Presence of Others: *Autos*, *Schole*, and the
Flourishing of Children in Nature-based Schools   225
  Glenn M. Hudak and William Fulbrecht

Chapter 15
Okinawa's Lesson for Peace and Democracy: Indigenous Values,
Political Tension, Military Contact Zones, and the International
Women's Club   239
  Kanako W. Ide

Coda
Creating an Equitable and Fruitful Contact Zone of
Philosophers and Teachers   253
  Cara E. Furman, Vikramaditya (Vik) Joshi, Meghan A. Brindley,
  Stephanie A. Burdick-Shepherd, Joy Dangora Erickson,
  Hillary Post, Michelle Johnson, Holly A. F. Lash,
  Kyleigh P. Rousseau, and Lindsey Young

Contributors   277

Index   283

Acknowledgments

First and foremost, we want to thank past president of the Philosophy of Education Society Ronald Glass who made space in the 2022 program for a preconference and then encouraged me (Cara) to run with the project. I so appreciated the guidance and space to explore. Additional thanks to then program chair Susan Verducci for supporting this project as it grew. Gratitude to a number of interlocutors who helped me think through what public philosophy broadly, and this project in particular, could be, including David Hansen, Jeff Frank, Chris Higgins, and Meira Levinson. Much gratitude to my co-editor, Tomas de Rezende Rocha, for his support, insights, camaraderie, and enthusiasm for this project from its very beginning. We are so grateful to all the authors who took a chance on this project and have given it so much care. You have shown the power of writing in and about various contact zones; working with you has been fun and meaningful. Thank you to Michael Gunzenhauser, Dini Metro-Roland, Ashley Taylor, Christina Lougee, and Hailey Hall, your work has been invaluable. Thank you to Mary Louise Pratt for her enthusiasm and endorsement of the project. We are grateful to the Modern Language Association for allowing us to reprint Pratt's 1991 essay, "Arts of the Contact Zone," first published in *Professions*. We have appreciated the encouragement and constructive reviews we have received from the editorial team at SUNY Press. Finally, gratitude to Ethan, Max, and Dan who support me in all possible ways. Tomas adds his thanks to Phil Bell and Carlos Martínez-Cano for commenting on early drafts, as well as his deep gratitude to Emily and Iris.

Foreword

MARY LOUISE PRATT

"Arts of the Contact Zone" was written at a critical moment of upheaval in American education, in the domains of both theory and practice. It was also inspired by that moment. In the 1970s and 1980s, school integration, affirmative action, and the democratization of higher education had transformed schools, colleges, and universities across the United States, making student bodies and teacher cohorts more heterogeneous and internally diverse than they had ever been. These developments put pressures of many kinds on conventional curricula, pedagogies, and educational philosophies. Most dramatically, perhaps, for many educators and educational thinkers, the challenge was no longer how to integrate a greater variety of students into established classrooms, curricula, institutions, and objectives, but how to transform all of those in light of the increased heterogeneity of the participants and the societal changes it reflected. More specifically: how could that dynamic diversification become a revolutionary educational asset, an opportunity to rethink what educational democracy was and could be? How could we develop the new forms of citizenship and belonging that those changes implied? "Multiculturalism" became the brand name of that project, a name that no longer conveys the excitement, boldness and emancipatory thought it generated at the time. The 1980s were also, of course, a time of right-wing retrenchment in the United States, as Reaganism took hold and neoliberal doctrines lay claim to the functions of the state. The retrenchment added urgency to the deepest questions of what society wanted its education systems to accomplish, what kind of citizens they were to produce. Reagan's celebrity secretary of Education, xii | Foreword

William Bennett, famously drove these questions to the forefront of public discussion, with explicit attacks on multiculturalism, and aggressive affirmation of "Western culture" as the only acceptable civilizational paradigm. The educational answer to heterogeneity was homogeneity. Bennett made Stanford University, the institution where I worked, a poster child for his critiques, and the struggle over multiculturalism and culture curriculum dominated our institutional lives there for several years.[1] But every scholar of my generation can recall how this battle, for it became one, played out in the institution where they worked.

"Arts of the Contact Zone" aimed to suggest the rich, fascinating possibilities the new heterogeneity offered for both teaching and scholarship. It originated as a keynote address for a conference whose design reflected the huge, democratizing shift that was taking place. It was a conference on literacy, cosponsored by the Modern Language Association, then the country's biggest scholarly organization, and the American Federation of Labor and Congress of Industrial Organizations (AFL-CIO), then its largest trade union—a collaboration that had never before taken place. Like this volume, the conference brought together scholars of literacy and letters with literacy practitioners who worked in elementary schools, high schools, trade unions, community literacy programs, and prisons. It was an unforgettable encounter. Writing the lecture was like nothing I had ever done before. What could a language-loving literary scholar contribute to this bold experiment, this unprecedented range of participants? I faced the challenge, I can see many years later, by writing simultaneously as a scholar, teacher, community member, citizen, and mother—a single bodied contact zone, as we all are. I finished pulling it together the night before, after the conference sessions gave me a sense of what was at stake. Delivering the lecture, I felt myself striving with mind, voice, and body, as I never had before, to connect with every person in the room. It was an unforgettable experience.

Teachers and Philosophy: Essays on the Contact Zone appears at another moment of critical upheaval in the US educational system. In some respects, alas, it is a reprise of the 1980s or perhaps a segue—a moment of even more extreme right-wing resurgence that includes aggressive legislative interventions to impose homogeneity and suppress heterogeneity in educational theory and practice. As in the 1980s and '90s, such interventions add urgency to the work of educational democracy, and also radicality and depth, because things once taken for granted—like the expertise and authority of teachers—no longer can be. The conversation

Foreword | xiii

has become foundational; futures are at stake. Many essays in the book refer to this moment. Like the Modern Language Association (MLA) AFL-CIO literacy conference, *Teachers and Philosophy* experiments with dialogic knowledge-making between thinkers who occupy different positions in the institutional landscape, and do different kinds of work. The conversations, notably between philosophers and practitioners, are held together by a shared commitment to education as a civic matter and an instrument of justice. Unexpectedly for many of us, these two fundamentals today need defending, as right-wing ideologies push to reframe education as a service accountable to families and religions rather than civil society, and as a tool of white supremacy and racial domination. In 1990 it was impossible to imagine that such proposals might be on the table in 2023.

As if this were not enough, the education system is emerging from the traumatic and unprecedented experience of the COVID pandemic, three years of radical disorientation, adaptation, experimentation, learning, and loss. We will spend the rest of our lives processing what took place over those three years and how it forever changed us. Some of the essays here do this work. And as if this were not enough, educators and students face a unique twenty-first-century predicament: the unfolding ecological catastrophe and the crisis of futurity it brings. To an unprecedented degree, the knowledge we have is no longer able to predict the future that lies before us, except to predict that it is unknowable and unpredictable. The lives of those who are now children, and the lives of their children, will be dramatically different, harsher, and harder than those of today's adults. And young people know this just as well or better than their elders. How can educators prepare people for futures unknown to all? What is the best way to know the unknowable—and more important, to live it? What will citizenship look like fifty or even thirty years from now? Can one imagine a greater challenge to educational thought and practice than this? We must approach it, I believe, as overwhelming and fascinating at the same time. Fear, horror, and grief must neither be suppressed nor allowed to displace joy, laughter, and a love of the world, for those, as Cree philosopher Tomson Highway reminds us, are what make life worth living.[2] The stakes in our work could not be higher.

"Concepts," says Australian philosopher Elizabeth Grosz (following Deleuze and Guattari) "are connected to problems, without which they would have no meaning."[3] Concepts "emerge, have value and function only through the impact of problems generated from outside." Concepts however, are not solutions to problems. Rather, they enable the search

xiv | Foreword

for solutions by opening up alternatives to the present, by enabling the imagining of possibilities. They do so by "transforming the givenness of chaos, the pressing problem, into various forms of order, into possibilities for being otherwise." We need concepts, Grosz says, to "think our way in a world of forces that we do not control," the more so because the solutions to our pressing problems inevitably lie "beyond the horizon of the given real."[4] At the same time, Grosz emphasizes, concepts are completely worldly. They are anchored in real events, experiences, and materialities; they generate agencies of all kinds—including the kinds of knowledge-making going on in this book. The changes they enable will also be real events, experience, and materialities. For Grosz, these worldly, problem-related, and future-generating dimensions of concepts make them indispensable to movements seeking radical change.[5] Contact zone is a concept in the way Grosz describes.[6] By shifting the point of view from the centeredness of homogeneity to the interactiveness and struggle of heterogeneity, it aimed to bring new futures into view, along with (and by means of) new ways of reading the past. This book proposes a kind of dialogic knowledge-making that explores possibilities for democratic citizenship and belonging in our unjust, disaggregated, divided, and media-manipulated society. I am pleased and honored that the idea of the contact zone has been of use to that work.

Notes

1. For an account, see Mary Louise Pratt, "Humanities for the Future: Reflections on the Stanford Western Culture Debate." *South Atlantic Quarterly* 89, no. 1 (1990): 7–25. Reprinted in Barbara Herrnstein Smith and Darryl Gless, eds., *The Politics of Liberal Education*, Durham, NC: Duke University Press; in Robert Atwan, ed., *Our Time: Readings from Recent Periodicals*, New York: St. Martin's Press, 1991; and in David H. Richter, ed., *Falling into Theory: Conflicting Views on Reading Literature*, Boston: St. Martin's Press, 1994.

2. Tomson Highway, *Dancing with the Trickster: On Sex, Death, and Accordions* (Toronto, ON: Anansi Press, 2022).

3. Elizabeth Grosz, *Becoming Undone: Darwinian Reflections on Life, Politics, and Art* (Durham, NC: Duke University Press, 2011), 78.

4. Grosz, *Becoming Undone*, 80.

5. Grosz, *Becoming Undone*, 82–84.

6. Mary Louise Pratt, "Mutations of the Contact Zone," in *Planetary Longings* (Durham, NC: Duke University Press, 2022).

Exactly What Is Needed

Editors' Introduction and Chapter Descriptions

CARA E. FURMAN AND TOMAS DE REZENDE ROCHA

> I came to theory because I was hurting—the pain within me was so intense that I could not go on living. I came to theory desperate, wanting to comprehend—to grasp what was happening around and within me. Most importantly, I wanted to make the hurt go away. I saw in theory then a location for healing.
>
> —bell hooks, *Teaching to Transgress*

"This was exactly what I needed." So said Hillary, a kindergarten teacher after engaging with a group of fellow teachers, philosophers of education, and other education practitioners to discuss philosophy and teaching at a preconference: *Writing within the Contact Zone: A Public Facing Philosophy PES Pre-Conference.*[1] Responding to Hillary's need and those of other educators, this book was founded in an urgent commitment to philosophy and education and based on the premise that such exchanges between philosophers and practitioners can be deeply beneficial for those who make their lives in schools (and beyond). In the epigraph, the American author, educator, and social critic, bell hooks, describes how she "came to theory" out of a powerful lived experience. In fact, for many, as exemplified by hooks and echoed by Hillary, "coming to theory" is life-saving and necessary for sustaining oneself and re-creating the world in more just ways.

This need for philosophical reflection on education is a common refrain among philosophers of education, who offer a diversity of views on what philosophy can and should do.[2] Despite this need, the cultural and material conditions for democratic, open-ended, and humanistic theorizing about education are at risk. A recent collection of essays edited by Andrew Colgan and Bruce Maxwell (2021), titled *The Importance of Philosophy in Teacher Education: Mapping the Decline and Its Consequences* explores this risk, beginning with an insightful social and historical overview of philosophy's "fall from grace" in colleges of education and teacher training programs.[3]

In diagnoses of this fall, Colgan, Maxwell, and others have identified various causes of philosophy's ailing health in institutions devoted to the education of teachers. These include (1) the marginalization of teaching and of a conception of teachers as autonomous professionals who exercise well-informed judgment, engage in ethical decision-making, and are afforded the time needed for reflection on practice;[4] (2) the expansion of policy directives related to punitive accountability, standardized assessment, and the curtailment of public education's critical democratic function;[5] (3) the rise of neoliberal corporatism, consumerism, and managerialism in university administration and a concomitant weakening of faculty's role in shared governance;[6] and (4) the erosion of the liberal arts and humanities in higher education more generally, as administrators promote subfields that help to bring in substantial research funding from private donors, further feeding the financial austerity discourse of modern public higher education.[7] For these and other related reasons, teacher education programs in our home country of the United States, as well as those in many other countries, have turned away from the study of educational philosophy as an integral part of teacher preparation.[8]

Despite the rather grim picture outlined above, we began the preconference (and this book project) by taking Colgan and Maxwell's optimistic and forward-looking guiding questions seriously: "How do philosophy of education and philosophical thinking feed into excellence in teaching today? How does a grounding in the philosophical and ethical dimensions of teaching, learning, and education systems contribute in meaningful ways to being a good teacher?"[9] We added a few more of our own: How does thinking philosophically help us to create better schools and classrooms? How does a training in philosophical analysis help teachers identify and navigate the prevailing complexities and heated public disputes surrounding matters of education? How is thinking philosophically a culturally sustaining, humanizing, life-giving practice for education practitioners? (Of note, although our focus is primarily on classroom teaching and teacher

Exactly What Is Needed | 3

education, the reader of this book will see that we regard "teaching" broadly in order to also consider the education that takes place in, for example, community organizing, women's clubs, and therapeutic relationships.)

We notice two things in bringing forth these guiding questions and concerns. First, we approach these questions from very particular orientations. Cara is a long-term early childhood teacher and teacher educator with a PhD in the philosophy of education. Her fundamental love is early childhood teaching and she believes that teaching well demands a commitment to ethics. Philosophical concepts, readings, and methodological approaches help her as a teacher to grapple with the daily conundrums of k–12 classrooms. For Cara, thinking dually through philosophy and education is important for ensuring that teachers do right by children and each other. Like Cara, Tomas's doctoral study also focused on the philosophy of education. Unlike Cara, his teaching experiences have taken place almost entirely in college and university classrooms and his students are usually neither current nor future teachers. Instead, his students often started as teachers but now intend to work in educational policy, programming, leadership, administration, or research. For Tomas, philosophy is a vital way to make meaning in and of the world; people grow and are enriched by its study, much like they are by art, music, literature, and other key cultural practices. Beyond this, though, he believes people working in education who are given the time and space to philosophize can more clearly understand and better overcome the problems they face. Simultaneously, academic philosophers benefit from being in close relationship with others working in education. Tomas sees how academics are grounded by these relationships as they are made aware of new social problems and supported in developing better accounts of them. For both of us, central to this project is a deep commitment to a more just world and the belief that we help advance justice when academic philosophers and practitioners are in genuine conversation and collaboration.

The second thing we notice when posing questions about philosophy and education is that there is something peculiar about the collective response to the "fall" of philosophy in light of Colgan and Maxwell's central claim (which we endorse) about the power of philosophy to positively influence teachers, teaching, and students. Namely, in our field, both the questions posed and the responses collected rarely come from *practitioners* and those who work most closely with them. Academic philosophers of education tend to maintain and dominate the platform for developing and sharing their answers to these questions. Further, while philosophers have certainly put effort into understanding what teachers gain from philosophy and what philosophers gain from working more closely with teachers, few scholars have asked teachers and practitioners (outside of the classroom) to engage in sustained philosophical inquiry *with them*, let alone to the point of coauthoring.[10] Anecdotally, at a recent philosophy of education conference, a panel on how to write *for* practitioners was standing room only. A year later, a panel on how to write *with* practitioners was sparsely attended. In her many years at various philosophy and education conferences, Cara has found similar patterns of attendance. These divisions can also affect the work and self-conception of the individual. For instance, those who both study philosophy and are grounded in teaching, like Cara and many of the authors in this book, tend to find that these areas of expertise are compartmentalized.[11] Scholars who inhabit both roles tend to be asked to assume one discourse over another and are rarely recognized fully as teacher-philosophers.

Why do these divisions persist? In our view, the tenor, language, structure, and purpose of many philosophy of education texts and classes are too often experienced by teachers as alienating and removed from their everyday professional experiences.[12] We do not know whether this is primarily a problem of instruction, of philosophy of education's "canon," or of students' expectations, preparation, or impatience, though anecdotally, we find many of these factors can be in play at once. What we can say more confidently is that, unfortunately, many students in our classes, and in many of our colleagues' classes, have previously experienced philosophy as an unfriendly space. They enter into the study of philosophy and do not see it as a space of open-ended inquiry, self-knowledge, solidarity, love of wisdom, or helpful problem-solving, but predominantly as a site of acute hierarchy between academic knowledge and practitioner knowledge. They do not anticipate practical guidance, insight, or a process of constructively questioning and unsettling their assumptions about the world. Instead, internalized feelings of inferiority and inadequacy are readily evoked. This is the impression of "Philosophy" with a capital *P* that our students often bring to the classroom, most frequently by those students who do not conform to the still widely prevalent cultural script of the white, male, heterosexual, cisgender, able-bodied, upper-class, Anglophone "Philosopher." Tomas recalls, for example, a recent conversation with a philosophically minded student who had dismissed the idea of working in the philosophy of education because "it's too white; that's why I'm not there." Likewise, Cara has had the experience with many scholarly minded female teachers and principals who described how academics, particularly academic philosophers, dismissed their ideas and treated them as foolish and ignorant.

Philosophical *practice*, on the other hand—by which we mean the bread and butter of philosophical reading, discussion, and writing—is almost always received as a beloved component of *any* preservice teacher's course of study. Likewise, philosophical reading and conversation are almost unanimously experienced as a deeply meaningful activity by all of the students with whom we have met, worked with, or learned about.[13] Anyone who has worked closely with teachers can tell you that education practitioners readily enter a philosophical headspace in the service of themselves, their students, and their profession.[14] To highlight just two examples, in recent volumes edited by Sonia Nieto, a regular refrain is that when teachers devote time to exploring their values and purpose, they are better able to navigate challenges and find meaning in their work.[15] In light of these realities, we worry that scholars miss far too many opportunities to substantively engage with practitioners on topics of shared philosophical interest. When practitioners see, hear, and read other professionals like themselves engaged in disciplined philosophical inquiry, the practice of philosophy appears immediately accessible. It is rendered into an everyday activity—one that can be practiced and informed by experts but is always open to anyone, at any level (as are drawing, music, sports, and so on).

Although we absolutely must solve the structural-material problems behind philosophy's decline in teacher training and in colleges of education, the additional observations we note above may suggest that the decline is not solely caused by neoliberal decay and the erosion of the institutional-systemic conditions needed to philosophize about education. It is also at least partially a symptom of how traditional approaches to philosophy can look and sound to teachers in an increasingly diverse and more inclusive country. In one of the rare articles to take this on directly, Nicholas Burbules and Kathleen Knight Abowitz have proposed reshaping the table around which teachers and philosophers gather to make it more inclusive of teachers.[16] We are obviously sympathetic, and in response to this call we offer in this volume a range of examples of substantive philosophical discussion, research, and writing done in partnership *with* practitioners, pursued both as an existential salve and as an avenue for *praxis*—that is, a vehicle for reflection and ameliorative action to solve the problems they face.[17]

Finally, before diving into our project, we briefly contextualize, pointing to similar attempts by colleagues in the field to give pride of place to the experiences of classroom teachers themselves, not merely as subjects but as authors of inquiry. Of particular influence, we note philosophers of education like David Hansen and Doris Santoro, who work closely with teachers to generate philosophical studies that blur the line between empirical and conceptual work.[18] In their studies, teachers are active participants in philosophical reading and discussion, which in turn shapes Hansen and Santoro's philosophical writing. (For our colleagues focused on empirical social science, this might be considered a blurred genre form of research-practice partnerships.) Their writing in these projects includes lengthy excerpts from extended interviews with teachers, further shaping the work. We note how, in these very same excerpts, teachers frequently express deep appreciation for this approach to educational philosophy.

That said, our project attempts to take one step in a different direction relative to what these thinkers have done. In this book, teachers and other education practitioners are not only brought to the table as philosophers in discussions and interviews but also welcomed as fellow philosophical writers. In the few chapters that do not feature such collaborations, we encouraged solo authors to bridge the internal divide between "teacher" and "philosopher" by giving themselves permission to speak from these dual roles equally.

How did we begin? In the fall of 2021, Cara issued a call for papers that required applicants to submit proposals as a *team* of philosophers and teachers. The call also borrowed from then society president Ronald Glass's upcoming Philosophy of Education Society (PES) conference theme, which asked aspiring participants to consider what it means to work within what the cultural theorist Mary Louise Pratt termed *contact zones*. In the original essay in which Pratt introduces the term, which we have reprinted in this book, contact zones are described as spaces in which "cultures meet, clash, and grapple with each other," often in the context of "highly asymmetrical relations of power."[19] One of our guiding assumptions was that the spaces where academics and practitioners collaborate can be experienced as contact zones.

In addition to bringing these groups together, a goal from the start was to use this space to write together. Traditional academic writing adheres to a code, at times almost like a recipe to follow. Writing from the contact zone does not come with such a formula, nor (arguably) should it. Writing collaboratively and speaking from a range of discourses is quite hard. It is also lonely. Knowing this, Cara wanted to create a space (the preconference) where a community interested in this work could come together, build bonds, and help one another. She also hoped that by developing and then sharing a range of ways to write from the middle, these authors would make tracks that others could follow.

Cara's call for papers elicited three responses: (1) Many academic philosophers of education applied to the project; they brought with them current colleagues, former students, or practitioners they had met and befriended when working in the field. (2) Some teams found that the lines between "philosopher" and "teacher" were blurry, whereas for others these distinct roles fit smoothly; where lines were blurred, teams tended to designate roles, arguing that for the purposes of this project, a given role fit one better than another. (3) Three applicants approached Cara without partners, with a request to participate solo; they felt that although the call for papers spoke to them deeply, they wanted to work through the division between philosopher and practitioner *internally*. In a spirit of inclusion and, being committed to multiple interpretations of the "contact zone," we welcomed a wide range of voices and entry points.

And so, six months later, in March of 2022, about thirty of us met in a hybrid setting, both on Zoom and in person at the PES conference in San Jose. Engaging mostly in mixed pairs or trios of philosophers and practitioners, we actively worked to reshape the table. As we introduced ourselves, almost everyone, including Hillary, quoted at the beginning of this introduction, shared stories of living and working in the "contact zone" between teaching and academic philosophy.

In supporting the resulting essays, we as editors have tried to capture some of the diversity of both the field of philosophy of education broadly and those working in this liminal teacher-philosopher space in particular. As such, you will see how the essays draw from a range of philosophical sources and traditions. In our commitment to welcoming a diversity of form as well as subject matter, we also welcomed variations in tone, organization, and style, with some authors leaning toward testimony and dialogue while others honed more traditional academic arguments. In reading this text, we hope that the diversity of styles and voices helps you to see multiple possible ways philosophers and practitioners might accompany one another. Where there is much to learn from the authors in terms of philosophies and practices, we see each chapter as contributing not so much an answer but rather an invitation to think about a topic. Activities and questions at the end of each chapter are intended to serve as provocations, encouraging further thinking. As you read you might find that, in some essays, the authors' navigation of the practitioner-philosopher contact zone was addressed explicitly and became a conceptual focus of the essay. Others, while still very much motivated by a desire to work in or across a contact zone, did not analyze or discuss Pratt's concept directly. As such, our final chapter is focused specifically on exploring what these

8 | Furman and Rocha

contact zone writing partnerships were like for our authors: we feature those who opted to reflect on their writing partnerships and offer advice for the success of future partnerships.

We would be remiss if we did not acknowledge that this book also first came together at the first gathering of PES after a period of absence due to the COVID-19 pandemic. For many, that gathering supplied a deep need for human contact that had been particularly unmet. At the time, aggrieved by failures of policy, leadership, and compassion around the world, many of us felt a renewed motivation to address structures and relationships that had too long been oppressive. The loss, pain, and revitalized joy and purpose of coming into contact in that moment, however cautiously, permeates our pages. (As we finish editing, now years later, we are struck by our authors' reflections from that time. They demonstrate a heightened need for community, safety, antiracist work, social freedom, and more, resonating now as much as then.)

One final note. A few months after the initial workshop, feeling inspired by the essays we received, Tomas reached out to Pratt, who welcomed our proposal to reprint her original 1991 essay. In that exchange, Pratt also pointed us to *Planetary Longings*, a recent book in which Latin American vernacular culture, literary fiction, and social movements are analyzed alongside critical discussion of modernity, neoliberalism, coloniality, and indigeneity.[20] In this new text, Pratt offers updated thinking on the contact zone and how the concept has changed for her over the past thirty years. A key to this revision, and exciting for us, is that Pratt now understands the contact zone as a space where humans and more-than-human life grapple with one another just as much as one where human cultures meet and clash. We encourage you to read her original essay on the contact zone and invite you to explore her exciting new work.

Chapter Descriptions

CHAPTER 1. COMPLICATING EDUCATORS' CRITICAL CONSCIOUSNESS: DESCRIPTIVE INQUIRY AS AN EQUITABLE CONTACT ZONE, BY RACHEL SEHER AND ALISA ALGAVA

What does it take to make a contact zone that is fruitful and equitable? This chapter explores how a process called Descriptive Inquiry can inform decision making about educational practice by bringing together faculty

Exactly What Is Needed | 9

from different ethnic backgrounds in an alternative urban public high school in meaningful conversation. The authors analyze the benefits and challenges of how the faculty use Descriptive Inquiry to develop culturally sustaining, antiracist pedagogy and curricula.

CHAPTER 2. REIMAGINING CONTACT AS A METHOD: PORTALS AND PORTRAITS IN THE CLASSROOM, BY VIKRAMADITYA (VIK) JOSHI AND MELISSA ROSENTHAL

A portal offers a way of seeing and sometimes a way through. Using portal as metaphor for a kind of witnessing, the authors of this chapter examine how educators can embrace the return of a classroom environment and social interactions with their students after the prolonged distancing of the COVID-19 pandemic. By sketching moments from a high school teacher's first year in this vocation and a philosopher of education's witnessing of this work, the authors spotlight the significance of curating a classroom environment and giving imaginative space for authentic student expression. In doing so, a portal is offered into the world of the teacher and student as artists.

CHAPTER 3. TEACHING WORMS: OBSERVATION AND CONVERSATION, BY CINDY BALLENGER

This chapter is a kind of meditation on interests—what they are and how they might work in relation to the learning of one particular student. It tells the story of a teacher who, faced with a puzzling child, set out to determine what she was interested in and, in doing so, found herself querying the philosophical nature of interests themselves.

CHAPTER 4. MAY WE BE ANGRY? TEACHING RESPONSIVELY DURING TIMES OF CRISIS, BY STEPHANIE A. BURDICK-SHEPHERD AND MICHELLE JOHNSON

What might rage offer in times of turmoil and how does it fit into hope? Two educators examine their feelings of rage during the height of the COVID-19 pandemic with their nation's approaches to teaching and learning in crisis. They articulate rage at schooling injustice and reflect on what it means to feel this emotion. They posit that pedagogies of play and dialogue can assist k–12 educators in negotiating the dynamics of rage while demanding widespread reform.

10 | Furman and Rocha

CHAPTER 5. "NO ONE WANTS TO DO THAT SHIT; NO ONE WANTS TO BE IN A CONTACT ZONE": ON THE GOALS AND STRUGGLES OF "CONTACT ZONE PEDAGOGY," BY TOMAS DE REZENDE ROCHA, JAMILA H. SILVER, AND EMILY S. L. SILVER

The authors seek to cultivate teaching and learning spaces that live out the liberatory potential of contact zones while recognizing the general absence and limits of such spaces. To do so, the authors explore the "contactless" zones of our classrooms (k–12 and higher ed) and workplaces. Themes of intellectual safety, courage, and curiosity are brought to the fore and examined in light of how racial capitalism creates contact zones but disincentivizes contact.

CHAPTER 6. LEARNING TOGETHER TO STAY WITH TROUBLE: SUSTAINING EDUCATORS ACROSS TIME AND SPACE, BY CARA E. FURMAN, HOLLY A. F. LASH, HILLARY POST, AND LINDSEY YOUNG

Donna Haraway uses the phrase "staying with the trouble" to describe how one takes on trouble by dwelling with it. The authors of this chapter describe "staying with the trouble" in three iterations. In telling their stories and how they rippled across with each other and Haraway, the authors highlight (1) the trouble that emerges for teachers trying to be responsive to their students; (2) the cascading effect and power of sharing a schema and stories of practice together; and (3) how sharing helped us stay with the trouble amid uncertainty, loss, and grief.

CHAPTER 7. IGNORING DIFFERENCE: HOW AN ANTIDIVISIVE CONCEPTS LAW CHANGED THE TRAJECTORY OF AN ANTIBIAS CURRICULUM PROJECT, BY JOY DANGORA ERICKSON AND KYLEIGH P. ROUSSEAU

Schools have a responsibility to support children's flourishing. They have an obligation to assist children in understanding and appreciating who they are that includes identifying other legitimate options for being that might complement their personalities. Assuming these to be worthy goals, it is important to think critically about limiting children's opportunities to explore their identities and the identities of others. In this chapter, the authors describe how they developed a series of antibias, antiracist, and civic early childhood curriculum maps that required changes when an antidivisive concepts law went into effect.

Exactly What Is Needed | 11

CHAPTER 8. FINDING A PLACE FOR PLAY IN SCHOOL:
RISK, AMBIGUITY, AND RESISTANCE, BY CHRIS MOFFETT
AND ELISABETH TAM

This chapter explores the ambiguity of the role of play in early childhood education. Given the general overt agreement on the value of play in principle, it is striking that it is often threatened from at least two related angles: it is either squeezed out to make room for other priorities, or colonized from within by gamifying curricular aims and content. We explore, from a teacher's perspective, the multiple contact zones that emerge around play across multiple school sites with diverse orientations—from standards-based international schools, to Reggio Emilia–informed schools, to forest and nature-based schools—with the aim of thinking not just about play as an object of study that needs situating, but also as a risky, ambiguous methodology of navigating and shifting contact zones themselves.

CHAPTER 9. *KATZI TXUMU'N*: CREATING A CURRICULUM
OF MESOAMERICAN SHORT STORIES FOR PHILOSOPHICAL
CONVERSATIONS WITH CHILDREN AND FAMILIES, BY
CRISTINA CAMMARANO AND KIMBERLY ARRIAGA-GONZALEZ

Curriculum is a live encounter of the new and the old, and this mixing can be emancipatory. Storytelling, story writing, and story discussing can offer an avenue for meaning making. This chapter presents a reflection on a creative project begun in a philosophy of education undergraduate course in which two students and an instructor created a curriculum of short stories for philosophical discussion with children, drawn from preconquest Mexican and Guatemalan traditions. The essay reflects on this experience in the specific local learning environment, and draws connections between storytelling as creative expression, learning, teaching, and curriculum creation as an emancipatory task.

CHAPTER 10. TAKING UP SPACE OR OPENING IT? RECONSIDERING
SPACE IN THE SOCIAL FOUNDATIONS COURSE IN TEACHER
EDUCATION, BY MEGHAN A. BRINDLEY

Due to increased accountability and accreditation requirements in teacher education, social foundations of education coursework is often viewed as taking up vital space in preservice teaching programs. The contact zone for the disciplines of teacher education and social foundations appears to be tied directly to the experiences of preservice teachers in required under-graduate foundations courses as opposed to an intentionally constructed overlap developed by faculty. As such where these courses still exist, a gulf tends to occur leading to a wide disconnect between foundations and methods. This chapter explores the contact zone between them and the missed opportunities for contact that arise between the two disciplines and their scholars.

CHAPTER 11. THE VALUE OF THERAPIZED EDUCATION:
EXPLORING THE STORY AND THEORY OF REFLEXIVE TENSION,
BY STEVEN ZHAO AND JESSE HABER

Education in recent years has seen the rise of a therapization of peda-gogy and student learning. Oftentimes, this can involve conceptualizing the process of learning as centered around experiences of psychological resilience/vulnerability. The pedagogical injection of therapeutic emphasis can spur both the support for its progressive educational potential and the resistance against its seeming erosion of intellectual seriousness in more "traditional" curriculum. The authors draw from teaching moments in a counseling class to approach therapization not as dichotomized from intellectual commitments but as constituting their very formation. By doing so, they reveal the ideal educative process as fundamentally defined by a reflexivity involving both therapeutic sensitivity and formative mastery.

CHAPTER 12. OLD WISDOM FOR CONTEMPORARY PROBLEMS:
A CIVIC REPUBLICAN APPROACH TO DIS/ABILITY IN EDUCATION,
BY KEVIN MURRAY AND JESSICA D. MURRAY

The civic republican tradition in political thought and practice advances a distinct conception of freedom—freedom as nondomination. In contrast with the liberal conception of freedom as noninterference, freedom as nondomination holds that freedom requires more than merely avoiding interference. The genuinely free person must be protected against the power of arbitrary interference—domination—even when it is not exercised. We draw on freedom as nondomination to develop a civic republican framework for animating and orienting educational thought and practice centered on dis/ability in schools.

Exactly What Is Needed | 13

CHAPTER 13. A HUMANISTIC BASELINE IN THE RURAL SCHOOL,
BY SARAH FREYE AND DINI METRO-ROLAND

Danielle Allen puts forth a humanistic baseline as a schema for developing just schools for a just society. A rural district could be the ideal setting for such a progressive, inclusive, and rigorous educational vision. Building on Allen, in this chapter the authors argue for and describe the potential of the rural school and showcase how efforts to conform to generalized educational practices interferes with the rural school's capacity to reach its potential.

CHAPTER 14. ALONE IN THE PRESENCE OF OTHERS:
AUTOS, SCHOLE, AND THE FLOURISHING OF CHILDREN IN
NATURE-BASED SCHOOLS, BY GLENN M. HUDAK AND
WILLIAM FULBRECHT

Autos, from the Classical Greek root for *autism,* is a mode of self-affirmation meaning being with oneself in the presence of others without defensiveness, such that one can relax in the world among friends. *Autos* is the ontological condition to coexisting in the same space while attending to one's own world. This chapter takes on concerns for children flourishing and a love of nature from the authors' two different perspectives: that of a longtime elementary educator and that of a father and philosopher of education. Together they ask, where and how does power manifest itself in the child's (and teacher's) engagement with nature? Can there be "contact" within nature without asymmetrical power dynamics? If so, does this relation of nonpower transform the contact zone into an autistic network characterized by "*autos*"?

CHAPTER 15. OKINAWA'S LESSON FOR PEACE AND DEMOCRACY:
INDIGENOUS VALUES, POLITICAL TENSION, MILITARY CONTACT
ZONES, AND THE INTERNATIONAL WOMEN'S CLUB,
BY KANAKO W. IDE

Yuimahru is an indigenous Okinawan idea of reciprocity, bound by friendship. This chapter discusses apolitical, feminine, and publicly open communities, nurtured by local and American military associates in Okinawa and operating in spite of political intensity regarding the existence

14 | Furman and Rocha

of American military in Okinawa. The chapter examines the educational meaning, paying specific attention to Yuimahru.

CODA. CREATING AN EQUITABLE AND FRUITFUL CONTACT ZONE OF PHILOSOPHERS AND TEACHERS, BY CARA E. FURMAN, VIKRAMADITYA (VIK) JOSHI, MEGHAN A. BRINDLEY, STEPHANIE A. BURDICK-SHEPHERD, JOY DANGORA ERICKSON, HILLARY POST, MICHELLE JOHNSON, HOLLY A. F. LASH, KYLEIGH P. ROUSSEAU, AND LINDSEY YOUNG

Authors draw on their experience of writing and partnering within the contact zone of philosophy and education. Where four of the authors center on partnerships with other people, one focuses on what it means to bring together into one voice the often antagonistic elements of herself (practitioner and philosopher). In pulling together themes from our experiences, we offer protocols and tips for facilitating partnerships in philosophy and education in a manner that addresses power differentials.

Notes

1. PES refers to the Philosophy of Education Society, the largest professional society for philosophy of education in the United States. We introduce "contact zones" toward the end of the chapter.

2. For just some of these accounts, see Maxine Greene, "Contexts, Connections, and Consequences: The Matter of Philosophical and Psychological Foundations," *Journal of Teacher Education* 32, no. 4 (1981): 31–37; Chris Higgins, "From Reflective Practice to Practical Wisdom: Three Models of Liberal Teacher Education," *Philosophy of Education* (2001): 92–99; Rene Arcilla, "Why Aren't Philosophers and Educators Speaking to Each Other?," *Educational Theory* 52, no. 1 (2005): 1–11; Nicholas C. Burbules and Kathleen K. Abowitz, "A Situated Philosophy of Education," *Philosophy of Education* (2008): 268–76; Harvey Siegel (ed.), *The Oxford Handbook of Philosophy of Education* (New York: Oxford University Press, 2009); Claudia Ruitenberg (ed.), *What Do Philosophers of Education Do? (And How Do They Do It?)* (West Sussex, UK: Wiley-Blackwell, 2010); John A. Clark, "The Place of Philosophy in the Training of Teachers: Peters Revisited," *Educational Philosophy and Theory* 45, no. 2 (2013): 128–41; Ruth Heilbronn and Lorraine Foreman-Peck (eds.), *Philosophical Perspectives on Teacher Education* (Malden, MA: Wiley-Blackwell, 2015); Nel Noddings, *Philosophy of Education*, 4th ed. (New York: Routledge, 2018); Paul Smeyers (ed.), *International Handbook of*

Philosophy of Education (Springer International Publishing, 2018); David T. Hansen, Megan J. Laverty, and Rory Varrato, "Reimagining Research and Practice at the Crossroads of Philosophy, Teaching, and Teacher Education," *Teachers College Record* 122, no. 4 (2020): 1–28; Liz Jackson, Kal Alston, Lauren Bialystock, et al., "Philosophy of Education in a New Key: Snapshot 2020 from the United States and Canada," *Educational Philosophy and Theory* 54, no. 8 (2022): 1130–46; Marek Tesar, Kathy Hytten, Te Kawehau Hoskins, et al., "Philosophy of Education in a New Key: Future of Philosophy of Education," *Educational Philosophy and Theory* 54, no. 8: 1234–55; Randall Curren (ed.), *Handbook of Philosophy of Education* (New York: Routledge, 2023).

3. Andrew Colgan and Bruce Maxwell, *The Importance of Philosophy in Teacher Education: Mapping the Decline and Its Consequences* (New York: Routledge, 2020), 1.

4. Chris Higgins, *The Good Life of Teaching an Ethics of Professional Practice* (Malden, MA: Wiley-Blackwell, 2011); Doris A. Santoro, *Demoralized: Why Teachers Leave the Profession They Love and How They Can Stay* (Cambridge, MA: Harvard Education Press, 2018).

5. Derek Gottlieb, *Democratic Theory of Educational Accountability: From Test-Based Assessment to Interpersonal. Responsibility* (New York: Routledge, 2021); Derek Gottlieb, *Education Reform and the Concept of Good Teaching* (New York: Routledge, 2016); Diane Ravitch, *The Death and Life of the Great American School System: How Testing and Choice Are Undermining Education*, rev. and expanded ed. (New York: Basic Books, 2016); Jack Schneider and Jennifer Berkshire, *A Wolf at the Schoolhouse Door: The Dismantling of Public Education and the Future of School* (New York: The New Press, 2023).

6. Wendy Brown, *Undoing the Demos: Neoliberalism's Stealth Revolution* (Brooklyn, NY: Zone Books and Princeton University Press, 2015); Gerardo del Cerro Santamaría, "A Critique of Neoliberalism in Higher Education," *Oxford Research Encyclopedia of Education* (September 30, 2019).

7. Martha C. Nussbaum, *Not For Profit: Why Democracy Needs the Humanities* (Princeton, NJ: Princeton University Press, 2016); Daniel Bessner, "The Dangerous Decline of the Historical Profession," the *New York Times* (January 14, 2023); Nathan Heller, "The End of the English Major," the *New Yorker* (February 27, 2023); Sarah Blackwood, "Letter from an English Department on the Brink," *New York Review of Books* (April 2, 2023).

8. Howard Robert Woodhouse, *Critical Reflections on Teacher Education: Why Future Teachers Need Educational Philosophy* (New York: Routledge, 2023).

9. Colgan and Maxwell, *The Importance of Philosophy in Teacher* Education, 7–8.

10. For a notable exception see Patricia F. Carini, *Starting Strong: A Different Look at Children, Schools, and Standards* (New York: Teachers College Press, 2001).

11. Furman, " 'Me and Socrates, We Are Tight Friends."

12. bell hooks, *Teaching to Transgress: Education as the Practice of Freedom* (New York: Routledge, 1994); Cara Furman, "'Me and Socrates, We Are Tight Friends': Co-Constructing a Polis of Teachers and Philosophers of Education," *ACCESS: Contemporary Issues in Education* 41, no. 1 (July 23, 2021): 36–51, https://doi.org/10.46786/ac21.8287.

13. Patricia F. Carini and Margaret Himley, *Jenny's Story: Taking the Long View of the Child: Prospect's Philosophy in Action* (New York: Teachers College Press, 2010); Cara E. Furman and Cecelia Traugh, *Descriptive Inquiry in Teacher Practice: Cultivating Practical Wisdom to Create Democratic Schools* (New York: Teachers College Press, 2021); David T. Hansen, *Reimagining the Call to Teach: A Witness to Teachers and Teaching* (New York: Teachers College Press, 2021); Meira Levinson and Jacob Fay, eds., *Dilemmas of Educational Ethics: Cases and Commentaries* (Cambridge, MA: Harvard Education Press, 2016); Meira Levinson and Jacob Fay, eds., *Democratic Discord in Schools: Cases and Commentaries in Educational Ethics* (Cambridge, MA: Harvard Education Press, 2019).

14. Cara Furman & Sharon Larsen, "Interruptions: Thinking-in-Action in Teacher Education," *Teachers College Record* 122, no. 4 (2020): 1–12; Mark Enfield and Bird Stasz, "Presence without Being Present: Reflection and Action in a Community of Practice," *Journal of the Scholarship of Teaching and Learning* 11, no. 1 (2011): 108–18; Pamela B. Joseph, "Ethical Reflections on Becoming Teachers," *Journal of Moral Education* 45, no. 1 (2016): 31–45; Doris A. Santoro, "'I Was Becoming Increasingly Uneasy about the Profession and What Was Being Asked of Me': Preserving Integrity in Teaching," *Curriculum Inquiry* 43, no. 5 (2013): 563–87; Mordechai Gordon, "Teachers as Philosophers: The Purpose of Foundation Courses in Education," in Joe L Kincheloe, Alberto Bursztyn, and& Shirley R. Steinberg (eds.), *Teaching Teachers: Building a Quality School of Urban Education* (New York: Peter Lang, 2004); David Hansen, "Among School Teachers: Bearing Witness as an Orientation in Educational Inquiry," *Educational Theory* 67, no. 1 (2017): 9–30.

15. Sonia Nieto (ed.), *Why We Teach* (New York: Teachers College Press, 2005); Sonia Nieto (ed.), *Why We Teach Now* (New York: Teachers College Press, 2015).

16. Burbules and Abowitz, "A Situated Philosophy of Education"; Two other recent efforts within our field to address this challenge include *Groundworks* and *Thinking in the Midst*. *Groundworks* is PES's new public-facing journal, of which Furman is the immediate past editor. *Thinking in the Midst* is PES's new podcast, cohosted by Cara, where philosophers of education talk about how their research can inform educational policy and teacher practice around current issues in the field.

17. For an example of the scholar/practitioner partnership in curriculum and instruction see Cochran-Smith, Marilyn, and Susan L. Lytle, eds. *Inside/Outside: Teacher Research and Knowledge* (New York: Teachers College Press, 1993) and Bentley, Dana Frantz, and Mariana Souto-Manning, *Pre-K Stories: Playing with*

Authorship and Integrating Curriculum in Early Childhood (New York: Teachers College Press, 2019). bell hooks, *Teaching to Transgress: Education as the Practice of Freedom* (New York: Routledge, 1994) offers a look into how these identities can live in one person, particularly in conversations the scholar, hooks, has with Gloria Watkins.

18. David Hansen, *The Call to Teach* (New York: Teachers College Press, 1995); Doris Santoro, *Demoralized: Why Teachers Leave the Profession They Love and How They Can Stay* (Cambridge, MA: Harvard Education Press, 2018).

19. Mary Louise Pratt, "Arts of the Contact Zone," *Profession* (1991): 33.

20. Mary Louise Pratt, *Planetary Longings* (Durham, NC: Duke University Press, 2022).

Arts of the Contact Zone

MARY LOUISE PRATT

Whenever the subject of literacy comes up, what often pops first into my mind is a conversation I overheard eight years ago between my son Sam and his best friend, Willie, aged six and seven, respectively: "Why don't you trade me Many Trails for Carl Yats . . . Yesits . . . Ya-strum-scrum." "That's not how you say it, dummy, it's Carl Yes . . . Yes . . . oh, I don't know." Sam and Willie had just discovered baseball cards. Many Trails was their decoding, with the help of first-grade English phonics, of the name Manny Trillo. The name they were quite rightly stumped on was Carl Yastremski. That was the first time I remembered seeing them put their incipient literacy to their own use, and I was of course thrilled.

Sam and Willie learned a lot about phonics that year by trying to decipher surnames on baseball cards, and a lot about cities, states, heights, weights, places of birth, stages of life. In the years that followed, I watched Sam apply his arithmetic skills to working out batting averages and subtracting retirement years from rookie years; I watched him develop senses of patterning and order by arranging and rearranging his cards for hours on end, and aesthetic judgment by comparing different photos, different series, layouts, and color schemes. American geography and history took shape in his mind through baseball cards. Much of his social life revolved around trading them, and he learned about exchange, fairness, trust, the importance of processes as opposed to results, what it means to get cheated, taken advantage of, even robbed. Baseball cards were the medium of his economic life too. Nowhere better to learn the power and arbitrariness of money, the absolute divorce between use value and exchange value, notions of long- and short-term investment, the possibility of personal values that are independent of market values.

Baseball cards meant baseball card shows, where there was much to be learned about adult worlds as well. And baseball cards opened the door to baseball books, shelves and shelves of encyclopedias, magazines, histories, biographies, novels, books of jokes, anecdotes, cartoons, even poems. Sam learned the history of American racism and the struggle against it through baseball; he saw the depression and two world wars from behind home plate. He learned the meaning of commodified labor, what it means for one's body and talents to be owned and dispensed by another. He knows something about Japan, Taiwan, Cuba, and Central America and how men and boys do things there. Through the history and experience of baseball stadiums he thought about architecture, light, wind, topography, meteorology, the dynamics of public space. He learned the meaning of expertise, of knowing about something well enough that you can start a conversation with a stranger and feel sure of holding your own. Even with an adult—especially with an adult. Throughout his preadolescent years, baseball history was Sam's luminous point of contact with grown-ups, his lifeline to caring. And, of course, all this time he was also playing baseball, struggling his way through the stages of the local Little League system, lucky enough to be a pretty good player, loving the game and coming to know deeply his strengths and weaknesses.

Literacy began for Sam with the newly pronounceable names on the picture cards and brought him what has been easily the broadest, most varied, most enduring, and most integrated experience of his thirteen-year life. Like many parents, I was delighted to see schooling give Sam the tools with which to find and open all these doors. At the same time I found it unforgivable that schooling itself gave him nothing remotely as meaningful to do, let alone anything that would actually take him beyond the referential, masculinist ethos of baseball and its lore.

However, I was not invited here to speak as a parent, nor as an expert on literacy. I was asked to speak as an MLA member working in the elite academy. In that capacity my contribution is undoubtedly supposed to be abstract, irrelevant, and anchored outside the real world. I wouldn't dream of disappointing anyone. I propose immediately to head back several centuries to a text that has a few points in common with baseball cards and raises thoughts about what Tony Sarmiento, in his comments to the conference, called new visions of literacy. In 1908 a Peruvianist named Richard Pietschmann was exploring in the Danish Royal Archive in Copenhagen and came across a manuscript. It was dated in the city

Arts of the Contact Zone | 21

of Cuzco in Peru, in the year 1613, some forty years after the final fall of the Inca empire to the Spanish and signed with an unmistakably Andean indigenous name: Felipe Guaman Poma de Ayala. Written in a mixture of Quechua and ungrammatical, expressive Spanish, the manuscript was a letter addressed by an unknown but apparently literate Andean to King Philip III of Spain. What stunned Pietschmann was that the letter was twelve hundred pages long. There were almost eight hundred pages of written text and four hundred of captioned line drawings. It was titled *The First New Chronicle and Good Government.* No one knew (or knows) how the manuscript got to the library in Copenhagen or how long it had been there. No one, it appeared, had ever bothered to read it or figured out how. Quechua was not thought of as a written language in 1908, nor Andean culture as a literate culture.

Pietschmann prepared a paper on his find, which he presented in London in 1912, a year after the rediscovery of Machu Picchu by Hiram Bingham. Reception, by an international congress of Americanists, was apparently confused. It took twenty-five years for a facsimile edition of the work to appear, in Paris. It was not till the late 1970s, as positivist reading habits gave way to interpretive studies and colonial elitisms to postcolonial pluralisms, that Western scholars found ways of reading Guaman Poma's *New Chronicle and Good Government* as the extraordinary intercultural tour de force that it was. The letter got there, only 350 years too late, a miracle and a terrible tragedy.

I propose to say a few more words about this erstwhile unreadable text, in order to lay out some thoughts about writing and literacy in what I like to call the *contact zones.* I use this term to refer to social spaces where cultures meet, clash, and grapple with each other, often in contexts of highly asymmetrical relations of power, such as colonialism, slavery, or their aftermaths as they are lived out in many parts of the world today. Eventually I will use the term to reconsider the models of community that many of us rely on in teaching and theorizing and that are under challenge today. But first a little more about Guaman Poma's giant letter to Philip III.

Insofar as anything is known about him at all, Guaman Poma exemplified the sociocultural complexities produced by conquest and empire. He was an indigenous Andean who claimed noble Inca descent and who had adopted (at least in some sense) Christianity. He may have worked in the Spanish colonial administration as an interpreter, scribe, or assistant to a Spanish tax collector—as a mediator, in short. He says he learned to write from his half brother, a mestizo whose Spanish father had given him access to religious education.

Guaman Poma's letter to the king is written in two languages (Spanish and Quechua) and two parts. The first is called the *Nueva corónica* 'New Chronicle.' The title is important. The chronicle of course was the main writing apparatus through which the Spanish represented their American conquests to themselves. It constituted one of the main official discourses. In writing a "new chronicle," Guaman Poma took over the official Spanish genre for his own ends. Those ends were, roughly, to construct a new picture of the world, a picture of a Christian world with Andean rather than European peoples at the center of it—Cuzco, not Jerusalem. In the *New Chronicle* Guaman Poma begins by rewriting the Christian history of the world from Adam and Eve (fig. 1), incorporating the Amerindians into it as offspring of one of the sons of Noah. He identifies five ages of

Figure 1. Adam and Eve. *Source*: Public domain.

Christian history that he links in parallel with the five ages of canonical Andean history—separate but equal trajectories that diverge with Noah and reintersect not with Columbus but with Saint Bartholomew, claimed to have preceded Columbus in the Americas. In a couple of hundred pages, Guaman Poma constructs a veritable encyclopedia of Inca and pre-Inca history, customs, laws, social forms, public offices, and dynastic leaders. The depictions resemble European manners and customs description, but also reproduce the meticulous detail with which knowledge in Inca society was stored on *quipus* and in the oral memories of elders.

Guaman Poma's *New Chronicle* is an instance of what I have proposed to call an *autoethnographic* text, by which I mean a text in which people undertake to describe themselves in ways that engage with representations others have made of them. Thus if ethnographic texts are those in which European metropolitan subjects represent to themselves their others (usually their conquered others), autoethnographic texts are representations that the so-defined others construct *in response to* or in dialogue with those texts. Autoethnographic texts are not, then, what are usually thought of as autochthonous forms of expression or self-representation (as the Andean *quipus* were). Rather they involve a selective collaboration with and appropriation of idioms of the metropolis or the conqueror. These are merged or infiltrated to varying degrees with indigenous idioms to create self-representations intended to intervene in metropolitan modes of understanding. Autoethnographic works are often addressed to both metropolitan audiences and the speaker's own community. Their reception is thus highly indeterminate. Such texts often constitute a marginalized group's point of entry into the dominant circuits of print culture. It is interesting to think, for example, of American slave autobiography in its autoethnographic dimensions, which in some respects distinguish it from Euramerican autobiographical tradition. The concept might help explain why some of the earliest published writing by Chicanas took the form of folkloric manners and customs sketches written in English and published in English-language newspapers or folklore magazines (see Treviño). Autoethnographic representation often involves concrete collaborations between people, as between literate ex-slaves and abolitionist intellectuals, or between Guaman Poma and the Inca elders who were his informants. Often, as in Guaman Poma, it involves more than one language. In recent decades autoethnography, critique, and resistance have reconnected with writing in a contemporary creation of the contact zone, the *testimonio*.

Guaman Poma's *New Chronicle* ends with a revisionist account of the Spanish conquest, which, he argues, should have been a peaceful encounter of equals with the potential for benefiting both, but for the mindless greed of the Spanish. He parodies Spanish history. Following contact with the Incas, he writes, "In all Castille, there was a great commotion. All day and at night in their dreams the Spaniards were saying 'Yndias, yndias, oro, plata, oro, plata del Piru'" ("Indies, Indies, gold, silver, gold, silver from Peru") (fig. 2). The Spanish, he writes, brought nothing of value to share with the Andeans, nothing "but armor and guns con la codicia de oro, plata, oro y plata, yndias, a las Yndias, Piru" ("with the lust for gold, silver, gold and silver, Indies, the Indies, Peru") (372). I quote these words as an example of a conquered subject using the conqueror's language to construct a parodic, oppositional representation of the conqueror's own speech. Guaman Poma mirrors back to the Spanish (in their language,

Figure 2. *Conquista*. Meeting of Spaniard and Inca. The Inca says in Quechua, "You eat gold?" The Spaniard replies in Spanish, "We eat this gold." *Source*: Public domain.

Arts of the Contact Zone | 25

which is alien to him) an image of themselves that they often suppress and will therefore surely recognize. Such are the dynamics of language, writing, and representation in contact zones.

The second half of the epistle continues the critique. It is titled *Buen gobierno y justicia* 'Good Government and Justice' and combines a description of colonial society in the Andean region with a passionate denunciation of Spanish exploitation and abuse. (These, at the time he was writing, were decimating the population of the Andes at a genocidal rate. In fact, the potential loss of the labor force became a main cause for reform of the system.) Guaman Poma's most implacable hostility is invoked by the clergy, followed by the dreaded *corregidores*, or colonial overseers (fig. 3). He also praises good works, Christian habits, and just

Figure 3. *Corregidor de minas*. Catalog of Spanish abuses of indigenous labor force. *Source*: Public domain.

men where he finds them, and offers at length his views as to what constitutes "good government and justice." The Indies, he argues, should be administered through a collaboration of Inca and Spanish elites. The epistle ends with an imaginary question-and-answer session in which, in a reversal of hierarchy, the king is depicted asking Guaman Poma questions about how to reform the empire—a dialogue imagined across the many lines that divide the Andean scribe from the imperial monarch, and in which the subordinated subject single-handedly gives himself authority in the colonizer's language and verbal repertoire. In a way, it worked—this extraordinary text did get written—but in a way it did not, for the letter never reached its addressee.

To grasp the import of Guaman Poma's project, one needs to keep in mind that the Incas had no system of writing. Their huge empire is said to be the only known instance of a full-blown bureaucratic state society built and administered without writing. Guaman Poma constructs his text by appropriating and adapting pieces of the representational repertoire of the invaders. He does not simply imitate or reproduce it; he selects and adapts it along Andean lines to express (bilingually, mind you) Andean interests and aspirations. Ethnographers have used the term *transcultura-tion* to describe processes whereby members of subordinated or marginal groups select and invent from materials transmitted by a dominant or metropolitan culture. The term, originally coined by Cuban sociologist Fernando Ortiz in the 1940s, aimed to replace overly reductive concepts of acculturation and assimilation used to characterize culture under conquest. While subordinate peoples do not usually control what emanates from the dominant culture, they do determine to varying extents what gets absorbed into their own and what it gets used for. Transculturation, like autoethnography, is a phenomenon of the contact zone.

As scholars have realized only relatively recently, the transcultural character of Guaman Poma's text is intricately apparent in its visual as well as its written component. The genre of the four hundred line drawings is European—there seems to have been no tradition of representational drawing among the Incas—but in their execution they deploy specifically Andean systems of spatial symbolism that express Andean values and aspirations.[1]

In figure 1, for instance, Adam is depicted on the left-hand side, below the sun, while Eve is on the right-hand side, below the moon, and slightly lower than Adam. The two are divided by the diagonal of Adam's digging stick. In Andean spatial symbolism, the diagonal descending from the sun marks the basic line of power and authority dividing upper from lower, male from female, dominant from subordinate. In figure 2, the Inca appears in the same position as Adam, with the Spaniard opposite, and the two at the same height. In figure 3, depicting Spanish abuses of power, the symbolic pattern is reversed. The Spaniard is in a high position, indicating dominance, put on the "wrong" (right-hand) side. The diagonals of his lance and that of the servant doing the flogging mark out a line of illegitimate, though real, power. The Andean figures continue to occupy the left-hand side of the picture, but clearly as victims. Guaman Poma wrote that the Spanish conquest had produced "un mundo al reves," "a world in reverse."

In sum, Guaman Poma's text is truly a product of the contact zone. If one thinks of cultures, or literatures, as discrete, coherently structured, monolingual edifices, Guaman Poma's text, and indeed any autoethnographic work, appears anomalous or chaotic—as it apparently did to the European scholars Pietschmann spoke to in 1912. If one does not think of cultures this way, then Guaman Poma's text is simply heterogeneous, as the Andean region was itself and remains today. Such a text is heterogeneous on the reception end as well as the production end: it will read very differently to people in different positions in the contact zone. Because it deploys European and Andean systems of meaning making, the letter necessarily means differently to bilingual Spanish-Quechua speakers and to monolingual speakers in either language; the drawings mean differently to monocultural readers, Spanish or Andean, and to bicultural readers responding to the Andean symbolic structures embodied in European genres.

In the Andes in the early 1600s, there existed a literate public with considerable intercultural competence and degrees of bilingualism. Unfortunately, such a community did not exist in the Spanish court with which Guaman Poma was trying to make contact. It is interesting to note that in the same year Guaman Poma sent off his letter, a text by another Peruvian was adopted in official circles in Spain as the canonical Christian mediation between the Spanish conquest and Inca history. It was another huge encyclopedic work, titled the *Royal Commentaries of the Incas*, written, tellingly, by a mestizo, Inca Garcilaso de la Vega. Like the mestizo half brother who taught Guaman Poma to read and write, Inca Garcilaso was the son of an Inca princess and a Spanish official, and had lived in Spain since he was seventeen. Though he too spoke

Quechua, his book is written in eloquent, standard Spanish, without illustrations. While Guaman Poma's life's work sat somewhere unread, the *Royal Commentaries* was edited and reedited in Spain and the New World, a mediation that coded the Andean past and present in ways thought unthreatening to colonial hierarchy.[2] The textual hierarchy persists: the *Royal Commentaries* today remains a staple item on PhD reading lists in Spanish, while the *New Chronicle and Good Government*, despite the ready availability of several fine editions, is not. However, though Guaman Poma's text did not reach its destination, the transcultural currents of expression it exemplifies continued to evolve in the Andes, as they still do, less in writing than in storytelling, ritual, song, dance-drama, painting and sculpture, dress, textile art, forms of governance, religious belief, and many other vernacular art forms. All express the effects of long-term contact and intractable, unequal conflict.

Autoethnography, transculturation, critique, collaboration, bilingualism, mediation, parody, denunciation, imaginary dialogue, vernacular expression—these are some of the literate arts of the contact zone. Miscomprehension, incomprehension, dead letters, unread masterpieces, absolute heterogeneity of meaning—these are some of the perils of writing in the contact zone. They all live among us today in the transnationalized metropolis of the United States and are becoming more widely visible, more pressing, and, like Guaman Poma's text, more decipherable to those who once would have ignored them in defense of a stable, centered sense of knowledge and reality.

Contact and Community

The idea of the contact zone is intended in part to contrast with ideas of community that underlie much of the thinking about language, communication, and culture that gets done in the academy. A couple of years ago, thinking about the linguistic theories I knew, I tried to make sense of a utopian quality that often seemed to characterize social analyses of language by the academy. Languages were seen as living in "speech communities," and these tended to be theorized as discrete, self-defined, coherent entities, held together by a homogeneous competence or grammar shared identically and equally among all the members. This abstract idea of the speech community seemed to reflect, among other things, the utopian way modern nations conceive of themselves as what Benedict Anderson calls "imagined communities."[3] In a book of that title, Anderson observes that with the possible exception of what he calls "primordial villages," human communities exist as *imagined* entities in which people "will never know most of their fellow-members, meet them or even hear of them, yet in the minds of each lives the image of their communion." "Communities are distinguished," he goes on to say, "not by their falsity/genuineness, but by *the style in which they are imagined*" (15; emphasis mine). Anderson proposes three features that characterize the style in which the modern nation is imagined. First, it is imagined as *limited*, by "finite, if elastic, boundaries"; second, it is imagined as *sovereign*; and, third, it is imagined as *fraternal*, "a deep, horizontal comradeship" for which millions of people are prepared "not so much to kill as willingly to die" (15). As the image suggests, the nation-community is embodied metonymically in the finite, sovereign, fraternal figure of the citizen-soldier.

Anderson argues that European bourgeoisies were distinguished by their ability to "achieve solidarity on an essentially imagined basis" (74) on a scale far greater than that of elites of other times and places. Writing and literacy play a central role in this argument. Anderson maintains, as have others, that the main instrument that made bourgeois nation-building projects possible was print capitalism. The commercial circulation of books in the various European vernaculars, he argues, was what first created the invisible networks that would eventually constitute the literate elites and those they ruled as nations. (Estimates are that 180 million books were put into circulation in Europe between the years 1500 and 1600 alone.)

Now obviously this style of imagining of modern nations, as Anderson describes it, is strongly utopian, embodying values like equality, fraternity, liberty, which the societies often profess but systematically fail to realize. The prototype of the modern nation as imagined community was, it seemed to me, mirrored in ways people thought about language and the speech community. Many commentators have pointed out how modern views of language as code and competence assume a unified and homogeneous social world in which language exists as a shared patrimony—as a device, precisely, for imagining community. An image of a universally shared literacy is also part of the picture. The prototypical manifestation of language is generally taken to be the speech of individual adult native speakers face-to-face (as in Saussure's famous diagram) in monolingual, even monodialectal situations—in short, the most homogeneous case linguistically and socially. The same goes for written communication. Now one could certainly imagine

30 | Pratt

a theory that assumed different things—that argued, for instance, that the most revealing speech situation for understanding language was one involving a gathering of people, each of whom spoke two languages and understood a third and held only one language in common with any of the others. It depends on what workings of language you want to see or want to see first, on what you choose to define as normative.

In keeping with autonomous, fraternal models of community, analyses of language use commonly assume that principles of cooperation and shared understanding are normally in effect. Descriptions of interactions between people in conversation, classrooms, medical and bureaucratic settings, readily take it for granted that the situation is governed by a single set of rules or norms shared by all participants. The analysis focuses then on how those rules produce or fail to produce an orderly, coherent exchange. Models involving games and moves are often used to describe interactions. Despite whatever conflicts or systematic social differences might be in play, it is assumed that all participants are engaged in the same game and that the game is the same for all players. Often it is. But of course it often is not, as, for example, when speakers are from different classes or cultures, or one party is exercising authority and another is submitting to it or questioning it. Last year one of my children moved to a new elementary school that had more open classrooms and more flexible curricula than the conventional school he started out in. A few days into the term, we asked him what it was like at the new school. "Well," he said, "they're a lot nicer, and they have a lot less rules. But know *why* they're nicer?" "Why?" I asked. "So you'll obey all the rules they don't have," he replied. This is a very coherent analysis with considerable elegance and explanatory power, but probably not the one his teacher would have given.

When linguistic (or literate) interaction is described in terms of orderliness, games, moves, or scripts, usually only legitimate moves are actually named as part of the system, where legitimacy is defined from the point of view of the party in authority—regardless of what other parties might see themselves as doing. Teacher-pupil language, for example, tends to be described almost entirely from the point of view of the teacher and teaching, not from the point of view of pupils and pupiling (the word doesn't even exist, though the thing certainly does). If a classroom is analyzed as a social world unified and homogenized with respect to the teacher, whatever students do other than what the teacher specifies is invisible or anomalous to the analysis. This can be true in practice as well. On several occasions my fourth grader, the one busy obeying all

Arts of the Contact Zone | 31

the rules they didn't have, was given writing assignments that took the form of answering a series of questions to build up a paragraph. These questions often asked him to identify with the interests of those in power over him—parents, teachers, doctors, public authorities. He invariably sought ways to resist or subvert these assignments. One assignment, for instance, called for imagining "a helpful invention." The students were asked to write single-sentence responses to the following questions:

> What kind of invention would help you?
> How would it help you?
> Why would you need it?
> What would it look like?
> Would other people be able to use it also?
> What would be an invention to help your teacher?
> What would be an invention to help your parents?

Manuel's reply read as follows:

> A grate adventchin

> Some inventchins are GRATE!!!!!!!!!!!! My inventchin would be a shot that would put every thing you learn at school in your brain. It would help me by letting me graduate right now!! I would need it because it would let me play with my freinds, go on vacachin and, do fun a lot more. It would look like a regular shot. Ather peaple would use to. This inventchin would help my teacher parents get away from a lot of work. I think a shot like this would be GRATE!

Despite the spelling, the assignment received the usual star to indicate the task had been fulfilled in an acceptable way. No recognition was available, however, of the humor, the attempt to be critical or contestatory, to parody the structures of authority. On that score, Manuel's luck was only slightly better than Guaman Poma's. What is the place of unsolicited oppositional discourse, parody, resistance, critique in the imagined classroom community? Are teachers supposed to feel that their teaching has been most successful when they have eliminated such things and unified the social world, probably in their own image? Who wins when we do that? Who loses?

32 | Pratt

Such questions may be hypothetical, because in the United States in the 1990s, many teachers find themselves less and less able to do that even if they want to. The composition of the national collectivity is changing and so are the styles, as Anderson put it, in which it is being imagined. In the 1980s in many nation-states, imagined national syntheses that had retained hegemonic force began to dissolve. Internal social groups with histories and lifeways different from the official ones began insisting on those histories and lifeways *as part of their citizenship*, as the very mode of their membership in the national collectivity. In their dialogues with dominant institutions, many groups began asserting a rhetoric of belonging that made demands beyond those of representation and basic rights granted from above. In universities we started to hear, "I don't just want you to let me be here, I want to belong here; this institution should belong to me as much as it does to anyone else." Institutions have responded with, among other things, rhetorics of diversity and multiculturalism whose import at this moment is up for grabs across the ideological spectrum.

These shifts are being lived out by everyone working in education today, and everyone is challenged by them in one way or another. Those of us committed to educational democracy are particularly challenged, as that notion finds itself besieged on the public agenda. Many of those who govern us display, openly, their interest in a quiescent, ignorant, manipulable electorate. Even as an ideal, the concept of an enlightened citizenry seems to have disappeared from the national imagination. A couple of years ago the university where I work went through an intense and wrenching debate over a narrowly defined Western-culture requirement that had been instituted there in 1980. It kept boiling down to a debate over the ideas of national patrimony, cultural citizenship, and imagined community. In the end, the requirement was transformed into a much more broadly defined course called Cultures, Ideas, Values.[4] In the context of the change, a new course was designed that centered on the Americas and the multiple cultural histories (including European ones) that have intersected here. As you can imagine, the course attracted a very diverse student body. The classroom functioned not like a homogeneous community or a horizontal alliance but like a contact zone. Every single text we read stood in specific historical relationships to the students in the class, but the range and variety of historical relationships in play were enormous. Everybody had a stake in nearly everything we read, but the range and kind of stakes varied widely.

Arts of the Contact Zone | 33

It was the most exciting teaching we had ever done, and also the hardest. We were struck, for example, at how anomalous the formal lecture became in a contact zone (who can forget Atahuallpa throwing down the Bible because it would not speak to him?). The lecturer's traditional (imagined) task—unifying the world in the class's eyes by means of a monologue that rings equally coherent, revealing, and true for all, forging an ad hoc community, homogeneous with respect to one's own words—this task became not only impossible but anomalous and unimaginable. Instead, one had to work in the knowledge that whatever one said was going to be systematically received in radically heterogeneous ways that we were neither able nor entitled to prescribe.

The very nature of the course put ideas and identities on the line. All the students in the class had the experience, for example, of hearing their culture discussed and objectified in ways that horrified them; all the students saw their roots traced back to legacies of both glory and shame; all the students experienced face-to-face the ignorance and incomprehension, and occasionally the hostility, of others. In the absence of community values and the hope of synthesis, it was easy to forget the positives; the fact, for instance, that kinds of marginalization once taken for granted were gone. Virtually every student was having the experience of seeing the world described with him or her in it. Along with rage, incomprehension, and pain, there were exhilarating moments of wonder and revelation, mutual understanding, and new wisdom—the joys of the contact zone. The sufferings and revelations were, at different moments to be sure, experienced by every student. No one was excluded, and no one was safe.

The fact that no one was safe made all of us involved in the course appreciate the importance of what we came to call "safe houses." We used the term to refer to social and intellectual spaces where groups can constitute themselves as horizontal, homogeneous, sovereign communities with high degrees of trust, shared understandings, temporary protection from legacies of oppression. This is why, as we realized, multicultural curricula should not seek to replace ethnic or women's studies, for example. Where there are legacies of subordination, groups need places for healing and mutual recognition, safe houses in which to construct shared understandings, knowledges, claims on the world that they can then bring into the contact zone.

Meanwhile, our job in the Americas course remains to figure out how to make that crossroads the best site for learning that it can be. We are looking for the pedagogical arts of the contact zone. These will include, we are sure, exercises in storytelling and in identifying with the ideas, interests, histories, and attitudes of others; experiments in transculturation and collaborative work and in the arts of critique, parody, and comparison (including unseemly comparisons between elite and vernacular cultural forms); the redemption of the oral; ways for people to engage with suppressed aspects of history (including their own histories), ways to move *into and out of* rhetorics of authenticity; ground rules for communication across lines of difference and hierarchy that go beyond politeness but maintain mutual respect; a systematic approach to the all-important concept of *cultural mediation.* These arts were in play in every room at the extraordinary Pittsburgh conference on literacy. I learned a lot about them there, and I am thankful.

Notes

1. For an introduction in English to these and other aspects of Guaman Poma's work, see Rolena Adorno. Adorno and Mercedes Lopez-Baralt pioneered the study of Andean symbolic systems in Guaman Poma.

2. It is far from clear that the *Royal Commentaries* was as benign as the Spanish seemed to assume. The book certainly played a role in maintaining the identity and aspirations of indigenous elites in the Andes. In the mid-eighteenth century, a new edition of the *Royal Commentaries* was suppressed by Spanish authorities because its preface included a prophecy by Sir Walter Raleigh that the English would invade Peru and restore the Inca monarchy.

3. The discussion of community here is summarized from my essay "Linguistic Utopias."

4. For information about this program and the contents of courses taught in it, write Program in Cultures, Ideas, Values (CIV), Stanford University, Stanford, CA 94305.

Works Cited

Adorno, Rolena. *Guaman Poma de Ayala: Writing and Resistance in Colonial Peru.* Austin: University of Texas Press, 1986.

Anderson, Benedict. *Imagined Communities: Reflections on the Origins and Spread of Nationalism.* London: Verso, 1984.

Garcilaso de la Vega, El Inca. *Royal Commentaries of the Incas.* 1613. Austin: University of Texas Press, 1966.

Guaman Poma de Ayala, Felipe. *El primer nueva corónica y buen gobierno.* Manuscript. Ed. John Murra and Rolena Adorno. Guadalajara, Mexico: Siglo XXI, 1980.

Pratt, Mary Louise. "Linguistic Utopias." *The Linguistics of Writing.* Ed. Nigel Fabb et al. Manchester, UK: Manchester University Press, 1987. 48–66.

Trevino, Gloria. "Cultural Ambivalence in Early Chicano Prose Fiction." Diss. Stanford U, 1985.

1

Complicating Educators' Critical Consciousness

Descriptive Inquiry as an Equitable Contact Zone

RACHEL SEHER AND ALISA ALGAVA

Our Practitioner-Philosopher Inquiry: Context and Theory

The 2020 to 2021 school year was a unique historical moment, one marked by global pandemic, national attention to racialized police violence, and frequently unpredictable transitions between blended and remote learning in local schools. Halfway through that school year and at a moment characterized by fragmentation and isolation, Rachel Seher, the principal of School without Walls (SWW),[1] an alternative public high school, worked closely with Cecelia Traugh, an experienced scholar and practitioner of Descriptive Inquiry, to convene an ad hoc schoolwide coordinating committee comprised of a cross-racial group of teacher leaders. The group's purpose was to build connections among various teacher-led initiatives. Through using descriptive processes in the very first meeting of that coordinating committee, the group identified a pressing need for the whole faculty to refocus their attention on implicit bias and racial equity with each other in order to challenge racial and economic injustice in their work with students. Alisa Algava, an urban education doctoral candidate at the City University of New York Graduate Center, an instructor in Bank Street College of Education's leadership programs, and a former school leader, was a weekly thought partner to Rachel throughout the school's endeavor. We both learned to use an approach to studying teaching developed by Patricia Carini in community, Descriptive Inquiry, through participation in yearly Summer Institutes facilitated by the Institute for Descriptive Inquiry and by participating in inquiry groups facilitated by Cecelia Traugh and other experienced practitioners in New York City and educators from across the country online.[2] We also both draw on an online collection of descriptive processes titled, *Prospect's Descriptive Processes: The Child, the Art of Teaching and the Classroom and School.*[3]

In this piece, we explore how Descriptive Inquiry as a "contact zone"[4] that reduces inequities (Pratt, 1991) can support and challenge educators to examine and reexamine their narratives about race and racism in their schools.[5] By lifting up a story from Rachel's own experience with Descriptive Inquiry—during one particular coordinating committee meeting—we hope to illuminate how learning via Descriptive Inquiry in the contact zone can be transformative for individuals and school communities. Through her experience of the group's collective space of critical reflection, Rachel complicates and deepens her own critical consciousness, supported by Alisa.

As coauthors—both of whom identify as white women committed to centering racial and economic justice in all of our work—we come to Descriptive Inquiry through both our personal and professional trajectories in education, as students, as teachers, and as school leaders. Descriptive Inquiry is a phenomenological, strengths-based, collaborative inquiry process that engages educators in democratizing the construction of knowledge. We believe what Carini believes, which is that "to describe teaches me that the subject of my attention always exceeds what I can see."[6] Descriptive Inquiry is a stance encapsulated by concrete practices, in that it teaches us how to respect and honor each child and adult with whom we learn and work. It teaches us how to see from different angles. We have learned that to "describe requires and instills respect."[7] As members of a group describe without judgment, without interpretation, we co-construct meaning and understanding of a phenomenon, problem, or issue. When we see the subject of our inquiry in its full complexity, we are better able to appreciate and honor it *as it is*, not for what it may become.

Schools that prioritize descriptive processes see adult learning as inseparable from student learning. Developed by teachers at the Prospect School in Bennington, Vermont, during the early 1970s, descriptive processes are used by educators to look closely and deeply at children, student work, and their own teaching practices, not to judge or evaluate but to better understand so that they may more substantively foster learning and growth. Descriptive processes are grounded in a set of beliefs including that all individuals are unique and whole, human capacity is widely distributed, knowledge is partial and incomplete, local expertise is valuable, learning and growth are best cultivated by building on strengths, and the growth of children, educators, and schools are intertwined.

In our collaborations, as a public high school principal (Rachel) and as a former progressive school leader and now researcher-activist (Alisa), we use Descriptive Inquiry as a philosophy and practice of collectivity that anchors us as we look closely, understand deeply, and co-construct knowledge which no one philosopher or practitioner could do alone. Mary Louise Pratt's original definition of contact zones is one which holds our Descriptive Inquiry work across multiple layers of context, community and self. Pratt writes: "I use this term to refer to social spaces where cultures meet, clash, and grapple with each other, often in contexts of highly asymmetrical relations of power, such as colonialism, slavery, or their aftermaths as they are lived out in many parts of the world today. Eventually I will use the term to reconsider the models of community that many of us rely on in teaching and theorizing and that are under challenge today."[8]

In the complex and often messy nature of the community-centering work we do as leaders and researchers in and around schools, we consider and reconsider the relationship between our principles and our actions. As white women who strive to enact antiracist leadership and critical self-reflexive practices, we constantly live and learn in the contact zone between our visions of anticolonial collectivity and the realities of the racialized and capitalist systems and bodies we occupy. We each define ourselves as scholar-activist-educators and we experience contact zones internally between and among these seemingly disparate identities, every single day. From these hyphenated realities—individually and together—we continue working to reimagine and re-create spaces in which educators can collectively build authentic communities that center racial and economic justice.

In the scenes below, Rachel shares one of many coordinating committee meetings that used Descriptive Inquiry to explore issues of racial literacy and justice at CWS. She then critically reflects on her own process of *conscientização*, that is, "learning to perceive social, political, and economic contradictions, and to take action against the oppressive elements of reality."[9] Throughout the group's experience of Descriptive Inquiry, Pratt's concept of contact zone lives on-the-ground as "ways for people to engage with suppressed aspects of history (including their own histories), ways to move into and out of rhetorics of authenticity; ground rules for communication crosslines of difference and hierarchy that go beyond politeness but maintain mutual respect."[10] While the perspective offered is partial, we believe that Rachel's narrative shows how Descriptive Inquiry can be used to facilitate problem-posing learning and to complicate how we come to critical consciousness as educators. Using Descriptive Inquiry can help us reimagine and remake schools as more just and liberatory places for *all* people who learn in them.

Descriptive Inquiry as a Form of Freirean Pedagogy

Having collaborated with Rachel for more than a decade at Bank Street College and more recently in a monthly Descriptive Inquiry Leadership group, Alisa is an educator-scholar-activist and one of Rachel's main thought partners who understands the praxis of progressive leadership, descriptive processes, action research, and problem-posing education. In our conversations, coteaching and collaborative writing throughout the years, we continually explore the inseparability of theory and practice in our own professional learning and lives. Descriptive Inquiry is one process that we have used to facilitate our own and others' transformational, problem-posing learning.

Like Paulo Freire's problem-posing education, Descriptive Inquiry is rooted in a deep belief in the practical wisdom of educators, parents, and children. Close description focused on the experiences and work of children is the foundation of knowledge-making and surfaces important themes, patterns, ideas, and questions to guide educators' work with children and youth in schools. Traugh explains how these processes become inseparable from an inquiry stance: "Descriptive inquiry is values in action . . . The trust in 'human capacity widely distributed' (Carini, 2001, p. 20), the effort to see a person and their work in their terms, the shared authority of participants in the processes, and the multiplicity of views and ideas that it invites result in democratic knowledge-making of a kind that supports individuals, builds community and develops practical wisdom. The descriptive stance also helps individuals and groups work within the tensions that emerge in schools—for example, the tension of working to build a democratic school within a hierarchical system."[11]

Descriptive Inquiry has allowed both authors of this piece to foster and experience transformational learning within contact zones in the

Complicating Educators' Critical Consciousness | 41

schools and educational spaces with which we are affiliated. The type of learning facilitated through Descriptive Inquiry in contact zones has many of the qualities of Freirian "problem-posing education." Problem-posing education characteristically begins with the lived realities of human beings, "the 'here and now' which constitutes the situation within which they are submerged, from which they emerge, and in which they intervene."[12] In contrast to the "banking notion of education," which simply imparts information on individuals like coins dropped into a piggy bank, problem-posing education presents material reality to individuals as "a problem," an "historical reality susceptible of transformation."[13] Social reality is not static but malleable and, therefore, can be re-created and transformed by the humans situated in it.

Dialogue is central to the process of re-creation and social transformation through problem-posing education. Dialogue, as defined by Freire, is "the encounter between [humans], mediated by the word, in order to name the world." Freire writes, "If it is in speaking their world that people, by naming the world, transform it, dialogue imposes itself as the way by which they achieve significance as human beings."[14] "Dialogue," he continues, "is thus an existential necessity . . . Dialogue is the encounter in which the united reflection and action of the dialoguers are addressed to the world, which is to be transformed and humanized."[15] Ultimately, this "naming of the world" is a liberatory "act of creation and recreation" that abolishes a "situation of oppression."[16] Dialogue is a shared "task of learning and acting" that requires specific qualities: "humility," "horizontal relationships," "mutual trust," "faith," "hope," and profound "love for the world and for people."[17] These attributes allow dialoguers to engage as egalitarian partners in true "critical thinking—thinking which discerns an indivisible solidarity between the world and the people . . . thinking which perceives reality as process, as transformation, rather than as a status entity—thinking which does not separate itself from action, but constantly immerses itself in temporality without the fear of risks involved."[18] Freire refers to dialogue as central to "praxis," the creative synthesis of theory and practice for the purpose of individual and social transformation. Without dialogue there is no meaningful communication, and without meaningful communication, "there can be no true education," education which is able to transform consciousness and in turn foster action intended to re-create the material world, which is "liberation."[19]

A key aspect of Freirian dialogue is the identification of "generative themes."[20] For Freire, "the program and content of education" must be

42 | Seher and Algava

"the people's 'thematic universe,'" in other words, "the complex of [the] 'generative themes'" that emerge from human beings' exploration of their material reality through dialogue.[21] Freire writes "consistent with the liberating purpose of dialogical education, the object of the investigations is . . . the thought language through which [humans] refer to reality, the levels at which they perceive that reality, and their view of the world, in which their generative themes are found."[22] A generative theme is specifically one that emerges from "limit situations," which are aspects of historical material reality that individuals themselves perceive as "an obstacle to their liberation."[23] The investigation of the generative themes inherent to individuals' "contextual reality" supports them in becoming more deeply aware of and thinking critically about the world they experience. Thus, inquiry and action must begin with people's lived reality and focus on "meaningful themes" identified by people themselves. If the themes explored are externally imposed as in the banking method, the learning process ceases to have a "liberatory character."[24] As Freire summarizes, "[t]hematic investigation thus becomes a common striving towards awareness of reality and towards self-awareness, which makes this investigation a starting point for the educational process [and] for cultural action of a liberating character."[25] Liberation through collective inquiry is at the core of our vision as educators, philosophers, and leaders.

We, therefore, connect Freire with Carini who points to the potential of Descriptive Inquiry to cultivate thinking, experiencing and, ultimately, critical consciousness in her seminal essay, "Making and Doing Philosophy in a School." Quoting John Dewey (1916/1997), she writes, "Philosophy might almost be described as thinking which has become conscious of itself—which has generalized its place, function, and value in experience."[26] Schools that use Descriptive Inquiry, Carini maintains, have the "great advantage" of locating the practice of a philosophic attitude in the work we do as educators every day.[27] As we surface and explore the pressing "philosophical questions" that live in our own work with children and young people, we embrace the contact zones among and within us.[28]

A key Freirian practice mirrored by descriptive processes is the Freirian culture circle. According to Mariana Souto-Manning, "culture circles are grounded in the belief that '. . . no educational experience takes place in a vacuum, only in a real context—historical, economic, political, and not necessarily identical to any other context.'"[29] Culture circles attempt to promote *conscientização* or "in concrete terms . . . a process of coding/decoding linguistic and social meanings," organized through specific steps. Souto-Manning explains,

Complicating Educators' Critical Consciousness | 43

> The first step is to generate themes from the community in which students live. The generative themes are socially and culturally relevant to individuals and communities. After the generation of themes, they are employed in dialogue circles. Specific steps are taken to achieve the process of reading . . . [which] consist of a process of decoding written words . . . from a coded existential situation. This connection to the real existential situation is . . . crucial . . . enabling students to use . . . knowledge to reconstruct their lives.[30]

Similarly, Descriptive Inquiry is a way for learners, whether young people or adults, to describe what they see and have experienced, surface and identify generative themes or patterns across their experiences, explore those themes, and, ultimately, consider and enact new ways of thinking and being in connection with them. This unique inquiry process supports educators in looking closely at and more deeply understanding children as well as their own educational practice, individually and collectively. Descriptive processes include reflections on a word (to reveal the layered meanings the word embodies), recollections (storytelling), reviews of work (for example, writing, artwork, a lesson plan), reviews of practice (pedagogies and curricula), reviews of a child (including their strengths and interests, educational experiences, relationships) and close readings of a text (for example, curriculum, philosophy, journal writing). Egalitarian, structured process is central to Descriptive Inquiry. Each descriptive process begins with a question raised by a presenter (an educator, parent, child) and entails looking closely and describing before moving to successive interpretive rounds. Participants take turns responding in an egalitarian manner so multiple perspectives are elicited. As Traugh writes, the "work of Descriptive Inquiry is given shape and direction through the enact-ment of process. The core idea is that process is about making something new out of already existing things and/or ideas. It is a systematic way of making, doing, thinking, and working to reach a goal. There are steps, done in sequence, and for the process to be reliable, each step is done consistently."[31] Both presenter and participants typically leave a review with new and multiple insights into the focusing question and additional ideas and approaches for supporting the holistic and academic development of children and young people in school. The collective generation of new knowledge in response to pressing questions through descriptive processes serves as a means for individual, community, and social transformation, as we see in the experience of the Coordinating Committee of teacher leaders convened at SWW.

School without Walls: Descriptive Inquiry as a Contact Zone

Contemporary public schools in the United States are contact zones. They are filled with real people each of whom is differentially situated in relations of power, each of whom is shaped by their personal history, language, and culture, as well as historical structural inequities related to race, gender, class, sexual orientation, and more. SWW is a public experiential learning school in New York City, originally founded in the 1970s as a school-without-walls. The school uses internship-based learning to reengage young people ages sixteen to twenty-one in formal education. SWW is more racially and socioeconomically diverse than many schools in New York City, which like most large United States cities is marked by de facto segregation. SWW is part of a network of progressive high schools in New York City, known as the Consortium for Performance-Based Assessment. Founded as part of the progressive movement in education all Consortium schools have a testing waiver with New York State; instead, students demonstrate college-readiness through projects known as Performance-Based Assessment Tasks (PBATs). The work of the Consortium is explicitly supported by Bank Street College of Education, where both authors have studied and taught, and is grounded by the ten common principles of the Coalition of Essential Schools, a national network of progressive high schools that existed from 1984 through 2017.

For the past several years, Rachel has guided the faculty of SWW, including herself, in using Descriptive Inquiry to see students more fully and holistically, build on student interests and strengths, tap into their own practical wisdom as educators, take multiple perspectives on questions of educational practice, and learn from each other. The faculty at SWW has used Descriptive Inquiry to deepen professional learning and make schoolwide decisions during faculty and team meetings since the 2016 to 2017 school year. For example, the faculty has utilized descriptive processes to describe decision-making in the school and subsequently create a framework for shared decision-making; to better understand challenges related to young people's substance use and develop more

Complicating Educators' Critical Consciousness | 45

supportive policies; and much more. Most recently, descriptive work has been led by the school's professional development committee (PDC), a group of teachers and formal leaders within the school that coordinates and facilitates whole staff professional learning each week.

Halfway through the 2020 to 2021 school year, Rachel, as principal, asked the school's teacher leaders and assistant principals to begin to meet as a Coordinating Committee in order to better align their work and support each other with it. The Coordinating Committee included nine members: two assistant principals, three teaching team representatives, one PDC facilitator, the parent coordinator, the restorative justice coordinator, and Rachel, as principal. Four members of the group identified as Black, two identified as Latinx, and three identified as white. By bringing together a cross-racial group of stakeholders from across our faculty, the Coordinating Committee functioned as a contact zone.

During its second meeting, the Coordinating Committee engaged in a close reading of the notes from the committee's initial meeting. The group wanted to return to the theme of race and antiracism, which had emerged quickly and strongly in the first meeting as a prominent generative theme for whole faculty work. The following description is written from Rachel's first-person perspective as captured in her meeting notes and articulates each step of the process used for this second meeting, which occurred on Zoom due to the pandemic. *We encourage the reader to pause at the end of each step and consider how they might respond to each prompt as a participant.*

STEP 1: ENTER THE ZOOM ROOM

One by one, faces appeared in the Zoom boxes on my computer screen. Once the group had virtually gathered, I read aloud the focusing questions from the meeting agenda, accessible to all in a shared Google Doc. The questions had surfaced during the first meeting in which we each had described the work we were leading and then made connections. The focusing questions were as follows:

1. What ideas from our discussion last time feel most pressing in terms of o\ur work together as a faculty to support our students for the rest of the year? What is missing that is important to add? What else has come up since the last meeting that is important to add or note?

46 | Seher and Algava

2. How can we ensure that our (emergent) shared principles and values as an antiracist, equity-focused school are reflected in and supported by all of our work?

3. Which of these ideas or strands feels most pressing right now in terms of our ability to work together in support of our students?

The second round, I suggested, would build on the first and focus on the following questions:

1. How can we build these various priorities as an antiracist, equity-focused school into our faculty meetings and other spaces?

2. What next steps make sense?

I then added that my hope, as principal, was that we would use the ideas from the two rounds, especially the second round, to create a meeting map for our faculty and team meetings that we would review and adjust at the next meeting of the Coordinating Committee.

Everyone then sat in silence on Zoom with our cameras off for about twenty minutes reading the notes from the first meeting.

When everyone was ready to go with cameras back on, I restated the focusing questions for the first round and suggested that we take turns speaking to the questions, ensuring that each person got to speak once. Sometimes, we might put an order in the chat for descriptive rounds, but my intuition as a facilitator of this particular meeting was for each person to speak as they were moved to do so, in order to better build on ideas. This group had significant experience with descriptive processes and they knew to take turns and not interrupt or directly respond to another person.

As a reader, consider pausing to journal in responses to some of the questions above, as if in preparation for a review based on your own experiences as an educator.

STEP 2: INQUIRY PROCESS ROUND ONE

Vina, who identifies as Afro-Caribbean, spoke first. She saw in our notes: "a desire to return to the work on ourselves and as a community around being antiracist, a desire to articulate the next thing in that work so that

Complicating Educators' Critical Consciousness | 47

we can be of better service of our students," as well as a "perceived tension between academic work and antiracist work that doesn't actually exist." She also articulated the theme of "equity" for faculty, "who holds the work and does the labor," adding that much of our schoolwide work was held by Black and non-Black Person of Color (POC) women.

Emma, who identifies as white, spoke next, identifying the theme of "resistance," specifically referencing white colleagues who express resistance to antiracist equity-centered work. She identified the importance of "keeping students at the center" and openly asked, "If you are resisting this work, antiracist work, and that's who we strive to be, is this the place for you?"

Salena, who identifies as Trinidadian American, spoke third, building on Emma's comments. She identified that some colleagues did not see the connection between their direct work with students and self-reflection around racism and implicit bias, "not realizing that they are one in the same." She suggested that supporting colleagues in making this connection was an important "lens through which we view the next step in our work," for example in "faculty-to-faculty skill shares," "talking about what our teaching looks like," and thinking about "internships" for next year. How do we focus on educator practice, she asked, while explicitly making it "clear that it's all part of the same work" to be an antiracist school?

Mara, who identifies as white, spoke next, envisioning "a diagram with students at the center and the antiracist work overlaying everything (our teams, PDC, teaching strategies, sharing our successes and what's working)," naming that she found it "strange to see that people see academic and antiracist in tension" with each other. She echoed Emma in asking: "Who are we inviting in to work with our students? How is this reflective of antiracist education? We really have to be cognizant of that."

Trinity, who identifies as Black, spoke fifth, articulating the importance of having clearly shared and stated "values and principles" as a "rubric for evaluating our decisions and actions, so that we are moving with integrity and ensuring that we are providing the best possible experience for our students." She offered the Young Lord's thirteen-point program as an example of this type of coordination. "Our students require that we move in coordination with each other," she added. She echoed the earlier point that we should connect all areas of practice to shared "principles and values," including antiracism.

Esperanza, who identifies as Latinx, built on the idea of addressing "resistance" among colleagues to work on antiracism and bias by clearly making the connection between "antiracist values" and "academic learning" for all of our students. She noted that she had heard some colleagues say that they did not see the "connection between strong learning and anti-racism" in other spaces. She added that she appreciated that within our Coordinating Committee on this day, we were making that connection. "It felt like right now everything came together, and I appreciate that," she stated. "I am seeing this work shifting and making its way into other spaces—even in spaces without anyone here," she noted. "I have seen this come up, the language in the document (our January 26 meeting notes) is in those spaces."

Carter, who identifies as Black, spoke next. He added the importance of making the work "concrete." "It would be useful to lay out our antiracist work with teachers," he noted, "so that people can see what that is and how it applies to them." He said that we need to "show people what they will experience and what we are looking for/moving toward," adding that this was a way to "make it concrete so that people know."

Riki, who identifies as Latinx, spoke last specifically on the topic of "coddling resistance." She challenged us to acknowledge that "resistance is going to be there" and to be "prepared to address it and not just pretend it's not there." "People should know," she vocalized "that we are doing intentional work to address [resistance] . . . so folx don't feel like it's just fine." "There needs to be a next step," she continued, "If you resist, you are inviting us to be in conversation with you—is that what you want?" "Resistance is an invitation to conversation," she closed.

As a reader, consider how you might respond in this first round, assuming that you were the last person to contribute, given the comments already made.

Step 3: Inquiry Process Round Two

I suggested that we move to the second round, focusing on the question: *Given what we've said, what are some ideas for concrete next steps? What lingering questions remain unanswered?* I did not respond to the first round because I was focused on facilitating and capturing my colleagues' thinking.

Esperanza spoke first in the second round, stating that the "Messaging around this" felt important. She specifically emphasized that we needed to communicate that "this is also work that is not going away; this is with us from now on." Jackson so spoke to the importance of having a way to evaluate and assess "our own accountability (each one of us)."

Trinity then spoke powerfully and clearly. "We cannot meet people where they are at on the path toward racial equity," she stated. "Equity is neither optional or negotiable, this is who we are as a school, these are the values to which we are held accountable, period." "People need support," she added, "and also there are some behaviors that need to be shut down." She suggested that an additional way to reinforce our commitment as a school to antiracism would be to "embed rituals into all of our meetings that will support everyone in making a connection to our principles and values," including antiracism.

Mara then shared that, as a white person, she needed help "understanding" what it looked like to be "antiracist" and what our "concrete next steps" could be.

Salena then wondered aloud, "Are we creating space for people who genuinely have questions? How do we do that without causing harm? We need to give people a space to ask questions." She suggested forming Racial Affinity Groups in which educators who identified with specific racialized groups (Black, non-Black people of color, and white) would gather separately in safe and brave spaces for reflection, learning, and support. The following year we initiated these affinity groups during our faculty meeting time.

The rest of the comments affirmed and built on these in some way. We were at the end of our ninety minutes, so I then stepped in as facilitator and as the principal of the school who convened the group, to summarize a list of possible next steps based on the comments made in the two rounds and in the previous meeting on January 26.

As a reader, consider your own response to the guiding questions for the second round: Given what we've said, what are some ideas for concrete next steps? What lingering questions remain unanswered?

STEP 4: INQUIRY PROCESS PULLING THREADS/SUMMARIZING

The first theme, I noted, was messaging. I emphasized that "we need a clear statement around our commitment to antiracist education and focus as a school," as well as a meeting map that showed "this is where we want to go this year, next year." "Establishing where we need and want to be" and that the work was "nonnegotiable" felt important. I also suggested that we "go public as a Coordinating Committee" working on antiracist education as part of our "messaging to the whole faculty."

50 | Seher and Algava

Some of the key ideas that I captured for the "messaging" included the following:

- We are going to make mistakes—accountability and redemption are important

- Creating a culture of antiracism—if people say something, it gets processed—this is a practice.

- Establishing a regular reflective practice (and clear set of actions) as part of all of our group meetings, one-on-one meetings, and in our individual work—this is accountability.

- Using an explicit framework (that had been shared in a districtwide equity team meeting) as a tool toward creating a shared definition of antiracist, multicultural school.

A second theme that I captured was the importance of creating time and space within racial affinity groups during faculty meeting time. A third theme was around building clear routines and rituals for continually integrating antiracist principles and values into our work with each other and our students and clear systems and processes for accountability. A fourth theme that I captured was the importance of having clear antiracist principles and values to hold us as a staff in our work with each other and our students.

I added that, at this point, we appeared to need support from an outside organization in moving forward work around antiracism, since none of us had facilitated racial affinity groups before. In the past, we had worked with the Center for Racial Justice in Education, a nonprofit partner organization that supports school communities in developing and implementing a framework and practices for teaching for racial justice. I readily agreed to reach out to them to see if they could work with our entire staff for the remainder of the 2020 to 2021 school year and into the next year.

As a reader, how would you have added to or amended the themes summarized, had you been a participant of the ad hoc Coordinating Committee?

STEP 5: REFLECTIVE JOURNALING

As a self-reflexive practice, I journal after many of our meetings. Journaling is an important part of how I reflect on my own unconscious biases and

Complicating Educators' Critical Consciousness | 51

examine and develop my stance as school leader. I wrote in my journal later that day my colleagues' candor during the review, especially the clarity and honesty of Black and non-Black POC teacher leaders, felt like a tremendous gift to me and to our school. I visualized a curtain being pulled back that I had momentarily been allowed to look behind, so that I could witness the conversations that might be happening in teacher offices and at lunch and meetings when I was not there, especially informal conversations among Black and non-Black POC staff members and possibly even students. I also felt powerfully compelled to respond to the call to action that had been expressed, to actually create a statement committing our school to antiracism, to cocreate a vision for antiracist education at our school, to more actively call in/out colleagues for racist behaviors, and to follow up when individuals acted in ways that were not aligned with antiracist principles and values.

I also knew that I myself and we as a group needed support. I had participated in racial affinity groups but had never facilitated them, and I still struggled to address certain behaviors effectively, especially given the constraints of the larger system within which we worked. I felt nervous to require participation in racial affinity groups, and I also knew that we needed to move in this direction based on the call for these spaces made by Black and non-Black POC teacher leaders and after hearing a white teacher leader say that she needed help knowing how to be antiracist.

I also left the meeting wondering what work was necessary for me. I often felt that because I committed to being antiracist I had arrived at that goal, but I also knew that I could not see my own biases and that colleagues might be more hesitant to call me in/out because I held the role of principal. I wondered how I could do my own internal work to become antiracist, what work was most necessary for me, and who could support me. I decided to start by having weekly conversations with Alisa, who I knew was also committed to taking an antiracist stance.

As a reader, consider taking a few minutes to journal your own reflections on the experience described in light of your own identity, positionality, and experiences as an educator.

Closing Thoughts: Embracing the Contact Zones among and Within

The example of the ad hoc Coordinating Committee meeting at SWW shows that, sustained over time, descriptive processes can foster the creation of learning communities that co-construct knowledge, reexamine the knowledge they construct, and engage in ongoing transformation of ideas and practices. Descriptive Inquiry is a set of democratic and inclusive processes that communities can use over time to engage in Freirean-style learning or -praxis that has the potential to transform individuals, groups, and organizations. Held by these processes, a community can surface and explore pressing questions and key generative themes, identify and uphold shared values, and foster the individual and collective transformation needed for all community members to thrive. In the context of the particular historic moment described in this piece of multiple pandemics converging (COVID, structural racism, income, and wealth inequality) combined with the uncertainties of remote schooling, Rachel and the ad hoc Coordinating Committee relied on their shared inquiry stance and the structure of descriptive processes, which they had used and cultivated over time, to surface and respond effectively to the generative theme of antiracism and racial equity in their school.

Descriptive processes allowed Rachel and teacher leaders at SWW to utilize the ad hoc Coordinating Committee as a contact zone, as described by Pratt, a space of inquiry in which members of the community brought *themselves*, shared different perspectives, identified differences of opinions and experiences, and navigated conflict generativity. In this example, educators' different backgrounds and lived experiences shaped their perspectives and beliefs, interpretations and analyses, and pedagogical commitments and practices, all within the sociohistoric context of systemic structures of power and inequity. Educators at SWW encountered *one another* within the ad hoc Coordinating Community as full humans who described practice and experiences in a way that allowed all participants to more deeply understand and act upon the phenomenon of race and racism at SWW. As they described and interpreted from multiple vantage points, members of the group created knowledge and more deeply understood each other and the community in which they worked and learned. In this instance, Rachel experienced her own transformative learning as a school leader. Her close listening with her colleagues in a space of a Descriptive Inquiry contact zone pushed her to interrogate her own positionality, assumptions and role as a white principal committed to antiracist leadership and schooling.

We draw from Rachel's story the ways in which praxis is constantly at work in the contact zone of Descriptive Inquiry spaces. Her antiracist

Complicating Educators' Critical Consciousness | 53

aspirations and whiteness, her reflections and actions are inseparable, just as her internal identities as scholar-activist-educator are inseparable. In that sense, we both enter the contact zones in our learning communities with intentionality and the desire to complicate our own critical consciousness, and we simultaneously experience the dialectical and transformative activist (potential of the contact zones inside each one of us. Our internal philosophers and practitioners are in constant conversation as we reflect and as we act. By making visible our internal and external contact zones, to ourselves *and* others, we know that we are, indeed, all in it together as we continue striving to make our schools and our world more just. Join us in the contact zone of collaborative inquiry that centers justice, requires collectivity, demands humility and humanity . . . it may be our only hope.

We, the authors, continue to contemplate two questions. First, what might we, the authors of this piece, not be seeing? How might our own perspectives and biases as white female progressive educators and leaders have shaped the narrative? How would this piece be written if the authors were Black or non-Black POC teacher leaders who participated in the ad hoc Coordinating Committee? How might the story be different, and would they have experienced the meeting as generativity as we describe it? Second, what are limits of Descriptive Inquiry within contact zones to facilitate transformational change within public schools, and when is a clear policy stance needed, especially in relation to the question of antiracism and racial equity? For example, the school year after this meeting took place, Rachel, as principal, used her positional authority to require all faculty to participate in ongoing workshops and training focused on antiracism and implicit bias facilitated by an external organization, the Center for Racial Justice in Education. While the need for such learning arose strongly as a generative theme within the ad hoc Coordinating Committee, some faculty members still only participated in antiracist learning because it occurred during mandated faculty meetings.

Questions for Discussion

- Reading through the teachers' discussion, what themes emerge for you? If you were a participant in these conversations, what might you want to bring up next?

Further Reading

Carini, Patricia F. *Starting Strong: A Different Look at Children, Schools, and Standards.* New York: Teachers College Press, 2001.

Himley, Margaret, and Patricia F. Carini, eds., *From Another Angle: Children's Strengths and School Standards: The Prospect Center's Descriptive Review of the Child.* New York: Teachers College Press, 2000.

Himley Margaret, Himley, Margaret, Lynne Yermanock Strieb, Patricia F. Carini, Rhoda Kanevsky, and Betsy Wice, eds. *Prospect's Descriptive Processes: The Child, the Art of Teaching and the Classroom and School,* rev. ed. North Bennington, VT: The Prospect Center, 2002.

Furman, Cara E., and Cecelia Traugh, *Descriptive Inquiry in Teacher Practice: Cultivating Practical Wisdom to Create Democratic Schools.* New York: Teachers College Press, 2021.

Activity

Consider how Descriptive Inquiry might be used to create a more equitable contact zone in their own institution or organization, especially if it is an educational setting. Consider taking a few minutes to jot down your own thoughts on how you might create a contact zone like the Coordinating Committee at SWW in which you and you colleagues with differing roles and types or levels of power use descriptive processes to explore pressing questions, surface and consider multiple perspectives, cocreate knowledge, and engage in ongoing transformation of ideas and practices.

Notes

1. This and all proper names listed as first names are pseudonyms.

2. "The Institute on Descriptive Inquiry Home Page," Institute on Descriptive Inquiry, last accessed May 1, 2023, https://sites.google.com/idiprocess.org/idi.

3. Margaret Himley, ed. *Prospect's Descriptive Processes: The Child, the Art of Teaching and the Classroom and School* (North Bennington, VT: The Prospect Archives and Center for Education and Research, 2011), https://cdi.uvm.edu/sites/default/files/ProspectDescriptiveProcessesRevEd.pdf.

4. Pratt, "Arts of the Contact Zone."

5. Pratt, "Arts of the Contact Zone," 7.

Complicating Educators' Critical Consciousness | 55

6. Patricia Carini, *Starting Strong: A Different Look at Children, School, and Standards* (New York: Teachers College Press, 2001), 163.

7. Carini, *Starting Strong*, 164.

8. Pratt, "Contact Zone," 34.

9. Paulo Freire, *Pedagogy of the Oppressed*, trans. Myra Bergman Ramos (New York: Bloomsbury Academic, 2014), 34.

10. Pratt, "Contact Zone," 40.

11. Cecelia E. Traugh, "Cultivating Practical Wisdom through Descriptive Inquiry: A Case of Caring of the Self," in *Descriptive Inquiry in Teacher Practice: Cultivating Practical Wisdom to Create Democratic Schools*, eds. Cara E. Furman and Cecelia E. Traugh (New York: Teachers College Press), 32.

12. Freire, *Pedagogy of the Oppressed*, 85.

13. Freire, *Pedagogy of the Oppressed*, 85.

14. Freire, *Pedagogy of the Oppressed*, 88.

15. Freire, *Pedagogy of the Oppressed*, 88–90.

16. Freire, *Pedagogy of the Oppressed*, 89–90.

17. Freire, *Pedagogy of the Oppressed*, 89–91.

18. Freire, *Pedagogy of the Oppressed*, 92.

19. Freire, *Pedagogy of the Oppressed*, 93.

20. Freire, *Pedagogy of the Oppressed*, 97.

21. Freire, *Pedagogy of the Oppressed*, 96–97.

22. Freire, *Pedagogy of the Oppressed*, 97.

23. Freire, *Pedagogy of the Oppressed*, 99.

24. Freire, *Pedagogy of the Oppressed*, 107.

25. Freire, *Pedagogy of the Oppressed*, 107.

26. Patricia Carini, "Making and Doing Philosophy in a School," in *Jenny's Story: Taking the Long View of the Child*, eds. Patricia Carini and Margaret Himley (New York: Teachers College Press, 2010), 156.

27. Carini, "Making and Doing Philosophy," 156.

28. Carini, "Making and Doing Philosophy," 158.

29. Mariana Souto-Manning, Mariana, *Freire, Teaching and Learning: Culture Circles across Contexts* (New York: Peter Lang, 2010), 17.

30. Souto-Manning, Mariana, *Freire, Teaching and Learning*, 18.

31. Traugh, "Cultivating Practical Wisdom," 33.

2

Reimagining Contact as a Method

Portals and Portraits in the Classroom

VIKRAMADITYA (VIK) JOSHI AND MELISSA ROSENTHAL

[It is] like an aquarium (but unlike the ocean), the classroom is both real and invented: classrooms are real places, inhabited by real people, but the meanings that children—and adults—find there are meanings they create themselves.

—Julie Diamond, *Kindergarten*

As coauthors, it is our responsibility to explain the perspective from which this paper is written. Owing to the extensive time commitments that a first-time teaching position involves, this paper is written from Vik's perspective. Melissa's voice is preserved throughout the text through the insertion of excerpts from interviews, conducted by Vik, coupled with the fact that the editorial process for completing this draft has been collaborative. We felt it important to offer this point of clarification as both authors are scholars and practitioners in their own right and this choice of perspective is pragmatic, not an expression of asymmetry. Further, we see the range of sympathetic and compassionate voices we introduce, via citation, in this chapter as additional scholar-practitioners dwelling at the intersection of philosophy and education.

58 | Joshi and Rosenthal

When we first embarked on this writing project, the ideal picture of this collaboration involved reading a range of books together, finding frameworks and theories to make sense of educational experiences, and writing this paper to exhibit the connections between theory and practice. But, if we have learned anything about ourselves, education, and the writing of philosophy and education, it is this: this work, as scholar-practitioner Bettina Love names it, is *messy*.[1] But the messy is real. If we *begin* from practice—the "messy" swirl of interactions, dialogues, and moments that a teacher bears witness to everyday—then we soon realize that our theories are in fact in need of remixing. Educators' testimonies, experiences, and actions will root us in the real lives and occurrences of classrooms. Theories—though powerful as a tool—need to be interrogated at their source. Where did they come from and how were they created? This is a paper that embraces the messiness of the real and our method—as much as our inquiry below—acknowledges that the classroom is a space in constant negotiation between the real and the ideal. This is why it's a contact zone.

Introduction: The Classroom as a Portal

When I asked Melissa Rosenthal, a first-time teacher at a small public school in Upstate New York, to show me around her ninth- and tenth-grade classroom, we both knew that this wasn't a possibility. Outside visitors were not permitted. If she began teaching a year prior in 2020, then *nobody* would have been permitted to be in the classroom—no teachers, no staff members, no students. We settled with a virtual walkthrough of the class, where Melissa became both narrator and guide. The camera was now recording from her perspective.

> When I first walked into the class before I put up decorations, I was really excited, and I loved the windows. The school and the classroom felt very old school and had a sort of old charm to it. I will say now, I do not love my classroom and it really does bother me. It does not produce the feeling I want. I am still figuring out exactly what that feeling is (mixture of calm and comfort) and how to express this feeling within the room. For next year, I want to make one of the walls of my room a student art wall so they can have a space that is 100% theirs. I also want to bring in some fun chairs like a couple of bean-bag chairs.[2]

Reimagining Contact as a Method | 59

There are five large windows across the back of the classroom. A teacher's desk—with a bottle of sanitizer, a sheaf of papers, and a small cactus bulb—sits at the right end of the space, facing three rows of tan desks and chairs spaced evenly. Melissa is *bothered* by her current classroom environment. It fails to create the "feeling" she desires—an unsurprising conclusion when a teacher's design principles prioritize reducing the transmission of a virus. This affects desk placement and arrangement. Students cannot work closely together in groups. A veneer of community barely covers the dictate: *stay apart.*

When John Dewey says that we educate *by means of the environment,* it would be inconceivable to think that so many of the decisions in shaping one's classroom environment would be taken away from the teacher.[3] The first thing you notice in Melissa's classroom is a desk covered in cleaning supplies: sanitizer bottles and sprays, rolls of paper towels, and disinfectant wipes stationed strategically next to the front door. Each day ends with a ritual precipitated by this ongoing period of *social distancing.*

> When I leave my classroom, I have a little routine. I first sanitize my desk, and my pens and pencils (especially if I was just grading). I will then sanitize the student's desks and place them back in their rows. I *have to* line up the desks back in their rows. It is a mental reset, and it lets me know that my desks are in order and prepared for my students to mess them up again the next day. Then I wash my hands, push in my desk chair, put on my coat, grab my keys and bag, sanitize my hands for good measure, kick the wooden door stop out the door and off I go![4]

Teachers are ethically motivated to keep not only their students protected but also to keep their colleagues and families safe from this virus. These daily decisions draw on a teacher's cognitive and emotional energy.[5] These rituals in service of bodily safety are repetitive. They do not need creative input to achieve their desired consequence. If surfaces are sanitized and masks are worn, then this ritual has served its purpose. At the same time, these penances pose significant constraints on the teacher's "expression" of values via the classroom environment.

Let's take the desks and chairs. Owing to social distancing—a term that has gained such currency that it requires no further explanation here—the desks and chairs are spaced apart in such a way that they take up *all the space* in the room. Remembering Julie Diamond's reflective

60 | Joshi and Rosenthal

teacher-narrative in *Kindergarten*—a moving first-person account of the rituals in her kindergarten classroom, offered by an educator who has spent twenty-five years teaching children in a variety of classroom settings—we see her [Melissa] curate the classroom environment with great care.[6] A student in that classroom learns to place their bag on a hook and put away items after use in specific drawers. The students are not discouraged from forming small groups, exercising their autonomy by inviting new members into their little societies, and then choosing to build norms that determine the way they play within these groups. Diamond describes the classroom environment, as we see in the epigraph of this chapter, in an evocative manner: "[It is] like an aquarium (but unlike the ocean), the classroom is both real and invented: classrooms are real places, inhabited by real people, but the meanings that children—and adults—find there are meanings they create themselves."[7]

We begin to see that the "real" during the pandemic became a source of unrelenting anxiety; masks improperly worn have "pulled" teachers out of their lessons immediately; and students and teachers were given the impossible task of imagining community in a virtual space that, unlike the classroom, is *disembodied*. However, Diamond's distinction between the ocean and the aquarium ("the classroom") offers an insight into the way contact zones can emerge despite these attenuating constraints on community building.

The ocean is vast and stretches beyond our perceptual horizon. By contrast, the aquarium is enclosed with clear boundaries that suggest finitude. Nevertheless, the metaphorical bridge between the aquarium and the ocean illustrates the imaginative potential that the classroom environment possesses. Consider the five windows in Melissa's class. They can be viewed, from the inside, as a symbol of separation from the world. The screen has fallen off the fifth window and her students often spend time with their hands outstretched to check the weather or to holler at their friends below.

For her students, these windows are not a symbol of enclosure but a *portal*. A portal is an opening to a new place of possibility. One can only look through a portal or step across the portal into a new place by seeing, by offering attention, by imagining the space anew. Stories, like portals, are an opening into the people we are and are becoming. Every surface in Melissa's classroom can, for her students, become a portal—a place to contribute to the story of this particular classroom. The whiteboards in the classroom are covered in student writing. Melissa writes the bell

Reimagining Contact as a Method | 61

schedule and the homework due on the board. Students cover this board in concentric circles of their names and calligraphic designs in a few corners. As Pratt says, students do not simply wish to be allowed in the classroom but sincerely seek belonging.[8] They may even demand it. As we slowly emerge from this pandemic, the call for students to be cocreators in the curation of classroom environments is a lesson that can only be truly learned if we begin to see our students for what they are and always have been: *artists*. Artists are not only painters, musicians, sculptors, writers, or dancers. To be an artist is to create *anything* that draws on our creativity, our inspirations, our sense of ourselves and the world. To recognize one's students as artists and the classroom as a portal is to embrace the real messiness—a place where the actual dreams, aspirations, and ideas of children meet the ideals of standards, reading levels, and the uptake of skills. To see this tension in the contact zone (that is, the classroom), let's meet a student who was seeking to be recognized as an artist.

Recognizing Stella, the Artist

Let's meet Stella.[9]

> One of my first memories of Stella is from the first day of school when she came stomping in, threw herself in her chair and paid little attention (or so I thought then—now I think she does indeed pay attention far more than most give her credit) to my introduction to our class. I recall giving a "do now" that asked what classes my students enjoyed, what classes they did not, and what music suggestions they had.[10] I remember for most of the "do now's" I gave her that week they were returned with an "I don't care" written as the response or thrown away in the garbage. I was curious about why Stella was so obstinate and needed me to see that she "didn't care." I recall finding it almost amusing how she would try to make it apparent to me and everyone else that she did not care, which suggests that she *actually did* care in some capacity.[11]

This is an example of what David T. Hansen calls "ethical tension."[12] Stella's sentence, "I don't care," creates tension owing to the possible interpretations Melissa can make from it. In one sense, it is a clear refusal of participation in the assigned activity; however, it is vital to recognize that not all tension is negative. The alternative interpretation, as Melissa outlines, is reading this ostensibly defiant act as an invitation to see what lies ahead in this story. A novel propels the reader forward by building narrative momentum with such tension. If Melissa responded to Stella's notes, which had "I don't care" scribbled on them or took the gesture of throwing assignments into the garbage as conclusions, rather than ethically tense *beginnings* of a narrative, then the story is over.

Teachers ought to recognize that a story is not an instrument of learning, but rather the *medium* in which learning occurs. When exploring the novels of J. M. Coetzee to gain insight into pedagogy, Megan Laverty highlights a common tendency to use stories as tools for ethical analysis.[13] By neglecting the literary elements that constitute the story in which a character—and their thoughts, feelings, relationships, and choices—appears, they fail to appreciate "the full measure of the intellectual provocation that these texts can offer."[14] A student meets a teacher in medias res. A student appears with a range of lived experiences. However, teachers may commit a temporal error in judgment by privileging the present over an unspoken past. By listening to students, posing thoughtful questions, or simply recognizing that a student comes to a new teacher with a reservoir of experiences, teachers become better readers of the unfolding novels in their midst.

Returning to Stella's portrait, we can see that her demonstrative acts of apathy—showing Melissa and the class that she does not care about the schoolwork—could only be understood in the greater context of a narrative. Melissa is recounting her *first* memory of Stella, not the last one. The impressions a human being, like Stella, chooses to leave on a first interaction with their teachers is fraught with a range of emotional considerations: *Will Ms. Rosenthal like me? What if she gives me a hard time? What can I do to show her how I feel about school right now?* These invaluable questions, often unheard and left unsaid by countless students during their first contact with a teacher, necessitate an orientation of bearing witness from the teacher—simply put, like a farmer who does not *wait* for the rain to arrive, but rather *waits upon* the weather's character to write the next chapter of this climatic narrative.[15]

> Stella always comes to school with her eyebrows perfectly shaped (a compliment I once gave her as she left my room, which resulted in her screaming to her friend, "Ms. Rosenthal likes

my eyebrows!"). It was not until I got to know Stella further that I could learn about her aspirations in life: hair stylist or makeup artist. In time, I also learned a little about Stella's past struggles. Stella once told me that she "had issues," specifically "anger issues." As the year pressed on, I came to know a different Stella than the one who first walked into my classroom. I came to know her passions, goals, humor, difficulties, mood swings, and how fiercely loyal and caring she is to those she lets in.[16]

bell hooks—the prolific and trailblazing author, activist-scholar, and educator—helps us realize that to enter a contact zone is to wish to know one's students. This is an "exciting" process.[17] Contrary to the "atmosphere of seriousness assumed to be essential to the learning process," we must let ourselves feel the excitement involved in the process of knowing.[18] To know your students, who are usually the ones confessing on command, is to balance this asymmetry by expressing yourself as a teacher. Teachers learn about students as they share through assignments or prompts, but the students do not typically hold the power to prompt or pose questions to their teachers. The consequent imbalance in students knowing little to nothing about a teacher's lived experience, thoughts, and aspects of their personality implies that this is a one-way street. What would it look like to simply express to one's students a genuine reaction, particular memory, or transformative personal story as part of a pedagogical practice? Melissa, for example, simply complimented Stella on her "perfectly shaped eyebrows." A student, like Stella, who was taking pains to illustrate her lack of care for any of the assigned schoolwork, could not ignore this moment of recognition from her teacher. It is not the perpetuation of certain "standards of beauty" or an act of flattery that has catalyzed Stella's reaction, but the mere fact that she has been *seen* by her teacher. A critic may disagree, suggesting that the student is responding precisely to this compliment on her appearance. We hold our interpretation, and our evidence lies in the fact that this moment of sincere recognition was *shared*. Stella's instinctual response was to recount her teacher's compliment to a friend. *She screamed to her friend: "Ms. Rosenthal likes my eyebrows!"* What significance might this innocent moment behold? It shows that Stella may or may not care what Ms. Rosenthal thinks of her schoolwork, but she evidently cares about this appreciation of her perfectly shaped eyebrows to such an extent that she needs her friends to know. This compliment has moved from a relation

64 | Joshi and Rosenthal

between teacher and student to being suffused through the student's social world of relationships.

Melissa's simple, yet delightfully thoughtful compliment deepened their relationship as teacher and student *before* we come to know that Stella is an aspiring makeup artist. What could have been written off as a polite expression of praise for a facial feature is now an attentive commendation of a student's artistic creation. For makeup artists, the human body is their medium. This is Stella's craft. Once she realizes that Ms. Rosenthal has an eye that can be sensitive to and appreciative of her artworks, then the *lived experience* she holds becomes a portal through which her teacher can choose to walk into. Stella's perception toward her teacher undergoes a *re-vision*. She sees her teacher anew and leaves the door of her being ajar. With time, Melissa is "let into" this world of her student. It is such an apt expression, for it conveys the sanctity of the process whereby a student brings into their vivid interior life a new presence. How extraordinary that Stella could move from throwing away her teacher's worksheets into the garbage to sharing her struggles beyond the classroom with her teacher. Melissa's compliment is an illustration of the growth of her teacher voice. This is a voice that moves as the student moves. It engages the student by invitation, not by force. As the days continue, this voice becomes attuned to the flow of the classroom and the students within it. This voice remains dynamic as the teachers and students return to the classroom every day. As hooks beautifully says, "The engaged voice must never be fixed and absolute but always changing, always evolving in dialogue with a world beyond itself."[19]

Emerging Creations in the Contact Zone

One day Stella came in for extra help to get caught up on missed work. I then found her sticking a small drawing of Squidward from SpongeBob onto her desk. I asked what that was, and she said it reminded her of a boy she was talking to but isn't anymore. Squidward remained on the desk for a few days. As I cleaned my desks at the end of class, I saw this Squidward and really enjoyed how it made the desk unique, playful, and most importantly, an extension of Stella. I thought about how I would like to have something on every desk. Later that day Stella walked into my classroom as I finished with another class and said she had made a few more characters because Squidward couldn't be alone. She asked if she could stick them on the desk and I said, "Why not." I then thought what an opportunity it would be to commission Stella to create a character for each desk. I asked Stella if she would be interested. She *glowed* and said, "Oh my gosh, yes!" From there, this project took on Stella's spin. She soon decided that she was going to think of a cartoon character that represented the person who sat there. I had her promise that she would not choose a character that was mean, and she said, "I would not put down a villain or anything," and off she went. Within days, she worked diligently during study hall, lunch, and even in class creating these cartoons. She remarked proudly, "I only have four more characters to come up with" before we left for break. So many students have asked, "Who created these?" with such curiosity and amusement. Whenever her good friend hears someone ask, she proudly replies: "Stella did, and she is making them to represent every student in the class."[20]

As described by Dana Frantz Bentley and Mariana Souto-Manning, "emergent curriculum" is engendered by the student's questions.[21] It *emerges* from them. When thinking of the contact zone, which Bentley and Souto-Manning recognize in both preschool and higher-education classrooms, it is in search of emerging models of community that the contact zone is born. The pedagogical arts that support the nourishment of contact zones include storytelling, composing narratives of history from multiple perspectives, experiments in collaborative critique, parody, and comparison of cultural forms, and, crucially for this paper, the development of an *approach to authentic expression.*[22]

Melissa notices Stella drawing. She is illustrating an existing character from a popular television show. This is an act of imitation—the creation of an imperfect substitute of the original. Elaine Scarry, in *On Beauty and Being Just*, explains that the rejection of such an act of imitation on the grounds that it simply begets an "imperfect version" of the original is an error.[23] She clarifies that there is a meaningful difference between the process of creation motivated by compulsion and this very process motivated by an "impulse toward begetting."[24] To beget is to birth *and* to reproduce. It is procreative and imitative. Stella, following her artistic impulse, is begetting characters through drawing. They are reproductions of existing characters and yet, they are her creations. If Melissa were to reject her drawings for their lack of originality or interpret this habitual drawing as wandering from the course set by the curriculum, then the *emergent* curriculum is lost. The contact zone cannot be imagined if we, following Scarry, "disparage beauty" on the basis of a misguided understanding of creation.[25] Melissa suspended any concern with imitation or departing from the formal curriculum and listened to the call of the emergent curriculum. She *commissioned* Stella to create an artwork for every desk in the class. This choice created imaginative space for Stella—the makeup artist, the visual artist—to find her authentic expression, to be in the contact zone.

Reimagining Contact as a Method

When reaching the conclusion of this chapter, I asked Melissa if there were any details missing from this portrait of her classroom or Stella. She offered two images.

The first is the whiteboard in her classroom. At the end of each day, she would erase the entire whiteboard as part of her end of the day "reset" ritual. Now, she leaves it for her students to erase if they wish. This change, she confessed, began because of laziness after a long day of teaching; however, she discovered that leaving the scribbles and unfinished sentences authored by her students on the board served as testimony of their shared time together.[26] Seeing the whiteboard blank now is strange. It became a symbol of disconnection from her students. In retelling this story, Melissa has given an enduring image of a key principle of contact as a method: the classroom environment has a *social memory*. To honor the participation and presence of one's students is to find ways in the contact zone that memorializes the work that is done in the classroom. Memories of feeling seen create safety. Memories of building friendships create safety. Memories of feeling like you belong create safety. To enact contact as a method is to cultivate an environment worthy of creating social memories. Pratt once wrote: The fact that no one was safe made us all involved in the course appreciate the importance of what we came to call "safe houses."[27] Safety is not a point of departure for inquiry, but an outcome of coming together with commitments of mutual recognition and care to create social memories. Contact zones beget social memories.

In this chapter, we have offered an illustration of *contact* as a pedagogical method. Readers may reasonably wonder, how is contact a method?

Let's briefly turn to W. E. B. Du Bois. Du Bois offers a method of education with the liberation of Black communities in mind: "The chief and great method, of course, by which a people come into the great social heritage of the modern culture-world and by which they gain close and efficient knowledge of the methods of the world's work is the training which comes primarily and essentially from human contact—a contact of those who know with those who are to learn."[28] Both Pratt and Du Bois understood the importance of contact as a method beyond technique. Method is often conceived of as an application of a certain approach or set of practices to reach a particular goal. However, drawing from the original Greek, we remember that a method (*methodos*) is a path to follow, to search, to wonder and wander along. When a teacher is teaching a lesson, method in its technical sense is dead, but method as a search is *alive*.

By walking alongside a high school teacher, this chapter offers an illustration, rather than a model or formula, of *contact* as a method. The portrait of a student sketched in these pages invites our readers to explore *contact* as a method for authentic expression—an essential constituent of a contact zone. As teachers, students, and staff return to classrooms across the world, it is imperative that we take this moment of reacquaintance with social contact to consider the possibility of contact as a method for intellectual, bodily, and artistic safety in our classrooms.

The second, and parting, image that Melissa shared is of Stella. While it is true that this student let Melissa into her world of art making and found an authentic expression of this artistic impulse in drawing characters for her fellow classmates, the picture is never so neat. Stella, Melissa explains, does not attend school with regularity, does not always take interest in the subject matter being taught, and does not consistently feel motivated to improve her academic performance.[29] The picture of the young student finding authentic expression is deepened, but not broken, by these new details. This larger portrait of Stella reveals the second principle of contact as a method: to be in contact is a *process of renewal*. Each day is new, and a teacher's students will return anew. Time will flow and days will pass, but the mystery of contact as a method lies in its resistance to treat mystery and uncertainty as a problem to solve. Human beings are not problems to solve. To be in the contact zone is to embrace these mysteries, to come closer together, to give space for authentic expression. But we mustn't forget to look at our classrooms as portals, as spaces of possibility, as ever-changing landscapes for teachers and children to become cocreators of a shared world.

68 | Joshi and Rosenthal

Questions for Discussion

- In what ways can a teacher invite students as cocreators of a classroom environment?

- When meeting students for the first time, after an extended break, or after a period of absence, what activities may help bring students back into the contact zone? How might these activities be rooted in who the child is?

Further Reading

Diamond, Julie. *Kindergarten: A Teacher, Her Students, and a Year of Learning.* New York: The New Press, 2011.

Furman, Cara. "Learning to Teach: Developing Practical Wisdom with Reflective Teacher Narratives." *Philosophy of Education Archive* (2016): 139–48.

hooks, bell. *Teaching to Transgress: Education as the Practice of Freedom.* New York: Routledge, 1994.

Activity: Re-Visioning Practice: From Portals to Portraits

Consider a character in a novel, film, or play. Write your impressions of a specific character in this work of art *from memory*. As you experience this form of art *again*, keep a writing utensil and paper with you. Log details about the character during the process. If you are reading, you may make notes in the margin. If you are watching a play or film, you may write notes in a journal. Notice details about the character—their gait, dress, style and manner of speaking, body language, and their presence in the scenes. Ask questions about the character: What are they motivated by or interested in? How do they interact with the world around them? What kind of relationships do they form with the people around them? In light of your reflections and questions, return to your account of the initial impression you formed about the character in your memory. Compare your notes to see the continuities and discontinuities from the past to the present. A practice of *re-visioning* offers an opportunity to recognize the way we learn about the characters that we come into contact with. Storytelling (through a variety of artistic media) is a portal through we begin to practice our attention and how our portraits of a character (person) changes across time. It also helps us recognize the limitations of sight as a metaphor and the value of accompanying perceptual modes—listening (auditory), contact (proprioception), and smelling (olfactory). When thinking of our students as whole beings, we can remember the value of re-visioning as a practice to see our students as changing every day, rather than as fixed images.

Notes

1. Bettina Love, "A Ratchet Lens: Black Queer Youth, Agency, Hip Hop, and the Black Ratchet Imagination," *Educational Researcher* 46, no. 9 (2017): 539–47.

2. Melissa Rosenthal, in conversation with the coauthor, February 12, 2022.

3. John Dewey, *Democracy and Education: An Introduction to the Philosophy of Education* (New York: Macmillan, 1916), 5.

4. Melissa Rosenthal, in conversation with the coauthor, February 12, 2022.

5. Cara E. Furman and Cecelia E. Traugh, *Descriptive Inquiry in Teacher Practice: Cultivating Practical Wisdom to Create Democratic Schools* (New York: Teachers College Press, 2021).

6. Julie Diamond, *Kindergarten: A Teacher, Her Students, and a Year of Learning* (New York: New Press, 2011).

7. Diamond, *Kindergarten*, 30.

8. Pratt, "Arts of the Contact Zone," 39.

9. This is a pseudonym used to protect the privacy, anonymity, and confidentiality of the student in question.

10. "Do nows" are brief opening or warm-up activities that occur at the beginning of a lesson. In contemporary pedagogical practice, "do now" activities are used across elementary, secondary, and higher-education classrooms. The activities may typically last between three to ten minutes. Examples include, but are not limited to, responding to a prompt; asking questions; engaging in a short quiz or game; or forming small discussion groups in response to a common idea or piece of content (article, painting, music video, etc.).

11. Melissa Rosenthal, in conversation with the coauthor, February 14, 2022.

12. David T. Hansen, *Reimagining the Call to Teach: A Witness to Teachers and Teaching* (New York: Teachers College Press, 2021), 18.

13. Megan Jane Laverty, "JM Coetzee, Eros and Education," *Journal of Philosophy of Education* 53, no. 3 (2019): 574–88.

14. Jay R. Elliott, *Character* (London: Bloomsbury, 2017), 246.

15. Martin Heidegger, *Discourse on Thinking* (New York: Harper Torch, 1969).

16. Melissa Rosenthal, in conversation with the coauthor, February 15, 2022.

17. bell hooks, *Teaching to Transgress: Education as the Practice of Freedom* (New York: Routledge, 1994), 7.

18. hooks, *Teaching to Transgress*, 7.

19. hooks, *Teaching to Transgress*, 11.

20. Melissa Rosenthal, in conversation with the coauthor, February 16, 2022.

21. Dana Frantz Bentley and Mariana Souto-Manning, *Pre-K Stories: Playing with Authorship and Integrating Curriculum in Early Childhood* (New York: Teachers College Press, 2019), 18.

22. Pratt, "Arts of the Contact Zone," 40.

23. Elaine Scarry, *On Beauty and Being Just* (Princeton, NJ: Princeton University Press, 1999), 10.

24. Scarry, *On Beauty and Being Just*, 10.

25. Scarry, *On Beauty and Being Just*, 10.

26. Melissa Rosenthal, in conversation with the coauthor, April 27, 2022.

27. Pratt, "Arts of the Contact Zone," *Profession* (1991): 33–40.

28. W. E. B. Du Bois, *The Education of Black People: Ten Critiques (1906–1960)* (New York: Monthly Review Press, 2001), 53.

29. Melissa Rosenthal, in conversation with the coauthor, April 27, 2022.

3

Teaching Worms

Observation and Conversation

CINDY BALLENGER

Many of us, throughout our professional lives as teachers, maintain commitments to ideas and practices that we rarely question. These commitments arise from our training, our own schooling and our experience. They seem obvious and natural to us, so much so that we can sometimes hardly see them. These habitual patterns of acting, of seeing, of valuing, of talking and making sense can be termed a "culture." Mary Louise Pratt famously used the term "contact zone" to describe the way classrooms can be places "where cultures meet, clash and grapple with each other."[1] I believe, as does Pratt, that what is often underlying these clashes are the assumed ideas that students and teachers bring to the classroom and what can make them especially difficult is not being able to name them, to make them visible.

Patricia Carini engages with this concern from within the tradition of philosophy; Carini does not emphasize Pratt's "clash" of cultures—her work is more focused on the individual child. She asks how we might break "the cake of custom and convention" in order to find the particular child beneath our inadequate and rigid "first looks."

These approaches are only a turn of the kaleidoscope away from each other, both using moments of clash, of puzzlement, of difference, of concern or failure to connect to see what is beneath the surface of classroom life.

72 | Ballenger

The practices of excavating beneath "the first look," in Carini's phrasing, developed when I was a member of a group of teachers who were committed to looking particularly at the words and the work of students who puzzled us. This group, the Brookline Teacher Researcher Seminar (BTRS), sought these puzzling moments, moments, as Pratt might say, which clashed with our expectations. In employing this practice, I found, on the one hand, that I saw the child more clearly and also with more feeling, and, on the other, that my own assumptions and assumed practices were made more visible to me, my own thinking became conscious of itself and more open to question.[2] I tell the story of this group in detail elsewhere.[3] Here I want to provide an extended example of one experience of observation and reflection deriving from these traditions of noticing. This story is intended both to describe how this activity can be an integral part of teaching and to explain the many things I learned from a student who challenged some ideas and interpretations that I had not questioned.

My account is based on what in the BTRS we came to call "field notes." Field notes are notes I make as regularly as I can during and after teaching. For me, they are a foundational practice of what Carini would call "doing philosophy" in schools, that is, making visible and thus subject to reflection, that which one would otherwise just accept. As Vivian Paley, a renowned teacher and author wrote, "If I don't write it down, I can't figure out what it means."[4]

These notes are often scribbles, hard to decipher, hurriedly written. They are not complete but contain remarks and moments that struck me. They remind me of questions that came up, or unintended directions we followed. I may add to them later, but even if I don't, writing seems to help me remember more of what happened and what was said and, in particular, what puzzled me, perhaps distressed me as well as pleased me. Taking these notes may sound like a lot of extra work, but actually it is not. These notes are often a part of my planning—they tell me what happened and where I need to go next. And in the moment, because I am taking them, I talk less as I teach. Thus the children talk more and I pay better attention to what they say that I don't quite grasp. Having the notes, as I hope the following account will show, also supports me in reflecting continually on what I am assuming about my own practice and about my students.

As I said above, I always find that I learn the most from children who seem, at least at first, the least like me. They may struggle academically, struggle with behavior, have various challenges; they may give me a

Teaching Worms | 73

hard time, and yet they are the ones who, as Pratt recognized, inevitably have the most to teach me. Jessica[5] was such a child. She was eleven years old. She had been diagnosed with autism. When I first watched Jessica in school all she did was pound her head with her hand and pick up teeny things (perhaps actually there, I was never sure) from her desk and from her shirt. She rarely spoke at all, and when she did she was very hard to understand. Her voice was very low and breathy. She made fleeting eye contact only. She did very little schoolwork.

Some of the specialists who saw Jessica one-on-one thought she was understanding more than it seemed. Others did not agree and regarded her as having a low intelligence. It was difficult to know. However, it was true that she had learned to read and write and had acquired basic math skills. Still she was so occupied with her head smacks that it seemed to me she could hardly hear or attend to those around her.

Choosing a Contact Zone

The plan was that I was to provide additional speech and language instruction and so I set out to determine what we were to talk about. My best strategy in these situations, I have learned over the years, is always to find something the student was interested in, a place for me to make contact with the real living child engaged with the world.

As John Dewey wrote, "I believe that interests are the signs and symptoms of growing power. I believe that they represent dawning capacities. Accordingly, the constant and careful observation of interests is of the utmost importance for the educator."[6]

I set out to uncover what Jessica was interested in. But how was I to identify the interests of a child like this, a child who seemed to engage so minimally with the world around her? It did not appear that she had any interests.

I soon witnessed that at recess she would spend all her time digging for worms. She would put on plastic surgical gloves and then squat in the school garden, raking through the dirt with her fingers, picking out tiny worms and other insects and dropping them on the sidewalk. Was this an interest, I wondered.

Carini's Descriptive Review process[7] directs us to include in our observations physical observations, observations of stance, movement, appearance. Clifford Geertz, the anthropologist, suggests that an aid

74 | Ballenger

to interpretation is to find a metaphor, something that the observer is reminded of in the event or the person[8] and then to make comparisons. Jessica made me think of a small, plump bird on a wire, balanced easily. She squatted all the way down, her bum just off the ground, and remained apparently comfortable in this position for up to ten to fifteen minutes, evidently oblivious to all else around her. She successfully kept her clothes immaculate. I saw her intentness, her focus, her balance. Her vision was like a sharp, alert bird. Was this part of being interested? Maybe. On the other hand, it also seemed possible that this activity might provide some physical comfort to this very tense child, or some stimulation that she craved? I wondered if raking the dirt was satisfying some need that she had and thus actually keeping her from engaging with the outside world. I really didn't know. Which was it? Or could both be true?

I began to join in. I would talk a bit, but she would not, other than to answer questions sometimes, with tight, highly abbreviated nods of her head. But when I suggested anything about being gentle with the worms, or wondered aloud about their behavior, for example, whether they might be cold where she left them exposed on the sidewalk, she wouldn't respond or indicate that she'd heard.

When I worked with her in school, we would do some of her class-work together as best we could—I used pictures and drawings, provided additional vocabulary work to prepare her for what she would encounter in class. I regarded this as "previewing," giving her some exposure ahead of class, and it was in my opinion very important at this stage. Sometimes, as we walked into class after our session, I was able to let the teacher know what Jessica had practiced, and so she would ask her a question and Jessica was sometimes able, and willing, to respond, out loud, in class. We teachers relished these moments, and Jessica would receive a lot of praise. What she thought or felt we did not know. She gave no indication.

At the same time I had purchased a worm bin and some worms and I kept them in my office. After we had done our class work, we would turn to the worms. We picked them up, felt them, and read about them in articles that I found. When I asked her to, Jessica would read, always silently; or I think she read—she would go awfully fast. We would write back and forth in my notebook as we worked since she still did not speak to me. I would ask her questions, but the questions were my questions. She didn't volunteer any questions, observations, or ideas and sometimes what she wrote in her answers to my queries appeared to be guesses. When I asked her to draw, the result was sloppy and rapidly done.

Sharing interests in my experience is usually an experience of connection, a contact zone. One feels the mutuality. But were we connecting? Had we made contact to use Pratt's turn of phrase. Jessica looked at me now and came with me willingly—her teaching team thought she was making progress, but I still didn't know what she might be thinking about worms or, even more importantly, I must admit that I wondered if she was thinking at all.

The Worm Apple Study

After a few weeks I decided to begin an investigation. I added an apple to the worm bin, and I wondered aloud if the worms would eat it. Jessica told me she thought so. She also nodded when I asked if she would share this question with her class. So we brought the worm bin into the classroom and asked each student to make two predictions: would the worms eat the apple and if so, how long would it take? Jessica filled out a chart I gave her, noting the guesses of each of her classmates. She sat up straight; she recorded each of her classmates' guesses, she corrected my spelling of one child's name. She did not rap her head. She did not look for tiny specks on her shirt or desk.

After a week, Jessica and I checked in on the worm bin and we saw that the apple was indeed being eaten. We decided to rejoin the class and show them. I took Jessica up front with me and we showed everyone the worms and the apple. The bin was also full of worm castings, worm poop, which looked just like dirt. Students made a variety of comments about decomposition and the worms eating the apple and also suggested there was dirt in the worm bin. Jessica told the kids out loud "no dirt" and then she explained, out loud "worms poop." Again no head rapping—she was up in front of the class in an easy stance.

We were all excited. No one had known that she would be comfortable in front of the class or that she would speak in response to the others. She seemed focused, her body calm. Everyone noticed her body and mentioned how present and calm she was.

A first step had been made. I was delighted. Where to go next? While there definitely seemed to be something wonderful about what happened with the apple investigation, I remained uncomfortable with how Jessica was functioning and/or how I was teaching. I wrote in my notes my distress that "she won't help me feed the worms." I regularly brought in food scraps and when I would suggest that she take a turn putting them into the bin, she always refused. And she seemed rough with them, perhaps not deliberately rough, but very offhand. And she still did not ask any questions about them or respond to the questions I asked: I would sit beside her, modeling my wondering—were the worms cold? Did they like the sun?—but she would ignore me from what I could tell.

Reflection

What is an interest anyway? How do we recognize interests? Dewey doesn't say. What are the features of an interest? I decided to explore my own experience with interests. I know some teachers will give students a survey in which they are asked to list their interests—I have never found this to provide compelling answers.

As I thought back on my experience with other children and their interests, I found that I was expecting, that Jessica, like others I had taught, would participate in my wonder, and would begin to ask her own questions in which I could participate in turn. I was also expecting that she would notice things—interested children often notice things that I have missed entirely, something I enjoy a great deal. And I hoped that she would care, that she would develop the various sorts of connections that I had seen other children develop with the things that interested them. In my experience these qualities, being curious, highly observant, and being in some sort of affective relationship with the phenomenon, were part of being interested, and Jessica was not showing me any of this.

Going On

In the rest of this paper, I will share my continuing observations of Jessica and describe the crucial role these notes and observations played in my understanding of this child and in my learning to recognize her interests.

The question arose from the other students, will the seeds from the apple grow in the poop. And from that question, another question arose among them, will seeds grow better in the poop or in plain dirt. Jessica predicted dirt. And when I asked her why, she wrote, "Poop is dirty." Other kids predicted poop—they said that there might be nutrients in it that would help growth.

Teaching Worms | 77

I wondered at the time and later, did Jessica care about this question or was she just going through the motions? I often found it hard to tell. But the following day she had changed her mind to agree with the class consensus that seeds would grow better in poop. At first, when she did this, I thought she was bowing to peer pressure. I laughed, thinking it was delightful and something new, but not particularly important in terms of engaging with the topic.

Months later, as I was reviewing my notes, I saw this episode differently. I think, whether it was Jessica responding to peer pressure or whether she was actually thinking through the other children's ideas, changing her prediction was a genuine move to engage with the group in a way I had not seen before.

We decided to leave the worm bin in the classroom rather than my office, and over the next few weeks Jessica negotiated a deal with her various classroom teachers that if she finished her class work, she could spend time with the classroom worms. During these explorations, she found a worm egg, which is very hard to do as they are very small. She noticed a worm that seemed about to lay eggs. She noticed one pooping. She shared each of these sightings with the other students who would crowd excitedly around her. Jessica was finding a unique place in the class. She was interacting with and paying more attention to the other students. But still she asked no questions. Or so it seemed.

Reflection with a Friend

I contacted a friend, Dirck Roosevelt. He is now a professor, but also a former teacher deeply schooled in the work of Patricia Carini.[9] He loves to think about kids. After describing Jessica, I asked him: "Is it possible to be interested without asking a question?" He pondered and then said, "Jessica may be questioning with her fingers." Hmmm.

Puzzling Moments

After our success with the worm-apple experiment, the teaching team suggested a few other opportunities for Jessica to get up in front of the class to present her work. As I said, I tried to note those moments when I was surprised or even distressed by what happened, and later to reflect on my response and on what my students did. I call these puzzling moments and I tend to remember them, especially if I have managed to write something down. Then later when I have some time, I try to take on the perspective of my students as best I can, to see what they might have been thinking that I was not expecting or planning on. The following three puzzling events were important in my understanding of Jessica and her engagement.

Jessica's science class was studying climate change and pollution, and so I gave her an essay I had simplified for her to read about how worms clean the soil. When I began with a simple comprehension question about the article, she answered "shark"; this was a reference to something written above the article, on the same page, but not what I had, clearly I thought, asked her to read. Not a good beginning to my plan. As we went on, she seemed to be nervously pointing to spots where she thought the answer was to my questions, looking at me for support. Did she read what I gave her? Was she derailed by some terrible anxiety to be right?

In some disappointment, I continued with the article, now explaining more, asking new questions, and acting out a good deal of the content as we went through it. Finally, we wrote back and forth what you see below.

CB: What dangerous things do worms eat?

J: Heavy metal.

CB: Are there dangerous things in the worm's poop?

J: No.

CB: How can we make our soil cleaner?

J: Worm poop helps the earth clean.

CB: If there is a lot of pollution and the soil gets dirty and full of dangerous things, how can worms help?

J: The worms keep the dirty stuff inside. They clean the earth.

The final sentence contains the point of the article—that worms can keep heavy metals inside their body, thus cleaning the soil. In the final sentence

Jessica used "earth," which I did not use, and her use of the word "stuff" again felt like her own word—this made me think that this was her own thinking, that she was not parroting what I had said. The last sentence was the longest sentence she had written to me to date. And I remember also that she appeared by then much less anxious, taking turns writing with me, looking at my responses.

But to get there I had done a lot of acting out and continuing to question her. My repeated questioning resembled what I call "pulling teeth," where teachers keep at their student until they get the answer they want. I disapprove of this style of interaction. I generally asked my students much more open-ended questions, and sat back and let them explain themselves. I began to see that my practice with Jessica was different, much more one-sided than usual. I attempted to change this pattern—waiting longer for her to respond—but I was not very successful. It seemed that I very quickly would begin to worry, to feel that that she needed help and I couldn't stop myself from providing hints in the form of further questions, physical enactment, and more information.

Later Reflection

However, much later, as I again reviewed these interactions in my mind, and questioned my seeming inability to change them very much, for the first time I wondered if Jessica felt that this was a problem. I have always imagined that students did not enjoy feeling interrogated, or questioned repeatedly until the teacher receives the desired answer. Did Jessica feel that I was poking at her, interrogating her, correcting her, telling her more? I realized that she often looked fairly relaxed as my interruptions progressed. Particularly as the year continued, I realized that she maintained eye contact and waited for me to respond, refining her answer at each turn as she did above. Was she perhaps using my questions as some sort of scaffold to express herself? Maybe, although I was doing something that I did not generally believe in, I was actually helping her put her thoughts into language and perhaps to process my words as well. Truly she was not practiced in putting her thoughts out there. From this time on, I tried to remain open to the idea that my impulse to give Jessica more information, to keep on her, was not always wrong. I tried to remain very aware of how she was responding and what my feelings and intuitions were, and to keep asking, her and myself whether I was helping her or not.

More Puzzling Moments

In the case above, it was the article's idea that I wanted her to understand; however I also was steadily worrying that I wasn't seeing her own ideas. I didn't hear her thinking, responding, commenting. I modeled this kind of "thinking outloud" but she, unlike other students in my experience, remained silence. To me, it appeared that she wasn't fully engaged, although she remained intent and seemed to be learning.

The following are two more puzzling moments. In these, again my observational notes helped me to see that she had taken more initiative than I recognized at first.

The first one occurred when Jessica was presenting in front of her class. She and I had read an article about communication among worms. It claimed that when they cluster together, they often then head out in the same direction, and that this indicates they have somehow made a group decision that they are able to communicate. We had seen worms do this clustering. We planned another class presentation. Once we were up in front of the class, though, and I asked her to tell the class what we had learned about what happens when worms cluster together, she told the class they do it because they are cold. This was true, but it was old information for us—we read it a while ago, and it was not the reason presented in the article we had just read. I was distressed, afraid she had missed the point of our reading. Later, when I reminded her of what we had read, she drew a picture of a cluster, and then of a couple of worms going off together, indicating, like the article had, that they have shared a plan.

She looked at me as if to say, "see," I think.

What's up here? I asked in my field notes.

In this next example Jessica and I had prepared to present ideas of convection to the class at her science teacher's suggestion—she had asked her to do this because she felt Jessica understood convection well.

We practiced observing the interaction of hot (red food coloring) and cold (blue food coloring) water in an aquarium. She agreed to explain to the kids that hot water rises. When we presented, she was focused and organized. The kids were thrilled to watch the demonstration and to feel the water. But when I asked Jessica to explain what was happening as the (hot) red hot water rose above the (cold) blue, she said "lava." I laughed and remonstrated and then asked very specifically, what is the hot air doing. Jessica said, somewhat stiffly, "It's rising." Then she was asked to draw a diagram of what had happened and she did it very well, with hot water rising, cool water sinking. Later I wrote to her, asking why she had said lava and she wrote, "It's red." She included a small drawing of lava spreading above what is evidently an erupting volcano.

Reflection

In thinking over these two puzzling presentations, my first realization was that I had an expected format for these presentations that we did together: I would ask the initial question and Jessica was supposed to answer as we had practiced. I was invested in this—I wanted her to look smart. She had not always looked smart in her school career. But clearly, she didn't always comply. And then I would feel that somehow we had failed.

Upon reflection, it seems in the case of the cold worms, she was perhaps almost feeling the worms being cold and then huddling and warming up; a very visceral idea. Perhaps she liked the imaginative feeling of worms when they huddle in comfort. When I paid attention to that idea, I felt that too. She seems to have made that feeling the focus of what she wants to tell the other students, rather than the idea that they communicate.

In reference to convection, she was fascinated by volcanoes. She had been studying the culture of Hawaii, and in science she had been looking at the ring of fire, at volcanoes, and at tectonic plates. One day, she asked me, "How was Hawaii made?" When I asked what she meant, she reworded this as"How did the islands form?" This was the very first questions I'd heard from her—she was asking about the role of volcanoes in the formation of the island chain. The hot water in our aquarium did rise and spread out, somewhat like a volcanic eruption. I believe she was putting together her interest in volcanoes and the demonstration of convection currents.

My point in both these two examples is that she seems to have been making comments that she chose, presenting connections that she wanted to offer. I did not initially see it this way—as I said, I found them puzzling and unclear and they worried me. I think my worry, and her way of making comments, combined to make it difficult for me to recognize what she was doing, made it difficult for me to grant genuine respect to her contributions. Without my notes, I am not sure I would have realized this. This realization changed how I heard her. I became more able to give her time, and I usually remembered to come back later to ask what she meant when I didn't.

Spring

By spring, her adviser told me Jessica was now using her voice in every class. She answered questions. She talked to the kids at lunch. And the other kids talked to her. She never hit her head anymore, or picked at her T-shirt. She made eye contact a good deal of the time. That she was intelligent had become clear.

Still . . . I continued to worry that she was rough with the worms or at least quite offhand.

One day, as we were poking some worms in my office, we were able to determine which end was the front by watching how they escaped from the poking. Jessica was excited and so we rejoined the class, and again set up in the front of the room. She demonstrated and the kids were fascinated, they came up to the front to see. Then during the poking, one big worm started to bleed. We stopped and returned it to the worm bin. I felt responsible since I had given Jessica a rough implement for her poking, rather than the plastic spoon we had used earlier, which I could not find. I didn't say so but I was kicking myself for being careless.

Two days later, Jessica brought me the same worm and showed me where it had healed. She was answering the worry of a few days earlier. Was it her worry? Had she felt mine? Or both? In any case, it was a true case of empathy.

There is much more to say about our worm studies and the turtles that we subsequently studied. But let me end by pointing to another aspect of Jessica's life in school. My notes remind me that by spring, she was getting angry often. She would stomp her feet. She broke materials a few times when teachers didn't give her what she wanted. And she began truly caring for the worms, for example, breaking open an apple with her bare hands to make it easier for them to eat, an idea all her own. And finally, she began giving me worms to carry; when she did this it felt ceremonial. I received a tremendously strong vibe of kindness; she moved me almost to tears.

Conclusion

What did I learn from this child? What did I learn about thinking?

Teaching is, to me, in many ways, the process of getting behind whatever categories and preconceived notions we may have in order to

Teaching Worms | 83

see the individual child in real interaction with the world. And it is a way to gain a truly open and complex idea of what thinking can look like. The practice of close observation almost always leads to the revision of familiar ideas as we see the individual more and more clearly.

Here, in particular, I gained appreciation for how seriously to take the composed, intent stance. I don't know what it always means, but it is always worth paying attention to. I had had many experiences that suggested to me how interested children generally look, as well as how being concerned or taking initiative might appear. I also learned from this experience to see deeper into the concept of interest and to see a greater variety of ways in which students might take initiative or make comments or show interest.

I learned a great deal as well about who Jessica was and how she learned. Of course, many new questions remain and others are yet to appear. "Each child, and each of us, [is] highly particular . . . and altogether unique in our interests, our passions, our yearnings."[10]

While this is a tale of revisions, and my understandings continually acquired new forms, I need to say that I don't feel it is a tale of errors. Working to find and include Jessica's point of view was perhaps the true strength of our relationship. Observation and searching interpretation is felt by both sides. As Andrew Kaplan says,[11] "Attention is a way of participating." Observing and interpreting each other, which together leads to new understanding, are at the core of many if not all relationships. I can't prove it but I believe she felt this as much as I did. Her enormous gains were a part of this process, and in my case, as with many others in my experience, this process brought me much closer to someone unlike me, which is a gift in endless ways.

Questions for Discussion

- Do you think this sort of observation and reflection could be incorporated into your teaching day? How might you try it?

Further Reading

Ballenger, C. *Teaching Other People's Children: Literacy and Learning in a Bilingual Classroom.* New York: Teachers College Press, 1999.

84 | Ballenger

Himley, M. *Prospect's Descriptive Processes: The Child, the Art of Teaching, the Classroom and the School*. North Bennington, VT: Prospect Center, 2022.

Activity

Do a few observations on a student who puzzles you. Try to get the physical stance, the feeling, as well as the words and activity. Jot down your ideas about what you see. Then share what you have seen, without your ideas, with someone else, maybe someone who doesn't know the student. See if you see the same things. What differences are there? Jot down your ideas again.

Notes

1. P. Carini. *Jenny's Story: Taking the Long View of the Child: Prospect's Philosophy in Action* (New York: Teachers College Press), 1990.

2. John Dewey, "My Pedagogic Creed," *School Journal* LIV, no. 3 (January 6, 1897): 77–80.

3. Cynthia Ballenger, *Puzzling Moments, Teachable Moments: Practicing Teacher Research in Urban Classrooms* (New York: Teachers College Press, 2009).

4. Vivian Gussin Paley, *The Boy Who Would Be a Helicopter* (Cambridge, MA: Harvard University Press, 1990).

5. This is a pseudonym with identifying details modified to protect the child.

6. Dewey, "My Pedagogic Creed."

7. Margaret Himley et al., eds., *Prospect's Descriptive Processes: The Child, the Art of Teaching and the Classroom and School*, rev. ed. (North Bennington, VT: Prospect Center, 2002).

8. Clifford Geertz, *The Interpretation of Cultures: Selected Essays* (New York: Basic Books, 1973).

9. Patricia F. Carini, *Starting Strong: A Different Look at Children, Schools, and Standards* (New York: Teachers College Press, 2001).

10. Patricia F. Carini and Margaret Himley, *Jenny's Story: Taking the Long View of the Child: Prospect's Philosophy in Action* (New York: Teachers College Press, 2010).

11. Andy Kaplan, Editor's Introduction, *Schools: Studies in Education* vol. I (Chicago, IL: University of Chicago Press, 2022).

4

May We Be Angry?

Teaching Responsively during Times of Crisis

STEPHANIE A. BURDICK-SHEPHERD AND MICHELLE JOHNSON

In this chapter, we examine our pandemic teaching experiences as an elementary teacher (Michelle) and an elementary teacher educator (Stephanie) in the Upper Midwest. We entered into this examination as interlocutors, working and learning together as educators during the COVID-19 pandemic, through lockdown, virtual schooling, and in-person learning, from April 2020 to March 2022.

Our discussion centers on one aspect of our shared experiences, our anger. We cheekily ask in our title permission to share this anger, but we implore our readers to consider what follows as a testimony of our experience—a serious examination that includes learning to name and give voice to an aspect of educational life we often find ignored. We also recognize that this experience centers on Michelle's elementary teaching experience because one purpose of this shared testimony is to consider the systemic power dynamics between the university academic and the practicing teacher. We have intentionally limited our citations in the following to only those core texts that helped us to frame our response. We did so to center the voice of practice. The voice of the practitioner is woefully underrepresented in academic writing, and we felt one component of this project was to magnify this aspect of education systems. Myisha Cherry's *The Case for Rage: Why Anger Is Essential to Anti-Racist Struggle,* grounded our theoretical exploration so that we could focus more on our experience and reflection on our experience of rage.

Questioning Rage

We—Stephanie and Michelle—connected during the initial phase of state and school lockdown to wonder (and worry) about the effects of the pandemic on young children. We were aware that this would be a crisis that would affect education, but we were less prepared for how much of a crisis this would be for ourselves professionally and personally. We quickly found ourselves not only physically locked down, but also locked away from our own beliefs and values about what children (and all people) need from their teachers and their educational institutions. We often would text messages to one another such as those below, checking in to see how yet another day of pandemic teaching had gone.

> (Michelle) "I'm so emotional today. I can't even. I can't stop crying. I have a student who is sick and can't find a way to get tested. . . ."
>
> (Stephanie) "I just finished parenting and schooling at home for 5 days. I am undone today."[1]

We danced around our frustration in these texts, sending Graphics Interchange Formats (GIFs) and virtual "hugs." But we always circled back at some point to how "stuck" and "frustrated" we felt in our educational institutions. Not only were we physically stuck at home, isolated from our normal routines and interactions, but we were also stuck and held fast by institutional norms and expectations.

During one long phone call, I (Stephanie) was counseling Michelle about an important meeting she had with a colleague. I remember telling Michelle to "take the long road," to go into the meeting not with anger but with data and cool rationality. Later, I reflected on this advice. Why were we not allowed to be frustrated in our meetings with colleagues? Why were people so afraid of educator anger in the face of this crisis? Are there ways in which the expression of full-on rage at injustice is not only emotionally appropriate but also an ethically valid response to the injustices of schooling and care?

Myisha Cherry's book long articulation of this question helps us recognize that women, especially Black women, are not allowed to be angry. Cherry problematizes the canon of moral theory on anger in philosophy, which always shows anger, *any* kind of anger, to be morally problematic. In Western intellectual and social spaces, anger is considered a vice, something that can never be thought of as just or virtuous. Though Cherry considers many points of view from Western philosophy, she most often interrogates Martha Nussbaum's 2016 critique of anger, *Anger and Forgiveness*. Nussbaum essentially argues that though there is a human tendency to act in anger and though this anger may have some (limited) instrumental purposes in human life, humankind now seems to be in a place where the more rational response is both possible and more positive. Nussbaum's point seems to be that humans have progressed so much in our history that we no longer need anger but should cultivate other emotions such as love to support further moral progress.

Interestingly, both Cherry and Nussbaum use the figure of Martin Luther King Jr. (MLK) as an exemplar of their reading of anger. But Cherry disagrees with Nussbaum's portrayal of MLK and other figures. She sees in MLK anger that is not morally problematic but instead something that is rich and worth holding on to. Cherry is suspicious of those like Nussbaum who see anger as a single, negative emotion, instead of a multifaceted one. Just as there are multiple types of love, so Cherry argues, there are multiple forms of anger. And one form of anger can be, in fact, morally just.

Cherry argues that if we spend some time defining types of anger instead of simply calling all rage "the same," we will find that there is one type of anger that is neither limited nor limiting and instead enacts possibility. Of this anger she writes: "Anger plays the role of expressing the value of people of color and racial justice; it provides the eagerness, optimism, and self-belief needed to fight against persistent and powerful racist people and systems; and it allows the outraged to break certain racial rules as a form of intrinsic and extrinsic resistance."[2] Cherry calls this "Lordean rage" giving credit to Audre Lorde's poetry and theory, which unlocks anger from an always "bad" emotion and leads to an emotional key that opens possibilities, particularly in the service of enacting radical racial justice in an imperfect world. As she describes, Lordean rage is the anger you feel when you recognize that "I am not free while any other is unfree. Lordean rage is aimed at change, the perspective is inclusive, and your response is justified to do the work, in that rage of this kind is appropriate to effect change. You use this rage to channel effective energy

88 | Burdick-Shepherd and Johnson

and it is focused and precise."[3] To be clear, we both walk through the world as white, middle-class, women and we wish to use Cherry's work to inform our work as allies for racial justice. We do not wish to use Cherry's concept of racially just anger as an appropriation for further scolding from the sidelines. As scholars and as practitioners we recognize that Cherry's work is primarily directed to unearthing the rightful anger that has been unjustly denied to Black women. Still, as Cherry points out, white allies can be (and must be) justly enraged at injustice. We believe that Cherry helps articulate an intersection of the denial of anger in regard to both gender and race, and we are grateful that Cherry's work recognizes the complications of this intersection.

We find that many elementary teachers in the US, who are primarily women, both white and Black, have had their rage around injustice silenced. These teachers have been painted as meek women in apple-printed jumpers running around with glue paste, cheerfully hugging children, and calling all the "kiddos" to the snack table. And while we hold nothing against apple-printed jumpers, we resist this burdensome stereotype that elementary school teachers (and those who teach them) are (and are told to be) passive women without a voice, an opinion, or the option to get angry at the injustices of the world.

We point out that if we hold our assumption true, that schools are contact zones where negotiations of justice and inclusiveness are always being fought and negotiated, then we doubt that the women (mostly) who work in those hallways and classrooms are unable to engage in the difficult conversations that must be had. We should also point out that Black women teachers have been especially silenced and marginalized in US schools as much of the injustice in the k–12 and higher education has been perpetuated against Black people. We want to question the view that anger in these contact zones is morally problematic. Although we denied ourselves many moments of public rage, our private rage boiled at the injustices of schooling and care against young children, their parents, and their teachers. We wish to interrogate what might be morally permissible and lauded in terms of our anger. And if, in fact, we should have raged publicly.

Raging

What distinguishes Lordean rage from other forms of anger is its drive for change, "[This] anger motivates us to fight against injustice."[4] The injustice, in our case, is the same as that discussed by Paulo Freire[5] and bell hooks[6]—the injustice that education distinctly *prevents* our society from cultivating agents of change. It is the job of the Lordean educator to use rage as fuel to help our students become critical thinkers in this society, a society that often fears this kind of thinking and often values submission. We see our work as educators is creating classrooms that transgress against the common narrative. Part of this work is recognizing that in some ways, our feelings of rage toward the events around us are appropriate. As Cherry helps us see, anger can motivate and sustain change toward justice.

The change I (Michelle), was driven to make stemmed from my inability to create space for students to truly be heard and seen within the virtual school format. Academics were a top priority, of course, but I couldn't help but feel academics were not my students' primary need. When I focused on determining what this primary need may be, I began to ask even more questions. How could I meet my students' needs when much of our instructional time was predetermined and highly structured? What power did I have to offer lessons and opportunities that meet these needs when other requirements were so over encompassing?

Frustration rose as I (Michelle) realized that to support my students in a multidimensional, whole-child framework, I would have to decide which expectations to break and which to uphold. How could I balance rigid curriculum expectations with making time to ensure my students knew they were valued as people with unique ideas, cultures, and insights? When all my time was dedicated to academic tasks, how could I begin to foster a sense of community and belonging across a computer screen? It is rage at this seemingly unfixable dichotomy that drove (and drives) me to answer these questions. It also planted a seed of hope that my changes could improve my students' ability to learn and grow throughout the pandemic. Yet, as I fretted over the impossibility of my schedule, I was forced to acknowledge how deserving my rage was, for this was a problem unfixable by me alone (and not limited to the COVID-19 pandemic).

Playing with Rage

Eventually, I (Michelle) concluded a few things: (1) my students needed authenticity, (2) my students needed community, and (3) my students needed freedom. I could not offer each of these in virtual math or reading lessons, in one-on-one Google Meets, or in Morning Meetings. Authentic learning, wonder, and creation would not occur in math class if my kids did not have manipulatives, even if I put their names in the word problems. The community wouldn't blossom in a Google Meet of twenty-nine second graders even if I managed to hear from half of them in a Morning Meeting. And freedom. Well, freedom was the most difficult to cultivate and the most common, as teachers were not free to follow the learning path students found most fruitful, but students were often free to choose if the school was worth attending that day or not. How could I nurture these three needs in a virtual classroom with scattered attendance, minimal tools, and twenty-nine unique homes and families?

I started with Wednesdays. Instead of discussing a social studies video that I could not ensure every student watched, we built things. Students were tasked with creating something from whatever tools they could find and sharing it with their classmates in a class meeting. In the afternoon we would meet again for a blend of philosophical thinking exercises and communal play, adding to and changing what we created that morning. Stephanie and I partnered together to bring her college students into this afternoon meeting to model and extend our conversations. We were building community. Learning together. Practicing freedom. Together on a screen, alone in our respective bedrooms or offices, connecting.

These Wednesdays were as much for the students as they were for me. Each week I (Michelle) found myself battling an ever-increasing frustration, a *rage*, toward the education system. I knew what my students needed—I knew what *I* needed—and it was not creating five-minute lesson videos to be followed by a worksheet. We needed each other, our community. These young minds needed to see that humans share this world, one person's pain is the pain of another—that "we are not free until we all are free," as Cherry says (2021, 93). I broke the rules when I planned our Wednesday meetings, I aligned them with no standard and gave no assessments. Yet I considered it, and still do, the most valuable class I taught throughout the week, because our learning objective was *seeing* each other.

But how far can a single educator go in this battle? Or in our case, how much change can a pair of educators, a schoolteacher, and a professor, create in reality? Stephanie and I had to carefully choose our battles. While we successfully implemented *Wednesday Build It* and discussion meetings, there were other moments just as powerful that had to pass by. I remember when February 2021 rolled around, and my second-grade teaching team created Black History Month–themed reading and writing tasks. Our lesson planning was highly delegated, so only one of our teammates was tasked with creating these lessons. Inevitably, the lessons fell flat and lifeless—without collaboration, proper time, and knowledge, it is hard to have expected anything else. Yet, the consequences of these lessons were tangible. Seeing misunderstanding and distress in one of my Black students, I was forced to address the flaws through an entirely inappropriate medium—email. Email to a second grader. It was fundamentally flawed, but I could not guarantee I would see them in class or, if I did, that I would have enough time alone with them to properly address the situation. And I needed to do *something*.

Eventually, I did get the chance to talk with them about it. Over video call, I chatted with a child dismaying over those who looked like them, explicitly wishing to be someone different. Completely limited to verbal responses, I gave words of encouragement ("You are perfect the way you are." "You can do *anything* you set your mind to.") while my heart broke. A dreadful awareness that I was not enough screamed at me. I am not just a single teacher trying to help a child, through a computer screen, grapple with the challenges of life. I am a white woman trying to help a Black child grapple with the complexities of being a Black student in America, and they are responding to thoughts triggered by lessons I allowed them to engage with. I texted Stephanie that day.

> "My heart hurts knowing that this is the whispering voice in this child's head, and it makes me doubly motivated to make sure the books I share in my class will show a more diverse life perspective."[7]

Looking back, I see the desperation I felt to *do* something about this. A fire burning within me, raging to just *fix it*, roaring with the knowledge that I could not. The best I could come up with was the thing I have the most control over—books. But books will not help students make sense of this world if most teachers are not prepared to have and engage with these conversations. Books will not fix the damage already done by centuries of racism. Books will not change the suffocating and violating system of racism that Black students and teachers live and work within every day. My heart broke, not from sadness but from anger. I was witness to and participatory in racial injustice. I lacked an appropriate educational response as a teacher and human. As Cherry helped me realize my feeling was rage and this rage was not only appropriate it was a way for me to

(1) name the injustice and (2) learn from and make change in my classroom spaces. Rage can be powerful, and I was learning to cultivate it in these moments rather than squash it down or allow it to turn to despair.

Rage can inspire powerful motivation. In Cherry's words, "anger motivates to fight against injustice. . . . Lordean rage, with its eagerness to approach its target and reach its goal, provides this fuel.[8]" I am grateful that this is the case, for without the rage I experienced toward the education system and my own inadequacies to make the actual systemic change during the height of the pandemic, I would never have found the motivation necessary to make the changes I did. Like many other teachers, I spent each day alone in a room with a persistent blue light headache, desperately trying to connect (on personal and technical levels) with tiny humans I had never actually met. A portion of my students arrived on time, even fewer a tad early, with a tidy and quiet learning space from which they could tackle the new day. Another portion joined while plopped on their couches in front of the television, Xbox controller in hand, chips in their mouth, and an unmuted microphone streaming in chatter from other family members in the room. Everyone else fell in between. Still, I knew that even those kids boiling ramen on the stove behind them during their lessons were doing their best. What else could we expect, anyway? The school was in their home. Home now came to school. We educators had the opportunity to see students in a new and personal way. But that required our virtual space to be safe, welcoming, patient, and responsive—extra responsive. My rage was never toward my students or their situations, but to the system that put them there. This distinction allowed me to use my rage as fuel to change that which I could, in order to make the learning experience better for my students.

Rage as an Act of Hope

My (Michelle) experience has been mirrored in many ways by our national story. Right now, communities around the country are limiting what students can read, what history they can learn, and how justice and injustice can be taught. We have seen politicians propose requirements for educators to publish a year's worth of lesson plans to be vetted by parents. Politicians and parents are fighting viciously against critical race theory (CRT) under the false presupposition that CRT teaches white students to be ashamed of their whiteness.[9] They claim American history, full of blatant racism and oppression, is too harsh for white students to learn about and should therefore be removed from classrooms. And their voices are *loud*. They are loud enough that districts, politicians, and teachers are listening to them, or at least, reluctant to counter their narrative. In the same way that rage was an appropriate response to my personal experiences, so is rage an appropriate response to this. In fact, it may be one of the best responses, due to the power of rage to motivate us into change-making action.

I was not alone in how my pedagogy directly contradicted the way schools around the country reacted to the pandemic. Educators shared similar experiences of being expected to create a traditionally full days' worth of instructional content. K–12 educators were expected to digitize each of their lessons but were not given extra prep time to do it. We quickly found this was next to impossible. For example, in a typical classroom, a discussion prompt just needs to be written on the board, but to put it online, one must create an assignment in our learning management software, type and format the question so preliterate students could "read" it (shout out to emojis!), move the file to an easily accessible folder with the same pattern as the assignments before it, and of course, not forget to publish it or the kids would never see it anyway. This is ignoring the time it took to teach students how to find said assignments, open them, respond to them, submit them, and see what other students said. In the virtual format, everything became exponentially harder. Discussions were no longer fun opportunities to learn social routines, explore learning, and make friends. They were a chore, a disconnected and stark negative of a traditional conversation. In some ways, that is what the entire virtual school experience was—a negative image of a responsive classroom. I took it as my responsibility to find ways to add a touch of color, a splash of emotion, and humanity, so the students had a respite from the otherwise suffocating experience.

My frustration at the futility of digitizing schools motivated me to develop other ways to build our classroom community. My change was to do away with pretending that our computers were portals into classrooms, where kids must follow school rules and ignore their home world existing behind them. Instead, we incorporated home into school. I invited students to find their building tools at home. I encouraged them to use things like recyclables, toys, pillows, and things that would otherwise be considered garbage—*anything* they had at home. Suddenly, the home was not just a background to blur, but a playground of creativity waiting for little innovators to explore.

Throughout the year, I witnessed some delightful creations. One student made a unicorn out of cereal boxes and oatmeal containers. This spawned an animated discussion about the characteristics of true unicorns and what differentiated them from other mythical creatures. Another few students made carlike structures moved by wind power. Others used toilet paper rolls to make a family of dolls with interchangeable outfits. Once the pattern of Wednesday Build It solidified, parents began building with their children. One family constructed a life-sized marble run out of a giant cardboard box and wood pieces. Another father-son duo constructed a car out of Legos. And after each child finished creating, they were so excited to share the product with their peers. They made videos acting out scenes while using their creativity and shared live during Morning Meetings. I never had a lack of volunteers to share on Wednesdays!

These meetings brought me hope. I hoped students would find ways to make friends with each other through the computer screen, find a love of learning through play, and build a sense of pride in their abilities to learn and grow. I watched as my shy group of girls slowly began to play together without needing me to guide them until I could eventually check in on them in a breakout room and be met with loud squeals and delighted giggles. I watched students who struggled in the virtual environment bond with others who were "good at school" because they were not required to abide by strict behavior expectations. Weekly playtime allowed this group of twenty-nine second graders to become something of a learning community.

Nevertheless, while I try to focus on the hope I found last year, I keep rounding back to anger. Of course, not all my students were able to engage with these lessons. Many wrote that they could not complete the "build" because their parents did not want them to make a mess or would not let them go outside. Others simply never went online to find the lesson and were upset when they came to the meeting without anything to share. Still, others just chose not to do it, for no reason other than they did not want to. All of this was expected—after all, this task was optional, not standards-based, and my creation was an experiment. I could not stand next to a resistant student and offer them the strength to give any task a try. I needed parents to trust that the tasks I gave were beneficial to their child's emotional and intellectual well-being, to remind them of their activities, and assist them in attending meetings. And we were all stretched so thin, expecting that from any number of families was optimistic at best, impossible at worst. These difficulties frustrated me immensely, but I was careful to focus my frustration at the source of the problem. Parent and/or student disconnect, tardy or absent students, and incomplete assignments are all frustrating, but these are symptoms of a bigger problem, not the problem itself. The true problem is that our schools and communities are not strong enough to support *all* our children, especially during a global pandemic. This of course is Cherry's main argument. The anger I must watch out for and contain is the anger of vengeance and despair; the rage I can healthily foster is focused on social change. Lordean anger keeps me hopeful because it reminds me that change is needed, and change is possible.[10]

My rage motivated me to try new strategies, to write this chapter, and to use my voice to push our community toward change. Without this intertwining of rage and hope, I would not have had enough emotional bandwidth to create these Wednesday Build-It lessons. Rage made room for hope to blossom, it helped our discombobulated group become something reminiscent of a community. But the source of our rage, the injustices students face from those who are expected to protect them, never went away. In fact, throughout the pandemic, we saw *more* reasons to feel rage at the system than reasons to feel hope. And so, as the virtual school year ended and I turned off my camera for the last time, I walked away with a powerful awareness of my limitations and a daunting view of the path ahead of us.

Raging into the Future

Whether we want to frame this time in which we now write, in 2022, as coming out of the pandemic, late-stage pandemic, or for those optimists in the room, postpandemic, we find ourselves still in crisis, still trying to figure this world out as teachers and learners and friends.

We are still in crisis.

Michelle and I (Stephanie) took the stance of closing our doors and "just" teaching in fall of 2021. We recognized the faulty connections of broken institutional practices and saw some power in being able to welcome students back into our classrooms with some new tech tools and a better understanding of what we needed and wanted to do as teachers. I knew that I needed to teach from a place of hope without giving away my rage, a hope that realizes there is no perfection, only the movement forward, of doing the work. But I still feel incredibly broken, fragile in a way that I know I do not wish to face fully. Just as an example, I could not remember entire episodes of teaching with Michelle last year as we sat down to write this. She told me it was a trauma response. Swallowing rage for two years is traumatic, grappling with your complicity in a system that continues to foster injustice does this to you as well.[11] Rage and hope are powerful and motivating, but the path we are on is a long one with endless obstacles littering the way.

Some will say that most of what Michelle and I went through is simply because we were forced to teach through virtual means. If we were to have opened schools and taught "normally" we would not be asking questions about how to hold on to both rage and hope at the same time. But resist this sentiment as too easy a claim. For though virtual learning was awful and went on for far too long, we think some virtual learning was probably necessary and that almost every child experienced a disruption in consistent schooling, regardless of mode of transfer. Fundamentally, virtual learning and disruptions to learning occurred because we were already grappling with a crisis of injustice of race and class in our educational systems for far too long.[12] We do not have a health-care system that makes folks healthy, we don't have an education system that provides ample resources, and we do not have a justice system that makes all people feel safe. What we do have is an economic and political system that disenfranchises many. In short, our system was not prepared for this global crisis on top of the always-constant crisis of inequality in our schools and nation. Our societal response to the pandemic was to digitize "what we've always done" so we could "just get through," when we could have taken it as an opportunity to address our nation's underlying inadequacies and inequalities.

Our experiences during the pandemic showed us that there was an overwhelming emphasis on presenting learning to children without seeing their complex variety as humans. Schools tried to universally present skills and content to young humans and in their attempt to provide something (the same thing) to everyone (at the same time) it denied the very humanness necessary to learning. Children (and undergraduates alike) simply cannot help but slip their humanness through. They resist attempts to flatten and erase the individual. We find that the best way to honor their resistance, in any space, in any mode, is through creativity, play, asking questions, being critical, and yes, even getting angry. These are the things that increase human connections, relationships, and growth. Even, and especially, when it is uncomfortable.

We are not sure that the pandemic or our experience gives us answers for how to achieve resistance to such flat pedagogy, but we may have learned to ask for more time to pursue questions in k–12+ that get us closer to what we hope learning spaces can be. And one thing that we have learned is that inquiring with anger, with others, is its own kind of positive response. A justified rage is a form of hope, for it means that you believe that there can be another way of being.

Teaching during a global pandemic taught us many lessons. For me (Michelle) the rage I felt then continues to motivate me, and the hope I feel for the future these children can create is stronger than ever. I have been able to push students to consider our world's inequities, oppression, and trauma from their perspective. I am currently (spring of 2022) guiding my students through a writing project comparing their choice of two books that discuss different forms of oppression and resistance in our world's history. I get surprised comments such as "This is interesting!" during discussions about power, freedom, equality, and human rights. Students request to stay "just a little longer" so they can finish the discussion or text before leaving for the next part of the day, and the whole class frequently exclaims "*No!*" at the prospect of pausing a discussion so we can attend to other aspects of learning. Lordean rage reminds me of the *necessity* of these conversations. I spent this year trying numerous strategies that have resulted in the community of learners we now embody. I am beginning to see the fruits of my efforts as students are taking on these issues for themselves. They are not regurgitating truths that I taught them, because it is not my job to give them truths. They are instead grappling with big issues and finding that they can construct understanding and opinions about them. When learning is about what it means to be human, students are suddenly eager to learn all they can.

Thus, "may we be angry?" is no longer our request for permission, but rather a powerful incantation: may we be angry. May our anger burn clear the road to our collective change.

Questions for Discussion

- We find that k–12 teachers are often permitted (or at least not reprimanded) to be angry in one instance and this is when their classes misbehave. In fact, many novice teachers are often coached to become more severe in their reprimands.

It is not unusual for a teacher to yell at a group of children to "be quiet" or to angrily retort something when the class clown once again "goofs" up. Research shows that children of color and children enrolled in special education are often violently harmed by teachers and administrators. Anger then is permissible in schooling but only that anger directed toward children who are derided as "out of control"? Why is this the case? Does this seem at odds with the purpose of education and the articulation of anger in society?

- Should children be educated about types of anger and how to manage being "angry" in different ways? Is there a way in which naming the emotion of anger (a common practice in Social Emotional Learning (SEL) curriculums in pre-kindergarten) can be expanded to encompass deep learning about the different kinds of anger Cherry describes and then ways that different kinds of anger require different forms of individual and collective work in terms of control and use?

Further Reading/Listening

Cherry, Myisha V. *The Case for Rage: Why Anger Is Essential to Anti-Racist Struggle* (New York: Oxford University Press, 2021).

Cherry, Myisha. "Anger Is Not a Bad Word." TED Talks. May 21, 2015. (17.45), https://www.youtube.com/watch?v=uysTk2EIotw.

Activity

- Loose-parts play can look out of place in many classrooms for those over age five, but we encourage anyone reading this who works in any age classroom to make time for loose-parts play with their students. You may choose to do it once a month or once week or once a day. But choose a regular time to try it out. There are many social media groups that put out ideas for multiple ages and grade levels. In our classrooms, our favorite items are cardboard boxes, pipe cleaners, popsicle sticks, and toilet paper tubes. We also use old socks, buttons, paper plates, and Styrofoam balls! One day we had students walk around outside and create "self-images" using only natural found objects such as dried leaves, sticks, stones, and moss. After providing your students with some "loose parts" such as these, provide them a challenge or question such as: Can you make a face? Can you make something that floats? Can you make a toy? As your students regularly begin to play with loose parts on a regular basis consider what aspects of your classroom are changing? Are your students working more cooperatively together? Do you notice different kinds of students leading activities? Is a student particularly "good" at loose-parts play who doesn't typically perform school well? As a challenge for yourself, can you construct something that "breaks" a barrier down in your classroom, the community, or your school? What was it? Why did it work? Was it difficult to create it? Do you think the time spent on loose-parts play helped you be more creative or see barriers in your school or classroom differently?

- Listen to Myisha Cherry in her TEDx Talk, "Anger Is Not a Bad Word"| TEDxUofIChicago, https://www.youtube.com/watch?v=uysTk2EIotw. As you listen, consider what it means to be "angry." What do you feel like when you are angry? Where (in your body) do you feel anger? How do you know that you are angry? Consider, as you do so, whether or not you also feel different kinds of anger and how you might be able to note the differences between one kind of anger and another. After listening and thinking about what anger feels like, take the next week to trace your own angry moments for a week. Take time at the end of each day to name and consider the kind of anger you are experiencing. When do you feel angry? Are there patterns in your anger? Are there events that often "make" you angry? Do you wonder why you are or are not angry at certain times? At the end of the week reflect on what happens to anger when we name it within our professional life. Consider how what you named may call for a response of anger (or something else).

Notes

1. S. Burdick-Shepherd and M. Johnson (authors), personal text, September 2020.
2. Myisha V. Cherry, *The Case for Rage: Why Anger Is Essential to Anti-Racist Struggle* (New York: Oxford University Press, 2021), 6.
3. Cherry, *The Case for Rage*, 23–36.
4. Cherry, *The Case for Rage*, 65.
5. Paulo Freire, *Pedagogy of the Oppressed*, 30th anniversary ed. (New York: Continuum, 2000).
6. bell hooks, *Teaching to Transgress: Education as the Practice of Freedom* (New York: Routledge, 1994).
7. M. Johnson (author), personal text, February 2021.
8. Cherry, *The Case for Rage*, 65–69.
9. Gabriel, T. and Goldstein D. "Disputing Racism's Reach Republicans Rattle American Schools." June 1, 2021. https://www.nytimes.com/2021/06/01/us/politics/critical-race-theory.html.
10. Cherry, *The Case for Rage*, 65–69.
11. Cherry, *The Case for Rage*, 65–69.
12. Jonathan Kozol, *Savage Inequalities: Children in America's Schools* (New York: Crown Pub., 1991).

5

"No one wants to do that shit; no one wants to be in a contact zone"

On the Goals and Struggles of "Contact Zone Pedagogy"

Tomas de Rezende Rocha, Jamila H. Silver, and Emily S. L. Silver

When literature and linguistics professor Mary Louise Pratt introduced the term *contact zones* in her 1990 address to the Responsibilities for Literacy Conference, she emphasized that these spaces—where "cultures meet, clash, and grapple with each other, often in contexts of highly asymmetrical relations of power"—are *social* spaces.[1] The scene evoked here, with the emphasis on "social," is one of flesh-and-blood persons, shaped by language and culture, coming into proximity (and then contact) with one another. When Pratt brings up artifacts as one type of contact zone, then, she is careful to emphasize the indispensably social phase or process of artifact-creation. It is not the lifeless artifact or object alone that qualifies it as a contact zone. It is the background set of social dynamics, the context of a physical object manifested in it—titanic, world-historical power differentials crystallized in tangible things. The sixteenth-century Quechua nobleman Guamán Poma's bilingual, bicultural chronicle, for example: a crystal of the Spanish conquest of the Americas. *Testimonios*, to take another example of a contact zone offered by Pratt, count as such because (perhaps only because) autoethnographic representation of the superexploited and extremely dispossessed often involves "concrete collaborations between people, as between literate ex-slaves and abolitionist intellectuals."[2] The social dimension of contact zone creation is highlighted once again.

Now, what spirit governs the social dynamics of, or within, a contact zone? Generally speaking, the "rules" of contact zones, at least in Pratt's telling, evoke something characteristically messy: *not* the orderly and utopian ideal speech situation (to borrow from Habermas), but rather a set of ambivalent and disorderly (chaotic, even) processes.[3] Pratt laments, for example, the absence of an open seat at the table for "unsolicited oppositional discourse, paradox, resistance, [and] critique" in the imagined community of her son's classroom.[4] Pratt faults the classroom teacher for failing to recognize or appreciate the subversive nature of Pratt's son's *transculturation*: he is genuinely engaging with the material of the teacher's dominant (adult) culture, but in a contestatory, parodic manner. These observations of classroom life lead Pratt to reflect on the inevitable costs and rewards of teaching in, from, or for the contact zone: we might get the exhilarating wonder, revelation, mutual understanding, and new wisdom afford by cross-cultural engagement, but often alongside moments of discomfort, rage, incomprehension, and pain. To what extent should we welcome the latter experiences in the hope of cultivating the former?

When discussing Pratt's essay, we tried to identify the presence of these experiences—wonder, understanding, rage, pain—in our own classroom and work-place pedagogy. On the one hand, we understood exactly what Pratt meant when she suggested that "contact zone pedagogy" (if we may coin a term) was the hardest and most exciting teaching she had ever done. We all underwent such experiences during our formal educations; since then, we have also witnessed them in our students and colleagues. On the other hand, we lamented the *absence* of these experiences in most of our everyday teaching and work. Contact zone pedagogy is predicated on difficult exchanges among persons who wield (or will likely learn to wield) different degrees of social power in accordance with a given social position. The baseline unfairness involved, paired with social niceties around aversion to conflict, can make such exchanges appear unpleasant. To quote one of the present authors during a study session: "no one wants to do that shit; no one wants to be in a contact zone." At the same time, the fact that a pedagogical activity can be unpleasant—an emotionally taxing lesson, exercise, or conversation—does not therefore make it undesirable or unimportant.

"No one wants to do that shit; no one wants to be in a contact zone" | 103

If contact zone pedagogy is valuable, then it is arguably worth an attempt to learn from moments of failure or of coming up short. Our essay explores the "contact*less*" zones of our educational spaces. How is contact *avoided* in spaces that could serve as opportunities for the kind of educational experiences Pratt is pointing to? How are the conditions for potentially constructive contact zones undermined? In other words, where does it go wrong? Our conversations and study sessions in preparation for this collaborative writing revealed at least two core, interrelated themes related to contact*less* zones: failures of trust and failures of curiosity—and perhaps thereby failures to overcome fear—in socially diverse classrooms and workplaces. Rather than acting as a manual on how to make contact, our essay will offer pedagogical considerations and educator reflection on contactless zones in the form of two philosophical vignettes, one each from Emily and Jamila. By blending personal reflection and social inquiry, we hope to offer a cautionary rendering of how contact zone pedagogy is sabotaged.

Emily on Avoidance within K–12 Contact Zones

I work as a social and emotional learning specialist at a grades six through twelve private school in a diverse city. Walking out of a cocurricular discussion group at my school one day, a student leader reflected: "Well, that conversation didn't go far. Nobody said what was really on their mind. Nobody wants to talk." Many schools aim to foster community conversations, difficult conversations, or some other variation on the theme of vulnerable dialogue, particularly among upper schoolers. These discussions, often student-led, aim to hold space outside of the academic curriculum to discuss "controversial" topics like leadership, political correctness, diversity, and more. The framing is often to practice "having hard discussions" about the "real world," a prelude to building a strong community later on. The student leader, frustrated and resigned, felt that students would not share beyond what they felt was the "right" answer, basically reiterating (in more school-appropriate language) our chapter's title.

There are a few reasons why students might not express themselves authentically: fear of saying "the wrong thing" and causing harm or being criticized; fear of facing requests for clarification they cannot answer and appearing uninformed or "stupid"; a more general lack of intellectual curiosity (itself arising from multiple possible causes); and a generalized feeling of exhaustion (especially in the upper–school years) that prevents students from taking any risks or exerting themselves beyond whatever is most useful for college admissions. The abolitionist educator Bettina Love reminds us that "schools reflect our political economy."[5] An economy that requires and perpetuates scarcity and precarity will manifest these ills in the school. The colonial-capitalist history of our country and the resultant political economy of our school systems have turned many classrooms into contact zones. In them, a desire for racially informed conversation and reconciliation rubs up against the miseducative effects of a political economy geared for the avoidance of genuine contact.[6]

A fear of failure is not a new phenomenon, though the stakes and context of this fear can change. Middle school teacher and author Kathy Greeley poses a question directly related to my observations: "What makes it difficult for teachers and students to take risks?" Her answer mirrors some of my own experiences: "Rather than being institutions that encourage risk-taking, learning from mistakes, and experimentation, schools have played a major role in inculcating that constant fear of failure [. . .] Even in schools that want to encourage inquiry and creative thinking, the culture of correctness can be difficult to overcome."[7] Indeed, the "culture of correctness"—fueled by the pressures of college admissions and politically correct evasiveness around power, status, class, and identity—can become a path of least resistance for students and educators who feel burdened with task completion and performance at the expense of democratic process and community building. Although a cocurricular space *could* be a zone of risk taking without the pressure of high-stakes evaluation, students ration their energies for spaces that "count" toward a more certain payoff. Love calls this the "educational survival complex, in which students are left learning to merely survive, learning how schools mimic the world they live in, thus making schools a training site for a life of exhaustion."[8] By perpetuating a dichotomy of curricular and cocurricular—one a space that matters deeply and one that, until recently, was (and sometimes still is) called "extra" (as in, "extracurricular")—we fragment students' possibilities for wholeness.

It is hard to take risks merely "for the sake of it" when students do not feel a sense of belonging in their communities, defined both by inclusion *in* and responsibility *toward* a group. Dena Simmons, the antiracist educator and founder of LiberatED, articulates the point like this in an interview with Loyola University Chicago:

> We cannot thrive without belonging. If only some people can belong and others cannot, then we have decided we are okay with inequity and we're deciding that it's okay that some children are not given as much belonging, and that some children go to school where they don't feel safe. We can't do anything, we can't take risks, we can't breathe freely without feeling like we belong. So if we really truly believe that all children should succeed, all children should thrive, then we have to start with belonging. Without it there's really little room for what we need in order to learn, which is to take risks, to ask questions, to challenge authority, to be creative.[9]

While Simmons is focusing on the experience of Black and brown students in American schools, the current manifestation of our ongoing culture war fuels a sense of fear and merely conditional belonging in students of *all* identities. Although a white student's fear of experiencing shame after saying something offensive is not equal to the apprehension that students of color might have toward racist micro- and macroaggression, a sense of threat will nonetheless pervade and hamper education without the proper support to work through emotions. Emphasizing student "safety" is generally considered reasonable when the goal is avoiding something as physically destructive as a school shooting. Yet what competent educator can deny that a baseline feeling of comfort (and, yes, safety) is required to adequately meet students' emotional, intellectual, and spiritual needs? No educator, and no education system, can guarantee absolute safety across any of these domains—an obvious observation that distracts from the main point: that security is a condition of trust and belonging, and trust and belonging a condition for the kind of intellectual risk-taking educators may rightly encourage in students. How might we structure our communities to pursue security, trust, and belonging, not just in rhetoric but in practice? How can we render contact zones as *desirable* (even if not always pleasant) spaces of struggle toward deeper learning, connecting, and healing? And to explore the point in a more suspicious register: Who ultimately gains power, comfort, or wealth from contactless zones?[10]

With security in place, students then must be ushered into a life of mattering, a civic project that roots Love's abolitionist teaching and wherein students "matter to ourselves, our community, our family, and our country."[11] This concept of mattering of course evokes the demand that

Black lives matter and pushes beyond rhetoric to think about the context and impact of what it means, where "mattering is civics because it is the quest for humanity."[12] When students of all identities understand that their voices and experiences matter intrinsically and especially to their school communities, they will feel ownership to hold themselves and their spaces with dignity and depth. "True ownership of that knowledge comes when students are given the opportunity to give voice to their own learning,"[13] and it needs to be modeled in all parts of a school community. The late Brazilian educator and philosopher Paulo Freire wrote, "Dialogue cannot exist, however, in the absence of a profound love for the world and for people [. . .] love is at the same time the foundation of dialogue and dialogue itself [. . .] love is commitment to others."[14] His foundational text invites us to see contact zones as zones of mattering and love, despite the highly asymmetrical power differentials that define them, and where we may nonetheless do good work toward healthy social connections and liberatory social systems. May we walk out of contact zones buoyed by gratitude and love, and bravely into future contact zones, dialectically moving toward deeper learning and deeper justice that over time undermines the creation of contact zones altogether.

Jamila on Policies that Eliminate Contact Zones for White Students

In this chapter's introduction, Tomas recounts the negative educational experience of Pratt's son, whose teacher failed to recognize the value of the transgressive, transcultural approach of his own learning. Whereas Pratt's son's classroom was *accidentally* turned into a contactless zone, a flurry of recent legislation in multiple states seeks to *intentionally* create zones of minimal contact. Legislation introduced in 2022 in the Florida Senate, for example, sought to limit the potential of contact zones for white students within schools. Florida Senate Bill 148 (SB 148), also known as the "Individual Freedom" bill, was an attempt to prohibit institutions of any kind from promoting a belief to the members of its institution, including workplaces and schools. The bill suggested that teaching a student something that they "do not believe" is not only problematic but also should be illegal.

SB 148, as reported by NPR, sought to prohibit educational lessons or training that cause people to feel "discomfort, guilt or anguish on account of their race."[15] It didn't name white people, but Florida Governor Ron DeSantis, who was for a while a major contender for the 2024 presidential race, claimed it would make sure no race is scapegoated in lessons or training influenced by critical race theory.[16] In *Race Talk and the Conspiracy of Silence: Understanding and Facilitating Difficult Dialogues on Race*, professor of counseling psychology Derald Wing Sue writes,

> Most people prefer to avoid discussing race for many different reasons. White Americans are fearful that whatever they say or do in a racial dialogue might make them appear biased and racist [. . . .] They (white people) may enter a conversation on race with great trepidation, be very careful about what and how they say things, remain silent and guarded, minimize or dilute the importance of the racial issues, profess color blindness, and voice their thoughts and opinions in politically correct language.[17]

In these interactions of avoidance, no one (neither the fearful white person nor the disappointed person of color) can be their full, authentic selves. Sue makes a strong case for the value of "race talk" in schools but writes within a context where conversation is a possibility. What if certain conversations are legally banned?

When we limit discomfort, how are we also limiting learning? We know students need to feel safe to learn, as described by Dena Simmons in Emily's vignette, but we also know that discomfort can lead to growth and learning, as recounted in Tomas's introduction. In prohibiting discomfort, education itself is prohibited. The moment we conflate discomfort, anguish, and trauma, we have already lost a sense of social and historical context; we have failed to consider Pratt's suggestion that "highly asymmetrical relations of power"[18] deeply shape the ways students experience school. The COVID-19 pandemic, for example, illuminated the power of schools as social spaces. What remote schooling could not replicate or emulate were the social aspects of waiting in a lunch line or attending sports games. Schools are where an enormous number of young people learn how to be in community with one another and how to engage civically. Schools are—and perhaps especially under unjust conditions, should be—zones, "where cultures meet, clash, and grapple with each other."[19]

The author and journalist Ta-Nehisi Coates's *Between the World and Me* is written as a letter to his son. Coates and his son are Black, and he dedicates his prose to telling stories about his moments of discovering and understanding race in America. It is written in an almost *testimonio*-like style (although Tomas might disagree—see "Tomas's Concluding Thoughts," below), explicating how racism has defined Coates's life and may define his son's as well. Establishing that difference and hierarchy are part of human existence, Coates writes that "race is the child of racism, not the father. And the process of naming 'the people' has never been a matter of genealogy and physiognomy so much as one of hierarchy."[20] He continues: "Difference in hue and hair is old, But the belief in the preeminence of hue and hair, the notion that these factors can correctly organize a society and that they signify deeper attributes, which are indelible—this is the new idea at the heart of these new people who have been brought up hopelessly, tragically, deceitfully, to believe that they are white."[21] This "telling it like it is" approach may seem, to some, inappropriate given his son's age, but the rawness is the reality Coates needs to convey. Coates continues pessimistically: "Perhaps there has been, at some point in history, some great power whose elevation was exempt from the violent exploitation of other human bodies. If there has been, I have yet to discover it."[22] He argues that the history of human beings is fraught, filled with contact, and that this is applied to any group, regardless of "hue." Coates reminds his son that there is no race devoid of this history, an insight that came to him in college during a moment of uncomfortable revelation as he comes to understand the purpose of education. Coates recalls, "It began to strike me that the point of my education was a kind of discomfort, was the process that would not award me my own special Dream but would break all the dreams, all the comforting myths of Africa, of America, and everywhere, and would leave me only with humanity in all its terribleness. And there was so much terrible out there, even among us. You must understand this."[23]

Not unlike Socrates's notion of learning through aporia—a frustrating impasse or contradiction in an idea or argument—Coates draws an inextricable link between discomfort, learning, and the truth. Our history is difficult. Education is difficult. We must understand and teach this. Reflecting on my own education, I can remember several moments of discomfort directly related to racial politics and racism directed toward me, but also to more universal experiences of failing a test or needing to rewrite an assignment. There were moments of discomfort in the cocurricular realm too: missing a shot during a game or being nervous during a flute solo. Educational spaces are filled with challenging moments, hopefully with the redeeming opportunity to learn. Racial struggle leading to racial transformation must involve discussing race—a process that bills like Florida's SB 148 seek to limit.

Legal barriers aside, what are some identifiable obstacles to interracial discussions of race (and other forms of contact zone pedagogy) in schools? Sue explains that professionals in education have historically valued an "academic protocol" rooted in poorly articulated and harmfully deployed discourses of "objectivity, rationality, and intellectual thought and inquiry."[24] Despite the availability of critical standpoint philosophies that emphasize, for example, the valuable objectivity gained by the incorporation of historically excluded standpoints, history shows that a particular discourse around inquiry-related concepts such as objectivity and rationality have and can be used as a cudgel to silence and exclude. Socialization into an academic protocol that is insensitive to the history of this discourse can be antithetical to race talk, which must make room for expression that is "highly subjective, is intense, relies on storytelling, and is emotive in nature."[25] Even though most educators report they want to support students' abilities to have difficult conversations on race, they feel "limited, fearful, and constrained from doing so."[26] Educators who have themselves been socialized into this academic protocol may find it particularly difficult to find an entry point into such conversations in a way that does not threaten their own desire for emotional stability.

The recently departed professor and public intellectual bell hooks echoes Sue's contention that in order for "multicultural education" to take place, educators must be prepared, since they themselves did not learn in such an environment: "Among educators there has to be an acknowledgement that any effort to transform institutions so that they reflect a multicultural standpoint, must take into consideration the fears teachers have when asked to shift their paradigms."[27] Even in the absence of legally enforced policy restraints, social anxiety and *fear* prevent teaching in a way that is multiculturally inclusive. hooks argues that excellent learners must learn to expect, or at least remain open to, confrontation. "We all know that whenever we address the classroom subjects that students are passionate about there is always a possibility of confrontation, forceful expression of ideas, or even conflict"[28]—or, in our historical context, and to borrow again from Pratt: *contact*. hooks recalls teaching a challenging course devoid of excitement, community, and contact. It inspired her to write not just to educators but to students as well, imploring them to be courageous in the classroom.[29] Teaching and learning for contact—and, in hooks's words, "excitement"—is critical to an engaging, meaningful, transformative education in an international community still struggling to recover from the transatlantic slave trade and the colonization of the Global South. Within this multicentury historical scope, hooks's words, merely twenty-five years old, resonate just as strongly in today's educational landscape.

In any conversation about American education in the 2020s, one would be remiss to ignore the impact of political geography and how conversations about race and ethnicity vary depending on a school's zip code. However, the fight for a robust public education with a diverse, inclusive curriculum is a national one. Ethnic studies professors Allyson Tintiangco-Cubales and Jeff Duncan-Andrade offer a history of the fight to include ethnic studies as a scholarly subject in schools and how the struggle continues today.[30] Despite successful efforts to establish ethnic studies curriculum and departments in k–12 and higher education across the country, including Arizona in the late 1990s, a backlash has resulted in various bans against the very same programs. The authors are very aware of the political pendulum shifts that in one moment enable the introduction of ethnic studies in public schools and in the next eliminate them.[31] While the metaphor of a pendulum aptly describes the oscillating nature of political and ideological change, it does not address what it feels like for educators and students to be in constant transition. Regardless of what "side" of the political spectrum one falls on—as related to ethnic studies, or multicultural education, or difficult conversations about race, or Black experiences in America—constant change of this sort creates, perhaps ironically, a type of confusion and instability that is not amenable to contact zone pedagogy. Nonetheless, teachers are tasked with creating these learning opportunities. What happens when teachers are prohibited, then permitted, then prohibited again from doing so? We know the obvious risk of legislating away the possibility of contact zones, but what about the risk of making it impossible for teachers to develop stable traditions and communities of inquiry around contact zone pedagogy?

Tomas's Concluding Thoughts

Part of what drew me to Pratt's essay was her mention of *testimonio* as a type of contact zone. In previous work, I've explored the nature and discourse of *testimonio* in education and educational research.[32] What challenged me there, and what challenges me now in working with Emily and Jamila, is to reimagine once again an expansion of *testimonio*'s traditional boundaries. *Testimonios*, traditionally conceived, include stark, graphic depictions of hardship and violence of a degree that is virtually impossible for many readers to imagine. In the 1990s, as scholars in the Global North became increasingly interested in this form of first-person accounting, an emerging conception of *testimonio* emphasized the "subaltern" status of a *testimonio*'s narrator. The idea in some circles, following postcolonial thinkers like Gayarti Spivak, was to see the term *subaltern* as referring, in a maximalist way, to those in a society who are *most* oppressed or *most* marginalized.[33] In other words, those whose suffering and exclusion is so great that their stories simply cannot emerge on their own without a kind of access mediated by the social and cultural power of a willing interlocutor: an academic, a journalist, etcetera.[34]

Now, consider the cases of Bettina Love, Dena Simmons, bell hooks, and Ta-Nehisi Coates, all of whom we cite in this essay. These thinkers and public intellectuals experience (or experienced) oppression. Yet their first-person accounts, to the extent that they are infused in their writings, would not constitute *testimonio* in the eyes of many *testimonio* scholars. When designing a curriculum for contact zone pedagogy, one that includes eyewitness testimony of oppressive suffering, is there any value in carving out a distinct space for those accounts that testify to the most egregious abuses of human dignity? There is something obviously obscene in the suggestion that we might rank suffering—equality in some sense must require that we attend to all injustice. Yet prioritarian principles of justice suggest we must indeed at times make determinations about who has suffered more relative to others.[35] Should these determinations be reflected, then, not just in our material distributive policies (for example, those that deal with taxes and school funding) but also in our consideration of whose stories get read and taught in our classrooms? It seems, still, an open question.

What appears much clearer is how individuals like Love, Simmons, hooks, and Coates are able to speak—in thoughtful, generative, moving ways—about the distinctive pains, strengths, and insights of being Black in the United States. This is why they are read and assigned by educators like Jamila, Emily, and their colleagues. For the person who wishes to "center the voice of the most oppressed" or "center those furthest from justice," the challenging question is something like the following: why should the intellectual work of these four authors take priority over the testimonies of the formerly enslaved (or the estimated forty million individuals caught in modern slavery today)? The question can be posed cynically, but we present it genuinely, philosophically.

For any given educator, we think the answer to the question of what to read or who to teach may actually depend less on an assessment of which authors are "furthest from justice." It may depend more on a nuanced, fine-grained ability to foresee how one's students will interact with a text or an author given a multitude of influencing factors: the contemporary political, economic, and cultural context; the demographic and linguistic composition of a classroom; what knowledge about oppression students already have, or their level of critical historical consciousness; what kinds of experiences they themselves have had (and which they are ready to learn more about); the legal and institutional boundaries placed on teachers and how far one can reasonably push them; and on a teacher's experienced sense of what sorts of reading assignments and discussions are more likely to captivate student imagination and provoke further inquiry and action.

In other words, it is quite possible that in some classrooms, a group reading of a *testimonio*, traditionally conceived, may not automatically result in the kind of communicative friction that Jamila and Emily yearn for in their vignettes. To the extent that it does, it may depend a lot more on preparing a more fertile ground for education along the lines they discussed: students' felt sense of trust and belonging, intellectual courage modeled by students and teachers alike, and so on. Is it possible that productive contact zone pedagogy can still happen in classrooms even if—perhaps sometimes *because*—the asymmetries of power involved are *not* as great as they possibly could be?

Questions for Discussion

- Have you witnessed, in your own experiences of teaching or learning, the distinction we make between "contact zone pedagogy" and "contactless pedagogy"? What are your thoughts on these two modes of teaching and learning? Do you aim to cultivate one or the other?

- In our essay we argue that some degree of intellectual safety is a prerequisite for intellectual risk-taking. Is this a paradox, or does it make sense to you? In the service of engaging in contact zone pedagogy, how can educators better distinguish between moments when intellectual safety and security are needed and moments when intellectual courage and risk-taking are needed?

Further Reading

Shulman, S. *Conflict Is Not Abuse: Overstating Harm, Community Responsibility, and the Duty of Repair*. Vancouver, BC: Arsenal Pulp Press, 2016.

Menchú, R. *I, Rigoberta Menchú: An Indian Woman in Guatemala*. New York: Verso, 1984.

Activity

CONTACT BALLOONS[36]

Participants will need inflated balloons and markers.

1. Ask participants to choose one word that reflects their heritage, a deeply held family value, a beloved tradition, or a staunch belief. (These can be kept in mind for now.)

2. Using a marker, each participant writes their word on a balloon.

3. Participants should silently keep their balloon afloat for one minute while moving around in a limited space. Balloons may not touch the floor or anyone else's balloon.

4. At your signal, ask everyone to stop moving and trade balloons with the participant nearest to them. Have participants read and contemplate the new word for a moment. (If there is an odd number of participants, the facilitator should participate as well.)

5. Invite the pairs of participants to discuss the following questions (approximately 10 to 15 minutes):

    - How did you feel keeping your word afloat?
    - How did you feel reading and contemplating my word?
    - Would you like to tell me the story behind your word?

6. Once every pair has had a chance to respond to these questions, ask the whole group to collectively reflect on the following questions:

- How do we keep our most important values, traditions, and practices afloat while not "bumping into" or "stepping on" others? Is it always possible?
- Are we as careful with others' balloons as we are with our own? Why or why not?
- How do we keep our experiences and identities afloat while dedicating some effort to carrying the experiences and identities of others?
- If you "step on" someone else's values, traditions, experiences, identities, and so on, how should you respond? How should they respond?
- How should we apologize for "stepping on someone's balloon"? How can we respond constructively in these cases?
- Are there any balloons in the room that shouldn't "enter into contact"? Why or why not? Can you imagine a situation where certain balloons shouldn't be in touch? Why or why not?

7. Invite participants to pose other relevant questions for group discussion.

8. Play as many additional rounds as the group would like, either with the same balloons or with new balloons.

Notes

1. Mary Louise Pratt, "Arts of the Contact Zone," *Profession* (1991): 33–40.

2. Pratt, "Arts of the Contact Zone," 35. Autoethnography can be understood as a fusion of autobiographical and ethnographic qualitative research wherein the researcher critically draws connections between personal experiences and wider social, cultural, political, and historical contexts. Though not universally understood in this way, *testimonios*, a form of autobiographical representation that Pratt mentions in her essay, can express features of autoethnographic research in part

because they traditionally and characteristically require collaborations between illiterate and literate individuals. The social, cultural, political, and historical context of the collaboration, and the oppressive nature of illiteracy in modern society, is often drawn out through the collaboration and thereby transforms a representation that is autobiographical into one that is more distinctively autoethnographic.

3. In the critical social theory of Jürgen Habermas, an "ideal speech situation" exists when participants in acts of communication are free to criticize the validity of claims of communication: intelligibility, propositional truth, moral rightness, and sincerity. To make communication more ideal in this way, differences between participants in things such as power, status, and ability should not be allowed to interfere with the articulation and force of their arguments—the interactions are orderly. By definition, contact zones are not ideal speech situations.

4. Pratt, "Arts of the Contact Zone," 39.

5. Bettina Love, *We Want to Do More Than Survive: Abolitionist Teaching and the Pursuit of Educational Freedom* (Boston, MA: Beacon Press, 2019): 17.

6. Here, some teachers may be reminded of Lisa D. Delpit's classic 1988 paper, "The Silenced Dialogue: Power and Pedagogy in Educating Other People's Children," published in *Harvard Educational Review*. In the essay, Delpit reflects on the implicit "codes" or "rules" of power shared (often unconsciously) among those participating in a "culture of power." Communication breaks down, argues Delpit, when members of different cultural groups do not share awareness of the codes of power. "Each cultural group is left saying, 'Why don't those people say what they mean?'" (283). Delpit's reflections in this paper contributed to her widely lauded 1995 bestseller, *Other People's Children*.

7. Kathy Greeley, *"Why Fly That Way?": Linking Community and Academic Achievement* (New York: Teachers College Press, 2000).

8. Love, *We Want to Do More Than Survive*, 27.

9. Maura Sullivan Hill, "The Power of Belonging," *Loyola University Chicago* (2019). URL: https://www.luc.edu/features/stories/academics/denasimmons/.

10. We purposefully ask "who gains power, comfort, or wealth" rather than "who benefits" because power, comfort, and wealth are not benefits if gaining them undermines our ability to enact joint flourishing and fulfill our relational responsibilities. See Nicolas Tanchuk, Tomas Rocha, and Marc Kruse, "Is Complicity in Oppression a Privilege? Toward Social Justice Education as Mutual Aid," *Harvard Educational Review* 91, no. 3 (2021): 341–61.

11. Love, *We Want to Do More Than Survive*, 7.

12. Love, *We Want to Do More*, 7.

13. Greeley, *"Why Fly That Way?"*

14. Paulo Freire, *Pedagogy of the Oppressed*, 50th anniversary ed. (New York: Bloomsbury, [1970] 2017), 89.

15. Greg Allen, "Fla. Bill Bans Businesses and Schools from Making Anyone Feel Guilt about Race," *NPR* (February 8, 2022): para. 7, https://www.npr.

org/2022/02/08/1079112803/fla-bill-bans-businesses-and-schools-from-making-anyone-feel-guilt-about-race.

16. Although SB 148 failed to pass in its original form, companion bills have moved forward, and Governor DeSantis recently signed the "Parental Rights in Education" bill into law, also known as the "Don't Say Gay" bill.

17. Derald Wing Sue, *Race Talk and the Conspiracy of Silence: Understanding and Facilitating Difficult Dialogues on Race* (Hoboken, NJ: Wiley, 2015).

18. Pratt, "Arts of the Contact Zone."

19. Pratt, "Arts of the Contact Zone."

20. Ta-Nehisi Coates, *Between the World and Me* (New York: Spiegel & Grau, 2017).

21. Coates, *Between the World and Me*.

22. Coates, *Between the World and Me*.

23. Coates, *Between the World and Me*.

24. Sue, *Race Talk and the Conspiracy of Silence*.

25. Sue, *Race Talk and the Conspiracy*.

26. Sue, *Race Talk and the Conspiracy*.

27. bell hooks, *Teaching to Transgress: Education as the Practice of Freedom* (New York: Routledge, 1994): 36.

28. hooks, *Teaching to Transgress*, 39.

29. hooks, *Teaching to Transgress*, 13–22.

30. Allyson Tintiangco-Cubales and Jeff Duncan-Andrade, "Still Fighting for Ethnic Studies: The Origins, Practices, and Potential of Community Responsive Pedagogy," *Teachers College Record* 123, no. 13 (2021): 1–28.

31. Allyson Tintiangco-Cubales and Jeff Duncan-Andrade, 22.

32. Tomas de Rezende Rocha, *Egalitarian Reverence: Towards a Cosmopolitan Contemplative Education*, PhD diss., Columbia University, 2020.

33. Gayarti Chakravorty Spivak, "Can the Subaltern Speak?," *Die Philosophin* 14, no. 13 (1988): 42–58.

34. The archetypal *testimonio* in this conception would be something like the 1983 *testimonio* of Rigoberta Menchú Tum, the K'iche' woman who describes the torture and execution of her brother, the killing of her father, and the kidnap, rape, and murder of her mother.

35. We thank an anonymous reviewer for pushing us to say more about why one might highlight (or even, in some cases, "rank") the suffering of one population over another, given our claim that "equality in some sense must require that we attend to all injustice." We never claim that we should highlight only certain kinds of suffering for certain populations. What we say is more narrowly and moderately about the necessity of comparing harm across social groups over time, if a society is interested in projects of social justice, restoration, and reconciliation. In our view, this is quite consistent with mainstream liberal prioritarian principles of justice along the lines of, for example, Rawlsian distributive justice.

In nonideal conditions (in the Rawlsian sense) and in conditions of material scarcity, such as the ones humans currently live in, it is not possible to attend equally to all injustices all of the time. (This is not an endorsement of current social arrangements but merely a description.) The systems and departments of justice in nation-states around the world regularly "triage" the administration of justice, often in accordance with some commitment to prioritarian principles. In order to do so, they need to make judgments about which social groups, on average, have suffered more or less harm over time. (The same is true about systems of education that make determinations about how to distribute limited resources.) We agree with another point by our anonymous reviewer: that social justice education ought not inflict unnecessary pain and that, prudentially, it should avoid provoking backlash. Absent argument to the contrary, we maintain that our discussion in this chapter has not proposed anything so counterproductive as what the reviewer might fear.

36. Adapted from Mariama Richards, head of Crossroads School, Santa Monica, California.

6

Learning Together to Stay with Trouble
Sustaining Educators across Time and Space

CARA E. FURMAN, HOLLY A. F. LASH, HILLARY POST,
AND LINDSEY YOUNG

I remember the first full week of school in fall 2021 being a time of tremendous joy in the classroom. At the end of the week, we sat together and reflected on how we felt being together again after we had spent most of the 2020 to 2021 school year remote. The conversation veered from happiness almost directly to many students speaking to the grief that they were still carrying about the pandemic and months spent in remote learning.

"I was so depressed! It was the worst year of my entire life!" said Willow,[1] as she teared up. "I had to start seeing a therapist!" At least six other children signed "me too."

"I just felt so sad all the time," Brian shared.

"My anxiety is kinda over the top," Jason offered.

"I'm tired of the whole thing. It makes me supermad," said Olla.

My assistant teacher and I looked at each other over our masks. We read this offering—what the children had chosen to share with us—as their way of asking for space to process together. This realization ended up changing the very direction of our curriculum as well as our relationship with our students.

These are Holly's words, one of the authors of this collaborative piece. Yet, it is a story that belongs to all of us. As philosophical teacher inquiry,[2] we tell of four seasoned educators operating amid steady pressure to keep students academically on track and remediate "learning loss" during the COVID-19 pandemic. Whereas responsive teaching is written into the Common Core Teaching Standards and is a hallmark of progressive education, meaningfully doing so can be extremely challenging. As such, we focus on how, guided by Donna Haraway's phrase "Stay with the trouble"[3] and each other's stories, we, like Holly, "chang[ed] the direction of our curriculum" to make space to grieve, explore, and make sense of a new reality and to be in meaningful relation with our students.

Karen Barad uses the concept of diffraction to describe how ideas like stones cast into water ripple across each other—sometimes influencing, sometimes acting in parallel.[4] With each stone, a new set of ripples is made—sometimes overlapping with those that came before. Over a period of a year in the midst of the pandemic, we gathered multiple times to toss our stories into a shared space. In doing so, we came to read our own daily classroom experiences through staying with the trouble and each other's stories.

After a brief description of staying with the trouble, we tell our story in three iterations, which we refer to, along with Barad, as "stones": First, we describe how with the help of Hillary and Lindsey, Cara presented a child study[5] at the Summer Institute on Descriptive Inquiry (IDI).[6] Second, we share how as teacher and staff developer respectively, Hillary and Lindsey re-presented Cara's story with staff at the beginning of the school year. Third, we share how we "stayed with" this perspective on trouble and grief through the fall of 2021, and into the spring of 2022. In telling our story, we highlight (1) the trouble that emerges for teachers trying to be responsive to their students; (2) the cascading effect and power of sharing a philosophical frame, "staying with the trouble," and stories of practice together; and (3) how such sharing helped us stay with the trouble amid uncertainty, loss, and grief.

The majority of this conversation took place over Zoom in preparation for the Summer Institute, at the Summer Institute, and in multiple follow-up conversations. We recorded our Zoom calls and lifted much of the language from those transcriptions. We also drew from detailed notes. In addition, we communicated through private and group emails, texts that included pictures, and the sharing of short readings.

Setting

In March 2020 when COVID-19 hit the United States, we all rapidly packed up our classrooms and abruptly shifted our teaching to almost entirely new methods. The permutations of the pandemic shifted constantly and with these shifts, the experience for teachers, parents, and children evolved—often rapidly and without time to prepare.

At the time of this writing, in the spring of 2022, Cara is a teacher educator in rural New England, former elementary school teacher, and the mother of two young children. Holly has been a teacher for over twenty years and currently teaches fifth/sixth grade at an independent school on the West Coast. Hillary has taught for ten years, now teaching kindergarten at the same school as Holly. Lindsey has recently moved from teacher into the role of administrator at the same school, supporting students, parents, and teachers, with ten previous years in the classroom.

We are all progressive educators and draw on our regularly reflected on values to make daily decisions in the field. With curricular flexibility, we are encouraged and expected to adapt to particular students, classes, and situations. Steeped in a shared philosophical approach to teaching, we have studied together for years at IDI. Having inquired together for many years and having witnessed each other's teaching practice, we came to this project, to use Haraway's phrase, "entangle[d]."[7]

Stone 1: Staying with the Trouble

In *Staying with the Trouble: Making Kin in the Chthulucene*, Haraway, begins by defining trouble as "'to stir up,' 'to make cloudy,' 'to disturb.'"[8] She then continues,

> We—all of us on Terra—live in disturbing times, mixed-up times, troubling and turbid times. The Task is to become capable, with each other in all of our bumptious kinds, of response. . . . The task is to make kin in lines of inventive connection as a practice of learning to live and die well with each other in a thick present. Our task is to make trouble, to stir up potent response to devastating events, as well as to settle troubled waters and rebuild quiet places.[9]

With both real-world and fictional examples, Haraway argues that staying with the trouble means leaning into the trouble in which we find ourselves amid. Doing so includes "entanglements," being drawn together and interwoven with others. Staying "entangle[d]"[10] with each other in the trouble leads to new and creative ways forward, what Haraway calls "*sympoiesis*" or "making-with."[11] In defining sympoiesis, Haraway emphasizes that "nothing makes itself."[12] Entanglement is therefore descriptive not aspirational, yet the nature of the entanglement can be strengthened through a more conscious cultivation.

Stone 2: Cara's Review[13]

A year into the pandemic, Cara found herself in the midst of trouble.[14] Specifically, she was having trouble "mak[ing] kin" with her four-year-old son's daily "response[s]."[15] Two things in particular baffled her: his intense tantrums and his absolute, full-bodied obsession with Transformers.[16] Cara saw the tantrums as a logical response to the isolation and fear of the pandemic. What baffled her was how to help the family live with tantrums. Though less jarring than the tantrums, she didn't like the violent and often misogynistic Transformers either, resisting being "entangled" through this play.

Staying with the Trouble rippled across her son's actions, offering a question: what would it look like to stay with his trouble? Cara believed that asking questions of her son's work among caring and insightful "kin" might help her stay better with him. She decided to present at IDI and asked Hillary and Lindsey to chair her study. They determined that Cara would share a gloss of Haraway's philosophy, anecdotes about her son's thinking with Transformers, and a collection of his Transformers artwork. Over three days, Cara presented her work to a small group of teachers, retired teachers, and teacher educators, many of whom were also parents, and grandparents. After reading her story and looking at the work, participants described back what they noticed. While much emerged from this session, a key piece that stuck with Cara was feedback that she and her child seemed deeply entangled and with that entanglement came care and joy but also the challenges of being so closely entwined with each other's emotions.

Stone 3: Staying with the Trouble at a School

Cara's story struck a chord with session chairs, Hillary and Lindsey, giving language to the complexity they anticipated in the return of school that fall. Deeply committed to nurturing the social-emotional lives of children, they believed the frame of staying with the trouble offered a distinct way to resist the dominant narrative of "learning loss" percolating in mainstream media at the time.

As described by Lindsey, they decided to bring the work back to their colleagues at beginning of the year staff meetings.

> Hillary and I began a session with a history of IDI and its deeply rooted connection to our school. We introduced the previous year's summer Institute theme, and shared the questions that framed our summer experience: *How do we provision for children, adolescents and teachers at a time that both offers narrowing structures and a time for possible opportunities. What does it mean to take care of each other in these circumstances? What have we learned about caring for our children and ourselves in the past year? How can we expand these lessons going forward?* We then shared the collection of Cara's son's renderings of Transformers. We did what's called a Reflection of the Word, in which everyone shared associations with the words *transform, transformer*.[17] After reading Cara's writing about her son and Haraway,[18] staff members shared passages that resonated with them in small groups. Returning to the full group, staff then shared reflections about staying with the trouble with other contexts and other children with a focus on our community.
>
> Before the students returned, I wrote to the parents and shared this staff work because I anticipated much anxiety and fear about how the school would talk about the pandemic. I knew parents felt concern about the many pandemic losses, including of life and lifestyle and safety in school as well as anxiety about kids falling behind academically. We wanted families to know that we were not entering the year as if nothing had happened, and that we all endured trauma, loss, and grief. We wanted to communicate that we would be intentional in how we were coming back together as a community.

Staying with trouble and certain passages from Cara's writing came up in staff meetings going forward and in casual settings as well, such as around the table at lunch. Here we trace influence on Lindsey, Hillary, and Holly by sharing a moment in January when together we revisited our ongoing conversation and shared how the work together had helped us stay with the trouble that year. Capturing the immediacy of the moment, we have kept the present tense.

Lindsey's Ripple

This year the focus of my work with parents has been different. It was clear even before the first day of school that the parents were going to need support in how to stay with trouble. I've really worked on educating the parents on how to show up for their kids. We've focused on acknowledging how hard it is and speaking directly about anxiety, fear, and grief. We brought in various speakers over Zoom in a critical attempt to bring this community together.

One of our most powerful parent sessions was titled "Naming, Normalizing, and Neuroscience." In all of the heaviness of the past two years, reigniting joy and hope in the community proved challenging. We began one parent meeting with each person naming something they admired about their child. Modeled after an activity we do with the staff and students at the start of the school year, we asked upper-grade parents to write a letter to their child to be opened in the near future, projecting their hopes and dreams. When parents came out of the breakout rooms, there were tears, so much emotion, as though a pressure valve had been released. They expressed so much gratitude for being in a school where emotions are attended to, named and seen, and where space is given to connect in an authentic and meaningful way.

When I think about a school, the interconnectedness and relationships between students, teachers, administrators, and parents are what define a community. Without empathy, compassion, and trust, we cannot begin to heal. So for me, staying with the trouble is holding the container for the parent community to connect and share their experiences, in the same way we have done with the teachers and the children.

Hillary's Ripple

I'm living through something right now that's really speaking to me. It's about Band-Aids, literally Band-Aids. At the beginning of the year, I was inspired by a colleague who ordered these Tru Colour Band-Aids that come in four different shades of skin tones. And I put them under the classroom sink and the kids were really into them. It felt validating because they could match their skin tone.

At the beginning of the year, kids had occasional needs for Band-Aids and they would come to me or my assistant teacher and point to something and want assistance putting on a Band-Aid. Then when we came back to school in January amid the Omicron wave of COVID-19, I suddenly felt like I didn't have enough Band-Aids because the need was constant. And what they were bringing to me were really small scrapes on their hands. When I looked more closely recently, I saw these are from dry skin from all of the handwashing we're doing because we're living through a pandemic. And so these Band-Aids are literally being applied to something related to the pandemic. They also feel like they have this huge emotional component.

Where I'm staying with the trouble is that I'm feeling such resistance to my role or my perceived role by the children as a healer. I am so broken from what this experience has been as a teacher that I resist giving the Band-Aids. I ask the students, "Do you really need a Band-Aid? That looks like it's healing. It looks like there's a scab on there. You're healing, your body doesn't need a Band-Aid." And then sometimes they insist that they do. And so I started shifting the Band-Aid responsibility to them. "You know where they are. I think you can put one on for yourself." So that's interesting too, because now there's this exodus from lessons to apply Band-Aids.

On the one hand, I feel like Band-Aids are in abundance and maybe they are healing themselves. On the other hand, this seems disruptive in so many ways and that's where some of the resistance was to me too. When these kids were coming up asking for these Band-Aids, I felt like I was a help desk and I didn't want to be the help desk. There's this resistance within me to fixing and helping, which I'm really wondering about within the landscape we are in.

It is starting to feel like resisting the fixing and problem-solving mode is the essence of staying with the trouble. I think as teachers we are used to jumping in to fix and problem-solve. And I feel like I'm not doing that exactly. Instead I'm in this limbo space with the kids and the Band-Aids, where I'm not jumping in but giving more space to simply watching what is happening in front of me. I've also been thinking a lot about healing and what's missing in the classroom. I'm thinking about something that is external for the kids to care for such as plants or gardening or Wuzzies.[19] I know people were doing that a lot at the beginning of the pandemic:

planting, gardening, caring for new pets, helping a neighbor care for their garden. So it feels like we're coming full circle. I'm thinking of talking more candidly. "It seems like we are hurting. What can we do when we're hurting? What are some things that might help?" So I'm staying with the trouble of Band-Aids. Resisting quick fixes and simple problem-solution paradigms and, instead, staying with the collective trauma of the pandemic.

Holly's Ripple

We had one student who after a couple weeks of school, maybe a month, was feeling upset that some students and teachers were not wearing their masks properly. One reaction would have been for me to just deal with it and put her at ease. But instead, we brought it to the class for a discussion.

Everyone affirmed her frustration but at the same time, the bigger thing that was brought up was, "Well, it's really hard to talk to people who are wearing their masks the wrong way because you don't want to make them mad at you and you don't want to make them feel bad." The bigger question was, what do we do as a community if we see that people aren't wearing their masks in the proper way? They tossed around ideas such as we can make a skit or we could go and give an announcement to each class, or we'll read a letter to each class. That grew into this bigger idea of making this play about why and how to wear masks properly. This was completely generated by the kids with a little help from the assistant teacher on the script.

It took over our class. Basically, we stopped all of the curriculum. Nothing really for about three weeks. Everything was focused on this. It was almost like a lens through which we processed. All came together in the play they wrote. The story goes like this: a kid wouldn't wear a mask and another person wanted to tell him to please keep their masks on, and then they had mask fairies that came to help. There was all this cool stuff about how to handle it but with a sense of humor. They even had a parody song about wearing masks. Kids who didn't feel comfortable onstage created the background music and the set and the props. So every child was involved in some way.

Then we announced to the school that we were going to do the shows, and then we performed it. Even that performance was the macroview of staying with the trouble because everything has to be thought about with the lens of COVID safety. We had to plan out how the kids were going to sit and one of the kids did this whole math problem: this many kids in this group and they have to sit a certain number of feet apart. And so how can we make this space work outside?

It was pretty cool in the end that they did that much work, and the kids loved it. We performed three shows and it brought the kids together and it made them feel like we were all in school together. It took out the heaviness and allowed us to say this is a ridiculous situation we're in. It let us cope with a sense of humor about what the pandemic is. They had been so frustrated with it.

It makes me so proud to think about how the emotional life of those children was supported by this particular experience, that they were able to use those feelings they had and those concerns and turn it into something that was art. It made this oldest group feel like leaders in school, like they had an impact in a way that they hadn't been feeling. Yet even though this is what it means to be a responsive educator and progressive, we (as teachers) were panicking about the curriculum we had planned. We were panicking about all of the things we had thought were going to be happening in that month. We were feeling that countrywide feel of the learning deficit and we were seeing those struggles in little ways, for example, with math. We had to keep reminding each other that is not what it has to be about. We had to take the chance to put aside our previous plans for a little while and really focus on this play. And I think it was the right choice. We stayed with trouble for sure, for sure.

Living Well with Trouble

Philosophy has the potential to guide us to live well,[20] and Haraway's theories did just that. As we listened to our communities, we heard the trouble. We also heard external pressures to push through. Repeating Haraway's phrase as almost a mantra, and bolstered by each other's stories, we consistently leaned into the trouble.

Our stories revealed us grappling together with each other—students, colleagues, and families. Just as Cara's son was bolstered by entangling others in his fascination with Transformers, we were all bolstered by stringing meaning around our capacity to stay with the trouble. Through this entanglement, one story rippled across another, leading us to make shifts in practice.

Another key element of our ripples was paying attention (often with others). Through Descriptive Inquiry, Cara listened carefully to her son's words and studied his artwork. Lindsey described listening to parents' anxiety and building on that listening to support them. Holly and Hillary described watching their students' as they played and listening as they talked—noting themes that emerged.

Upon listening, each of us reflected on how we might provision. Haraway repeatedly offers rich and varied moments of creativity that bolster those involved and entangle them together. For us, part of Haraway's offering was the encouragement of creative expression and play. Lindsey guided the parents through writing a loving letter to their child. Holly described the transformative effect for the school community of writing and sharing the play which, in Lindsey's words, was "the first moment of levity" of the year. After telling her Band-Aid story, Hillary and Cara texted about the potential of adding materials for doctor play into the dramatic play area. The next day, Hillary wrote, "A few of the doctors from earlier this morning transformed into Gods/Goddesses by late morning. Most children played doctor by the end of the day."

Haraway writes story upon story, building an ethos on staying with the trouble. In adding our own stories as stones to the tangle, we document the power of staying with the trouble as an ethos and add our own ripples into the mix.

Questions for Discussion

- What meaning, associations, and/or stories does the phrase "stay with the trouble" bring up for you?
- Think of a time when a frame or philosophical idea helped you work through a situation? What was the idea and the situation?

Further Reading

Carini, Patricia F., and Margaret Himley. *Jenny's Story: Taking the Long View of the Child: Prospect's Philosophy in Action.* New York: Teachers College Press, 2010.

Haraway, Donna Jeanne. *Staying with the Trouble: Making Kin in the Chthulucene.* Durham, NC: Duke University Press, 2016.

Little, Tom, and Katherine Ellison. *Loving Learning: How Progressive Education Can Save America's Schools*, 1st ed. New York: W. W. Norton, 2015.

Activity

Recollection is one of the Descriptive Processes that serves as "a usual starting place, for when we take time to recall and share experiences that had a shaping effect on our own learning (or that helped shape our way of seeking the world, or that connected us with values that widened our horizons), when we recall and share play that absorbed us in childhood, our perceptions of these inherently human experiences, attune us to their meaning in children's lives."[21]

Gather in a small group of six to eight people. Begin by each individually reflecting on the prompt. Consider a few different stories you would be comfortable sharing with a small group—stories that can be told in under ten minutes. Perhaps jot some notes to yourself in preparation for the telling.

- Consider a time when you "stayed with the trouble" as a teacher or as a student.

- Describe the surround: the location, the time, the context.

- Describe moments of conflict (internal and/or external) and moments of resistance.

- What thoughts and internal dialogue transpired for you? How did you move through the experience? What stays with you now?

Designate a chairperson. The chairperson will be responsible for taking thematic notes and maintaining confidentiality guidelines. Each person in the group takes a turn sharing their story, uninterrupted, and without comments from participants in between stories. When all stories have been told, the chairperson comments on themes across the stories. Participants are then invited to add themes they noticed across the stories and other reflections based on the experience of telling and listening.

Notes

1. This and all children's names are pseudonyms.

2. Patricia F. Carini and Margaret Himley, *Jenny's Story: Taking the Long View of the Child: Prospect's Philosophy in Action* (New York: Teachers College Press, 2010).

3. Donna Jeanne Haraway, *Staying with the Trouble: Making Kin in the Chthulucene* (Durham, NC: Duke University Press, 2016).

4. Karen Michelle Barad, *Meeting the Universe Halfway: Quantum Physics and the Entanglement of Matter and Meaning* (Durham, NC: Duke University Press, 2007).

5. Margaret Himley et al., eds., *Prospect's Descriptive Processes: The Child, the Art of Teaching and the Classroom and School*, rev. ed. (North Bennington, VT: Prospect Center, 2002).

6. An annual gathering of teachers who use a process called Descriptive Inquiry to study and grow their practice.

7. Haraway, *Staying with the Trouble*, 13.

8. Haraway, *Staying with the Trouble*, 1.

9. Haraway, *Staying with the Trouble*, 1.

10. Haraway, *Staying with the Trouble*, 13.

11. Haraway, *Staying with the Trouble*, 58.

12. Haraway, *Staying with the Trouble*, 58.

13. For a fuller version of this story that includes the review she presented at IDI, see Cara E. Furman, "An Ethos of Wander Time: Staying with the Trouble to Make Sense during Crises," *Studies in Philosophy and Education* 42, no. 1 (February 2023): 17–32, https://doi.org/10.1007/s11217-022-09859-z.

14. For a fuller version of this story that includes the review she presented at IDI, see Cara E. Furman, "An Ethos of Wander Time: Staying with the Trouble to Make Sense during Crises," *Studies in Philosophy and Education* 42, no. 1 (February 2023): 17–32, https://doi.org/10.1007/s11217-022-09859-z.

15. Haraway, *Staying with the Trouble*, 1.

16. These are animated robot-trucks in television shows, movies, and toys.

17. A Descriptive process where people take a few minutes to write down their impressions of a word and then each person shares. The chair then restates what has been shared noting themes.

18. Revised and published Furman, "An Ethos of Wander Time."

19. The Wuzzies are part of a curriculum developed by Joan Bradbury in which children care for handmade cotton-ball creatures and cocreate an imaginary world. The curriculum has many opportunities for studying about community, building empathy, and creative writing. Joan Bradbury wrote about the program in an unpublished piece, "Adventures in Wuzzyville: Real Life in Third Grade" and in Cara Furman et al., "Teaching for Human Dignity: Making Room for Children

and Teachers in Contemporary Schools," *Educational Philosophy and Theory* 56, no. 9 (July 28, 2024): 885–98, https://doi.org/10.1080/00131857.2024.2323566.

20. Pierre Hadot, *Philosophy as a Way of Life: Spiritual Exercises from Socrates to Foucault*, trans. Arnold I. Davidson (Malden, MA: Blackwell, 1995).

21. Margaret Himley et al., eds., *Prospect's Descriptive Processes: The Child, the Art of Teaching and the Classroom and School*, rev. ed. (North Bennington, VT: Prospect Center, 2002).

7

Ignoring Difference

How an Antidivisive Concepts Law Changed the Trajectory of an Antibias Curriculum Project

Joy Dangora Erickson and
Kyleigh P. Rousseau[1]

To live a flourishing life—a life that largely goes well—individuals must find ways of living that are in harmony with their "particular personalities."[2] Put differently, each person should come to understand who they are and have a foundational awareness of a variety of legitimate ways of living from which they can select those most compatible with their personality. According to Harry Brighouse, schools have a responsibility to cultivate the flourishing of the children they serve. They have obligations to assist students in understanding and appreciating who they are and to help them recognize other legitimate options for being and thinking that might complement their evolving personalities.

Engaging children in civic, antibias, and/or antiracist programs is one way schools support children in better understanding themselves and others. Within such programs children often take a closer look at who they are and what they believe (that is, they work to recognize aspects of their cultural, social, and personal identities), and they compare and contrast these facets of their identities with those of others. For example, kindergarten children might examine their own and others' physical appearances (including skin color, hairstyle, clothing, and assistive technologies), gender, ethnicities, traditions, and hobbies. This kind of inquiry can assist children in (1) understanding and describing who they are and (2) appreciating other legitimate ways of identifying. Additionally, many civic, antibias, and/or antiracist education approaches (for example, P4C,[3] Anti-Bias Education[4]) invite children to co-construct an understanding of fairness and to practice applying this understanding to a variety of situations. Programming that encourages children to examine their own identities alongside those of others and/or invites conversations about fairness supports children in learning about themselves and recognizing other legitimate ways of being and thinking.

Consequently, it is important to recognize that denying or limiting opportunities for students to explore their identities and the identities of others, is likely to slow or impede their developing awareness of legitimate ways of being and thinking—interfering with their flourishing. In an effort to support children's developing awareness of themselves and others, the authors of this chapter in collaboration with other experts and in reference to relevant frameworks, developed a series of antibias, antiracist, and civic early childhood curriculum maps over the course of the 2020 to 2021 school year that were to be piloted in a preschool and kindergarten classroom in the Northeast in the 2021 to 2022 school year.

Map 7.1 (see fig. 7.1), which is firmly rooted in an antibias education and focused on aiding young children's development of a healthy sense of self, was scheduled to be implemented in classrooms in September of 2021. However, the passing of the New Hampshire state budget in June of 2021 forced the creation of an alternate version of map 7.1—one that dramatically reduced opportunities for students to engage in identity work and discuss issues of fairness.

The New Hampshire legislation is part of a range of legislative actions and broad parental protests against what the public schools teach and what reading materials are available in the classroom and the school library. The current controversy taking place in legislative halls and once typical bland school board meetings has been characterized as a "moral panic," chilling teacher classroom speech.[5] The divisive concepts legislation limiting teacher speech has been dubbed "gag orders" and will be discussed below.[6]

In this chapter we describe three specific changes made to map 7.1 in response to this legislation, and we consider how these changes deprive students of opportunities for self-exploration, developing an appreciation for different ways of being and thinking, and constructing and applying an understanding of fairness. We conclude that extreme forms of legislation that function to restrict classroom discussions of ideas and topics considered divisive by some, impede worthy schooling efforts to support children in understanding themselves and others and in choosing ways to live that are compatible with their personalities.

Schools Have a Responsibility to Support Children's Flourishing

According to Brighouse, "The school should see itself as having an obligation to facilitate the long-term flourishing of the children."[7] Schools should play a fundamental role in supporting children's flourishing because the degree to which they flourish impacts the individual and the nation. A flourishing life can be described as one that mainly goes well for the individual. There are infinite possibilities for realizing a good life. However, Brighouse maintains that to flourish, (1) one must deeply identify with the life they are living, and (2) the life should contain objective goods.[8] Daniel DeNicola adds a third criteria, namely, that to flourish one must function in the world with "excellence and effectiveness."[9] We offer these criteria not to suggest that they are comprehensive or absolute, but to assist the reader in grasping this broad and contested concept. Research suggests living a good life usually requires having a satisfactory amount of money to avoid poverty, a healthy social network, and being able to work on advancing certain skills that are appropriately challenging for the individual. Two additional educational goods that Brighouse and colleagues maintain contribute to a flourishing life are (1) the capacity for personal autonomy and (2) the capacity to treat others as equals.[10]

The capacity for personal autonomy permits children and adults to "engage in activities and relationships that reflect their sense of who they are and what matters to them."[11] Autonomy aids individuals in truly identifying with the life they are living; it supports them in making choices that promote their inner peace. Brighouse and colleagues offer religion as an example, when people benefit from having knowledge of a variety of religious and nonreligious views; autonomous people are able to select religious or nonreligious ways of thinking and acting that align best with who they understand themselves to be and their values. As mentioned in the introduction, civic, antibias, and antiracism programs designed for young children often introduce them to a variety of ways of thinking and behaving. For example, in such programs children may learn new ways to dress, style their hair, eat, play, and so on. They may also learn about family routines, rituals, and traditions that differ from their own. These opportunities and many others contribute to children's knowledge of alternate legitimate ways of thinking and being in the world; they are made aware of a multitude of options from which they can choose to try out and adopt if they mesh well with their individual personalities. Selecting the ways of being and thinking that best match their personalities can assist children in living a happy life.

The capacity to treat others as equals is another educational good required for flourishing according to Brighouse and colleagues: "The experience of slights grounded in assumptions of superiority—as with gender, sexuality, or physical or mental abilities—undermines the self-respect and self-confidence of the slighted, making it harder for them to flourish."[12] Indigenous children, and children of color specifically, can come to believe that white people are superior when their racial and cultural identities are not acknowledged and appreciated inside and outside of the classroom.[13] Nurturing children's capacities to treat others as social and moral equals supports not only the flourishing of the individual but also the flourishing of the group. Civic, antibias, and antiracist programs aid young children in appreciating a wide variety of differences including, racial differences, gender differences, and physical differences. They also often engage children in discussions and applications of fairness. For example, they assist children in defining what it means to be treated fairly and practice applying their definition to both real and imagined scenarios. These programs arguably support children's developing capacities to treat others as equals.

Four Goals of Early Childhood Antibias Education

Though a variety of antibias, antiracist, and civic frameworks and resources were consulted before and during the map-making process, the four core goals for antibias work emphasized in Louise Derman-Sparks and Julie Edwards's framework served as the anchors for this project primarily because they were created for use with young children.[14] These four goals are as follows:

1. Identity
2. Diversity
3. Justice
4. Activism

The first goal of identity involves supporting children in feeling good about who they are personally and socially. Developing self-awareness and pride in one's home culture without needing to feel superior to others is a primary objective of this first core goal. The second goal, diversity, aims to support children in recognizing, feeling comfortable with, and appreciating people's similarities and differences. Being able to respectfully and accurately describe how people are alike and different is a primary objective of this second core goal. The third goal, justice, aims to support children's developing capacities for having empathy and understanding fairness. Specifically, children learn to recognize biases and injustices and come to believe that people should be treated fairly. The fourth goal of Derman-Sparks and Edwards's antibias framework is activism. This final goal aims to cultivate in children the strength and wisdom necessary to stand up against biases and injustices impacting themselves and/or others. Goals one, two, and to a lesser extent three, influenced the development of curriculum map 7.1 (see fig. 7.1), while goals three and four were centered in later maps.

Our Project

Our project began in the summer of 2020; late summer through the beginning of fall, the first author (teacher educator) and the two teachers who planned to implement the antibias curriculum maps completed a collaborative autoethnographic self-study that prompted them to explore their individual cultures and implicit biases and compare and contrast them with those of others.[15] Mid-fall through the winter months, the team reviewed a range of literature on antibias, antiracist, and civic education.

The group of early childhood educators had a collective knowledge base going into this work; however, they reviewed their understandings and sought out input throughout the process from several diversity, equity, inclusion, and belonging experts.

The group drafted map 7.1 (see fig. 7.1) in the spring of 2021. Derman-Sparks's and Edwards's first and second (and to a lesser extent third[16]) antibias education goals anchored this first map; *building positive identities* was the overarching theme of map 7.1.[17] Louise Derman-Sparks's and Patricia Ramsey's learning themes and strategies, which are aligned to these goals, further guided the map's development.[18] The four branches or learning themes coming off of the overarching theme included, *developing my own knowledge base, exploring individual similarities and differences, learning about our own and others' families and the community*, and *developing dispositions for caring, connecting, and cooperating*. Off of each subtheme are potential classroom activities and mentor texts the group thought might be useful in their settings. Some of the activities were inspired by the antibias support texts, while others came from the teachers' own experiences (for example, teaching abroad, observing colleagues, reading professional journals, and attending conferences).

With regard to implementation, the team decided that they would begin the unit in the fall of 2021 by observing and listening closely to children, taking care to notice how the children appeared to perceive themselves and others in daily experiences. After this initial four-to-six-week observation period, the teachers wanted the freedom to select their own starting points on the map and adapt the experiences coming off of each branch to better align with their teaching style and children's strengths, needs, and interests. For example, one teacher thought it best in her situation to begin working off of the branch titled, "Learning about Our Own and Others' Families and the Community," because she typically taught about families at the start of school. Another teacher thought she would be more likely to begin with the branch titled, "Exploring Individual Similarities and Differences" because she thought it might benefit her students to focus on identifying their own and their peer's characteristics before family or community characteristics. Similarly, the teachers had their own preferences specific to the mentor texts they planned to use to spark conversations and introduce activities. For these reasons, the activities coming off of each branch on map 7.1 are intended to support teachers in identifying the kinds of activities that might be used to help students reach the antibias goals of map 7.1,[19] namely, to help children feel good about who they are, appreciate similarities and differences in how they identify and how others identify, and begin to construct an understanding of fairness.

Modifications Made in Response to New Hampshire's Antidivisive Concepts Legislation

In June of 2021, while the team was planning for fall implementation of map 7.1, the governor of New Hampshire signed into law legislation that restricts how teachers talk about issues of inequity, including racism, sexism, and discrimination. The enacted series of statutes (House Bill 2) include what is commonly referred to as the "Divisive Concepts Statute," and is legally known as the Prohibition on Teaching Discrimination Statute (NH Revised Statutes Annotated § 193.40). The statute allows "aggrieved" persons to sue school districts (NH RSA § 193.40 [III]) and provides a basis for the State Board of Education to consider violations of the educator code of conduct (NH Board of Education Ed501.01 et seq.). The statute, while sounding somewhat reasonable on its face, is pernicious in its application and effect—sowing uncertainty and fear among many educators in the state.

For example, when Governor Chris Sununu signed the legislation ten of the seventeen members of the state's Council on Diversity resigned. The resignation letter, stated in pertinent part, "You signed into law a provision that aims to censor conversations essential to advancing equity and inclusion in our state, specifically for those within our public education systems, and all state employees. . . . Given your willingness to sign this damaging provision and make it law, we are no longer able to serve as your advisors."[20] In addition, the New Hampshire Department of Education created a website in which "those who believe that they, or their child, was discriminated against because their child's school was teaching and/or advocating" subjects prohibited by the New Hampshire law, can file a complaint.[21] The New Hampshire American Federation of Teachers (AFT) president, Deb Howes, characterized the New Hampshire Department of Education as declaring a "war on teachers," and stated,

It was bad enough that the law tried to find a problem that doesn't exist—no teacher in New Hampshire teaches that any group is inherently superior or inferior to another. That false flag has now been made worse with Education Commissioner Frank Edelblut launching a webpage to encourage parents to file complaints against teachers who allegedly teach so-called divisive concepts. . . . Edelblut has declared a war on teachers, a war that the overwhelming majority of N.H. parents will find repulsive.[22]

Though the New Hampshire law and the state guidance about it does not outwardly ban all discussions of race, and fairness in classrooms, it has been repeatedly criticized for its vagueness and for discouraging teachers from engaging students in conversations about discrimination and systemic racism.[23] Furthermore, it encourages parents to report a nonexistent problem. The potential consequences of being found in violation of the law (for example, losing one's teaching license) have intimidated school districts and teachers so much so that some are largely avoiding discussions related to race and/or inequality altogether in the classroom. Map 7.1 was amended in collaboration with school administrators and legal counsel to protect the teacher, school, and district from being accused of operating in violation of the law.

Three specific changes the second author made to map 7.1 are described below before discussing how those changes might limit children's opportunities to learn about themselves, others, and conceptions of fairness.

CHANGE NO. 1

A majority of the changes made to map 7.1 were done to decrease young children's opportunities to engage in discussions that focus on similarities and differences among individuals specific to race. One alteration was to eliminate the learning experience, artful explorations. The objectives of this activity are to (1) guide children's self-exploration and (2) affirm their individual identities. Children are provided paper, paintbrushes, paint palettes, mirrors, and paint jars filled with washable paints. As children mix the paint colors they are invited to discuss their skin tones and compare them to the skin tones of their peers and others. This was one of the first activities eliminated when revising map 7.1; encouraging the kindergarten children to engage in an activity that explores the idea that skin colors are made up of different tones and vary from one individual to the next, was deemed to be a potential violation of state law.

CHANGE NO. 2

Engaging with high-quality literature is another way children can increase their awareness of different ways of being and thinking. Reading books can prompt children to think critically about a topic and provoke rich discussions that further expand their understanding of who they are, who their community members are, and who they might want to become. In all three maps the team intentionally selected mentor texts to support the map's primary learning objectives. Mentor texts for map 7.1 are included in figure 7.1 (see Appendix). When reexamining map 7.1 through the lens of the New Hampshire law, it became evident that many of the mentor texts listed in the map could potentially lead to classroom discussions that might be understood as violating the law. For example, in our experience when a group of kindergarteners reads the book *We Are All Alike . . . We Are All Different* by Cheltenham Elementary Kindergarteners, they enjoy comparing and contrasting themselves to their peers and to the children represented in the text. The book highlights similarities and differences between people's physical attributes, their homes and communities, their family structures, and their interests, among other things. It introduces children to a range of ways to behave and think and fosters an appreciation and respect for others and the surrounding community. Similarly, through the children's book, *Same, Same, but Different* by Jenny Sue Kostecki-Shaw, children learn about two pen pals who live in different countries (United States and India). The young pen pals use the language "same, same but different" to compare and contrast how they live and to strengthen their respect and understanding for each other. This specific language has supported young children in the second author's previous classes in articulating their own thinking and actions and in describing, comparing, and appreciating those of others. However, when considering these texts and others alongside the New Hampshire law, it is foreseeable that discussions of similarities and differences could center on race and thus be interpreted as a violation of the law. Because educators may not be able to control what children say in group discussions and the topic of conversations may be considered divisive to some, these texts and all mentor texts on map 7.1 were removed.

CHANGE NO. 3

A third revision to the map was the elimination of the section that directed teachers to "pay careful attention for signs of superiority or entitlement" in the classroom, and the rephrasing of the statement encouraging teachers to notice "how children divide themselves during play" to "observe how children choose friends." The original phrases were included to assist educators in developing their own knowledge of the classroom community and in exploring any potential inclusion and exclusion play biases the children might hold. These observations could then be used to facilitate discussions and learning experiences related to fairness in ways that are particularly relevant to the children. As educators make note of these influences in the classroom community, they gain insight into how to further support children's construction and application of concepts of fairness and friendship. The New Hampshire law specifically prohibits teachers from acknowledging and discussing bias—both conscious bias and unconscious bias—in the classroom. As such, the removal and revising of these phrases from map 7.1 were deemed necessary to comply with the law.

POTENTIAL CONSEQUENCES OF MODIFICATIONS

The modifications made to map 7.1, in response to New Hampshire's antidivisive concepts law, limit opportunities for young children to learn about themselves, others, and the conceptions of fairness. When children explore the concept of skin color through intentional art explorations they can see themselves and others more fully; they are made aware of and given the language, time and space to practice respectfully depicting and describing their own physical attributes and physical attributes of others—they are seen and heard within their community and they see and hear others in their community.

When children are not permitted to engage with mentor texts that explore facets of identity including *We Are All Alike . . . We Are All Different* and *Same, Same, but Different*, they again are being denied opportunities to affirm their own identities and also opportunities to appreciate the identities of others. Additionally, they are restricted from learning about other ways of thinking and behaving that might fit their individual personalities and bring them joy. For example, in our experience, children have gained language and ideas from engaging with these texts that have inspired them to try out and sometimes adopt different modes of dress, hairstyles, problem-solving strategies, language, and games, among other things.

All too often in our careers we have seen children excluded from play schemes for a variety of reasons. Sometimes, girls are told they cannot play a game the boys have created. Other times, children with high energy levels, those who speak loudly, and/or those who actively seek out sensory feedback (for example, are more physical) are left out of calmer activities. When educators notice children being excluded during play and/or other signs of children potentially expressing superiority or entitlement, it is critical to respond with a developmentally appropriate, antibias approach. This might involve discussing conceptions of fairness and deciding as a classroom community how to treat one another. The second author has repeatedly observed kindergarten students dividing themselves by gender in their play schemes. She has also noticed them conforming and promoting traditional gender roles—girls only playing with and allowing girls to play at the dramatic play kitchen space, for example. Similarly, she has observed boys restricting girls from playing in the block area and heard both boys and girls claiming that one group is "better" than the other. In years past, the second author would have immediately jumped at these opportunities to provoke children's thinking with carefully crafted intentional questions (for example, "I am noticing that sometimes in our play friends may say to another friend, 'You cannot play because you are a boy' or 'You cannot play because you are a girl.' I am wondering what you think about this?") and listened carefully to each child's perspective before supporting the classroom community in defining what constitutes fair play. However, the new law functions to discourage teachers from taking action. They must deeply consider whether and how to approach these kinds of conversations to avoid violating a particularly vague yet highly threatening law. Failure to notice children's potential biases and engage them in discussions about unfairness and fairness may further harm those who are being excluded while at the same time stymieing children's developing understanding and applications of fairness.

Conclusion

In light of Brighouse's and Brighouse and colleagues' understanding of flourishing—specifically their position that schools have a responsibility to support children's flourishing by building their capacities for personal autonomy and treating others as equals, the alterations made to map 7.1 in response to New Hampshire's antidivisive concepts legislation, are concerning at best.[24] The changes discussed here are only three of many that were made to avoid violating the law. It is fair to say that the children experiencing the revised map are missing out on a multitude of opportunities to learn about themselves, others, and fairness—opportunities children experiencing the original map are not missing. When adults restrict children's opportunities to better understand themselves and others, they forgo worthwhile chances to affirm children's individual identities. The elimination of mentor texts that facilitate discussions centered on difference deny children exposure and the option to select from alternate ways of behaving and thinking that might better match their personalities and, in turn, support their happiness. Finally, when educators are prohibited from observing, acknowledging, and discussing unconscious and/or conscious bias in the classroom, children are denied opportunities to address any biases that may interfere with their abilities to play and work harmoniously with others as moral and social equals. Research examining the short- and long-term impacts of antidivisive concepts legislation is needed to determine just how detrimental they may be to children's developing capacities for personal autonomy and treating others as equals.

Questions for Discussion

- What do you believe you need to flourish? Compare your requirements with those of at least two other people. Where do the requirements converge? Where do they diverge? What can you infer about flourishing from this mini-experiment?

- What about teacher flourishing—do school leadership and the agencies governing schools (for example, district administration, state department of education) have a responsibility to support teacher flourishing? Explain your reasoning.

Further Reading

Derman-Sparks, Louise, and Julie Edwards. "Understanding Anti-Bias Education: Bringing the Four Core Goals to Every Facet of Your Curriculum." NAEYC. Accessed March 19, 2023, https://www.naeyc.org/resources/pubs/yc/nov2019/understanding-anti-bias.

Brighouse, Harry. "Education for a Flourishing Life." *Yearbook of the National Society for the Study of Education* 107 (2008): 58–71.

Activity

Digging into Self-Censorship

Think of a time when you avoided or changed some aspect of teaching (for example, content, text, instructional approach) for fear that it might upset others (for example, parents, school administration) and/or threaten your job security. Place the event at the center of a concept map and explore through mapping your rationale(s) for making your decision to censor yourself. The following prompts may be of use in the mapping process but are not required; feel free to map in a way that makes the most sense to you. Some find it useful to include images or doodles in addition to words. The goal is to be as honest and expressive as possible.

a. Who were you thinking about specifically when you made your decision?

b. Who were you most afraid of? Why?

c. Which aspect(s) did you believe to be most problematic?

d. What potential consequences to doing things as you originally intended did you envision?

e. Which one scared you the most? Why?

f. Would you censor yourself again in this way today? Why or why not?

Appendix

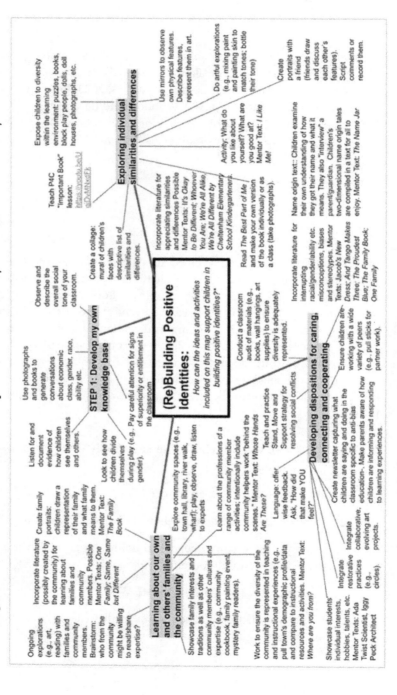

Figure 7.1. The first antibias curriculum map created and executed by the team. *Source:* Created by the author.

Notes

1. The authors would like to thank all those who commented on a previous draft of this chapter presented at the Philosophy of Education Society annual meeting preconference (2022) and Professors Todd A. DeMitchell and Winston C. Thompson for their support of this project and for feedback on previous drafts.

2. Harry Brighouse, "Moral and Political Aims of Education," in *Handbook of Philosophy of Education*, ed. Harvey Siegel (Oxford, UK: Oxford University Press, 2012), 35–51.

3. Steve Williams, "P4C: What, Why and How?" P4C, accessed March 14, 2023, https://p4c.com/about-p4c/.

4. Louise Derman-Sparks and Julie Olsen Edwards, *Anti-Bias Education for Young Children and Ourselves* (Washington, DC: NAEYC, 2020).

5. Todd DeMitchell, Richard Fossey, and Terri DeMitchell, "A Moral Panic, Banning Books, and the Constitution: The Right to Direct the Upbringing and the Right to Receive Information in a Time of Inflection," *West's Education Law Reporter* 397, no. 3 (2022): 905–928.

6. Jeffrey Sachs and Jonathan Friedman, "Educational Gag Orders Target Speech about LGBTQ+ Identities with New Prohibitions and Punishments," PEN America, accessed March 12, 2023, https://https://pen.org/educational-gag-orders-target-speech-about-lgbtq-identities-with-new-prohibitions-and-punishments/.

7. Brighouse, "Moral and Political Aims," 39.

8. Harry Brighouse, *On Education* (London: Routledge, 2006), 11–61.

9. Daniel DeNicola, *Learning to Flourish: A Philosophical Exploration of Liberal Education* (London: Continuum, 2012), 53.

10. Harry Brighouse et al., "Educational Goods and Values: A Framework for Decision-Makers," *Theory and Research in Education* 14, no. 1 (2016): 3–25.

11. Harry Brighouse et al., *Educational Goods: Values, Evidence, and Decision-Making* (Chicago, IL: University of Chicago Press, 2018), 24.

12. Brighouse et al., *Educational Goods*, 26.

13. Beverly Tatum, *Why Are All the Black Kids Sitting Together in the Cafeteria? And Other Conversations about Race*, New York: Basic Books, 2017), 111–30.

14. Derman-Sparks and Edwards, *Anti-Bias Education*, 15–18.

15. Joy Dangora Erickson et al., "Collaborative Autoethnography as a Tool for Developing Social-Justice-Oriented Preschool Experiences," *Kappa Delta Pi Record* 58 (2022): 43–48.

16. Fairness is centered in later maps.

17. Derman-Sparks and Edwards, *Anti-Bias Education*, 15–18.

18. Louise Derman-Sparks and Patricia Ramsey, *What If All the Kids Are White? Anti-Bias Multicultural Education with Young Children and Families* (New York: Teachers College Press, 2011), 61–88.

19. Activities listed on project maps are not intended to be used as a script; they are instead intended to guide and support teachers in selecting, designing, and implementing learning experiences that facilitate each map's goals.

20. Jenny Whidden, "Half of Governor's Diversity Council Quits over 'Divisive Concepts' Restriction in Budget," *Monadnock Ledger-Transcript*, accessed March 19, 2023, /https://www.ledgertranscript.com/Half-of-governor-s-diversity-council-abruptly-quits-41216250.

21. "Right to Freedom from Discrimination in Public Workplaces and Education," New Hampshire Department of Education, accessed March 19, 2023, https://www.education.nh.gov/who-we-are/deputy-commissioner/office-of-governance/right-to-freedom-from-discrimination.

22. Peter Greene, "New Hampshire and Moms for Liberty Put Bounty on Teachers' Heads," *Forbes*, accessed March 19, 2023, https://www.forbes.com/sites/petergreene/2021/11/12/new-hampshire-and-moms-for-liberty-put-bounty-on-teachers-heads/?sh=2e3af4c4a4bf.

23. "FAQ: What Is the "Divisive Concepts" Language in the NH Budget?" ACLU New Hampshire, accessed March, 19, 2023, https://www.aclu-nh.org/en/news/faq-what-divisive-concepts-language-nh-budget.

24. Brighouse, *On Education*, 11–61; Brighouse, "Moral and Political Aims," 35–51; Larry Brighouse et al., *Educational Goods: Values, Evidence, and Decision-Making* (Chicago, IL: University of Chicago Press, 2018).

8

Finding a Place for Play in School
Risk, Ambiguity, and Resistance

CHRIS MOFFETT AND ELISABETH TAM

Infinite play is inherently *paradoxical*, just as finite play is *inherently contradictory*. Because it is the purpose of infinite players to continue the play, they do not play for themselves. [. . .] The joyfulness of infinite play, its laughter, lies in learning to start something we cannot finish.

—James P. Carse, *Finite and Infinite Games*

Introduction: Getting Started

There is a fundamental risk in thinking and talking about play, much like the well-known paradox of trying to explain a joke. If you find yourself having to explain a joke, then something has gone awry. Rather than letting this risk bringing our conversation about play to a halt before it has even begun, we can instead use it as a way in, an invitation to play with talking about play, and an invitation to explore together the strange difficulty of getting play started. Play is perhaps a bit like falling asleep. While we may abstractly know something of it ahead of time, and even desire it, we know it practically and intimately by finding our way into and sustaining it. Likewise, few if any would argue, in the abstract, against the value of play, or even more specifically its value in education. And yet, in contrast, we must be struck with the evident and pervasive practical challenge of introducing and sustaining play in actual schools. What are we to make of this contrast?

In Brian Sutton-Smith's influential 1997 work, *The Ambiguity of Play*, he identifies seven distinct abstract frames for arguing for play.[1] Of these, the rhetoric of "play as *progress*" is most commonly deployed in education to advocate for play as the mode by which children "develop." As he notes, however, at a practical level we encounter any number of ambiguities that challenge a simple notion of progress. And this framing of progress comes in tension, or contact zones we could say, with other possible frames such as what he calls "the rhetoric of frivolity." Frivolity often destabilizes notions of progress by evoking forms of play that elude clear goals. The play of children "goofing off" in the classroom easily comes in tension with a curricular game they may be assigned for their learning development. This tension reflects a thornier ambiguity of play than a teacher may be prepared to wrestle with in the moment (which may in some way be the very reason it tends to recur so often in the classroom). Indeed, any attempt at a complete understanding of play is confronted with similar deep, intricate, and perhaps unresolvable ambiguities. Play eludes us, even as we engage in it.

Indeed, what Sutton-Smith shows us is that play itself expresses a flexible—and even contradictory, paradoxical, or ambiguous—form. There is, we could say, a play of play itself. This suggests two things. The first is that how we move into, or introduce, play is itself paradoxically a playful process that cannot be determined in advance. We feel our way into it by playing at it. The second is that we never play in general—play always involves responding to the specificity of the participants, circumstances, materials, and rhythms. And this shifts from moment to moment. How a cat instigates play with us is different than how it continues the play, which is different in some important way from the last time it happened.

Mary Louise Pratt points out the challenge of modeling, at a general level, the interactions of schooling as games: "Despite whatever conflicts or systematic social differences might be in play, it is assumed that all participants are engaged in the same game and that the game is the same for all players."[2] Pratt suggests that it is all too easy for *the idea of playing nicely* to mask the differences of class, culture, and authority that are at difficult play. She quotes her son's astute analysis of his new school: "They're a lot nicer, and they have a lot less rules. But know why they're nicer? . . . So you'll obey all the rules they don't have."[3] Against this generalizing and masking tendency, we could say that, on the one hand, the very conditions for play emerge out of these difficult contact zones, as we find a way to play together. On the other hand, the contact zones themselves might be part of the play, or even—as in the son's case?—the very thing being played with itself.

Given the ambiguity and situatedness of play, we should begin this foray into the challenges of introducing play in schools by introducing and detailing some of our own contexts, paths, and predilections. We (Elisabeth and Chris) first met through a mutual interest in an early childhood, play-based curriculum being developed in Anji, China, called Anji Play. With a MEd in Early Childhood Education, Elisabeth had been teaching early childhood in different settings, first in an urban field-based independent school, then in a Reggio Emilia approach forest school, and then teaching in a standards-based international school in Vietnam. (At the time of writing this, Elisabeth was teaching in an outdoor nature-based preschool in Seattle, but is now teaching at the Singapore American School, in Singapore.) Chris's doctoral work was in philosophy of education, with an emphasis on how educational practices are shaped at the intersection of embodied experience and deep historical metaphors of space, such as the way classroom architecture and practices often emulate earlier mythic tales of sacrificial descent into an underworld. He was teaching in higher education on the aesthetics of the educational imaginary—how we envision and make sense of what we are doing when we inhabit educational spaces. Drawn to Anji Play's unique interplay of play and space, he had spent a considerable amount of time researching in Anji, over multiple visits. His research increasingly focused on play and art. (At the time of this writing, he was teaching art education and foundations of art, and is currently a research scholar at the Digital Futures Institute at Teachers College of Columbia University.) This short summary hopefully suggests both the diversity and limitations of the contact zones in play in our own collaboration and experience.

Encountering Play

Out of our conversations together, both in the US and China, we began to explore questions about the nature and value of play, and particularly the challenges of introducing play in educational contexts where it is not the norm. Although Anji Play is the shared context for our conversations, we have time only for a brief description of it here. Developed over the last eighteen years, in Anji and outside of a Western context, Anji Play is the public education kindergarten model for the entire county and is now being piloted nationally. It is based on the premise of providing the maximum amount of freedom for children to determine their own play. This play takes up a considerable portion of their day as well as becoming subject matter for drawing and discussion afterward. It typically involves outdoor engagements with their environment, and abundant large-scale loose materials such as ladders and barrels.

Upon visiting an Anji kindergarten, a visitor is typically struck by the scope and enthusiasm of the play in a way that is difficult to describe. For an educator, this provokes something of a crisis of contact zones. What are we to do with this experience? Either we find ways to fit it within the paradigms and practices that we already know—*Oh, we do that already*—or the contrast becomes troubling—*We could never do that*. While it is clearly not impossible (since you are seeing it), the next line of defense is that it is impossible *where I am*. A more hopeful educator might begin to speculate (although not without the risk and anxiety)—*What would it take to do something like that where I am?*

It is this cluster of questions, challenges, and ambiguities suggested by the play encounter in Anji that we would like to explore in more detail. On the one hand, what happens when play is encountered? What does it invite or provoke? On the other hand, what happens when it is absent or even actively suppressed? How can play be initiated within educational contexts where play is largely absent or—perhaps as challenging—where it is already present, but circumscribed and limited in specific ways?

The Risk of Play: General Objections

If we think of play not as a discrete, definable, and knowable condition, but as an elusive, emergent possibility that is always in the making, then we could say that it is always something that we encounter as arriving. Play is always something of a surprise (even, or especially, when it is in full swing). Which is also to say that play, by its arriving, is always disrupting or interrupting something else. And since school is in the business of education, whatever it is that play is interrupting—it goes almost without saying—*is* this business (even, or especially, when it is in the service of it? What, after all, is recess but a withdrawal or departure?). To accept or welcome play is to let go. Play, in this sense, is a risky business.

Regardless, we encounter play as arriving, as in some way already underway as a surprise. From the perspective of a teacher in a school, how is this arrival felt? It can arrive as something that is happening: children are playing, of their own accord, with or without the intention of the adults. Or it can arrive as an idea or curricular proposal, ahead of itself: formal or informal, welcome or threatening, clear or barely registered—in which case, we draw on memories or abstractions, to make sense of the possible arrival. What will it look like? Every potential arrival calls for a response, be it a welcome or an objection.

As a teacher, this is constantly felt and negotiated. If children are playing, how do we know? What can or should we do in response? Do we not feel play? Where might we expect it from or seek it out? And what does it ask of us as teachers? More often than not, this is ambiguous, even if we have strong tendencies. For example, in Elisabeth's first teaching job, in first grade in an urban private school that organized itself around field experiences, the usual parameters of school were expanded, and they were able to explore diverse experiences, while at the same time these encounters were often framed around the need to be attentive and polite guests. Likewise, a small unused space in the school was able to be converted into a garden, but at the same time, it found itself being used for enacting supervised botanical observation rather than something more playful. Meanwhile, her next school aligned with the Reggio Emilia approach. Developed in Italy, this approach reflects a constructivist view of children's development, and emphasizes the self-guided experiential learning of the child.[4] In Elisabeth's school, the children already had extensive access to forests and other spaces where they were free to roam and play. The encounter with play here was markedly different, expansive, and enthusiastic. The questions revolved around the best ways to support the experience. Her next school, by contrast, was an international school in Vietnam where she initially taught first grade, and it is here that we see the strongest tension. The school's curriculum was standards-based, academic, and oriented to college as an outcome. Play was felt as a kind of lack, and it is in this context that the tension between a commitment to play as a necessity of childhood and the school's scholastic commitments unfolds.

Whether teachers already have a strong sense of the possibility of play or it is simply being evoked as a possibility, in common circumstances like this, there is a general objection (one that is, we can safely assume, largely accurate): *I can't do that.* There is no time or space for it. Or, specifically, it's not allowed. Or more vaguely, what if I am seen not actively teaching? How will administrators or parents respond? Or, when will I teach *X*? Whether they are felt as frustrations or defenses, objections or laments, we should acknowledge them first as responses to the ambiguous potential of play. Play arrives—even or especially, where it is not sanctioned—and asks us to respond.

The Play of Play

In the epigraph to this essay, from a work that remains unfortunately largely ignored in the theory of play, James P. Carse distinguishes between two modes of play: finite and infinite.[5] Put simply, finite games are composed of fixed rules designed to bring the play to a close with a specific outcome, while infinite games are designed and perpetually modified in order to continue the play for its own sake. We can see the felt conflict between these two distinct agendas most acutely in the contexts in which education is increasingly framed as a finite game. It's not that there is simply no time for (infinite) play, but that another mode of play is actively at work staving off the instabilities that it would introduce. But more difficult to see is the ways in which play runs through both of these forms. For Carse, they are diametrically opposed in all matters but one. In both modes, whoever plays, plays freely. In finite games, this precondition is often hidden or externally constrained, and the coercive forces at play deserve much closer scrutiny. And Carse never develops the conditions by which we move into, out of, or between forms of play in detail. Nevertheless, it leads to an interesting paradoxical insight: the condition of play is not the removal of constraints, while at the same time it always begins with an essential freedom.

As the game designer and theorist Ian Bogost, puts it, freedom is not freedom from constraints, but "a practice of working within adopted constraints" in order to "pursue a greater respect for the things, people, and situations around us."[6] Again, what we still need is a way of thinking about how we might go about this paradoxical free adoption of constraints. It clearly cannot mean a simple resignation in the face of coercive or uninteresting games. Instead, what we are proposing with the idea that *play arrives* is that we need to be sensitive both to the ways in which we are asked to respond to the conditions of play, and to the play within those conditions themselves (and what they make possible or not.) Play arrives everywhere, and at the same time, not all play is the same. Nor is it always clear what the differences are. Or to put it another way, there is a play of play. Play is a way of finding the conditions of play. And the conditions for finding ways of sustaining play often, if not invariably, have to do with the constraints or diverse contact zones in which we find ourselves.

This is the paradox: on the one hand, play needs time and space; while on the other hand, time and space are not the preconditions for play. Playgrounds are great in the abstract, but they are not necessary, nor guarantees of play. Quite the opposite, the fixed structures of so many playgrounds are often discarded by children for places that provide more interesting wiggle room.

Stepping Back and Seeing What Happens

Frustrated by the lack of opportunity for play in the international school, Elisabeth voiced her frustration to the head of school, and while the school was not simply going to change its approach like that, she was given the opportunity to move to kindergarten. In other circumstances, different opportunities might have been available, such as changes to the curriculum, schedule, or roles. But perhaps the biggest challenge that a teacher faces is stepping back and seeing what emerges. This is most evident in the classroom, where there are many internal and external motivations to interfere in children's play. Not doing something, or choosing to support what is actually emerging, can be felt as a risk. Indeed, there are often real reasons for fear, but these are also often imagined to be bigger or different than they actually turn out to be. And the value of the initial risk is that it can create the conditions for its own minimization. Discovering that things were fine after all allows for play to move past its uncertain beginnings and see what can flourish.

As a teacher, this might mean stepping back in two directions: What space can you find to step back in your classroom, to see what emerges? And where can you find space to see where things might shift with the school itself? In Elisabeth's case, she looked for opportunities with her class: What's really keeping us from going outside when it's raining, to study the weather more directly? What other spaces can we find? But also, where is there room around the curriculum to approach it differently? When all of the classes were required to do projects around health and the body, she asked her students how they wanted to approach it, and they said "Robots!" Rather than steering toward a more adult-legible direction, she encouraged it, and the students took the concept of robots and ran with it. In the end, the difference in the students' creativity and engagement relative to the other classes was evident to the other teachers and visitors.

Elisabeth also reached out to other teachers and invited them to talk and visit the classroom to see what was going on. She would also document what was happening and show the principal. Maybe you have a principal that you sense might be open, or maybe not. Oftentimes, the visiting teachers would express reluctance. It's not about a particular response, though. An invitation to visit the classroom is not an expectation that you will have to do or feel anything specific. It's about playing with the possibilities, and stepping back to see what resonates. By creating the conditions for play to emerge, both inside and outside of the classroom, however, you create more opportunities for a felt response to play, and an experience of the difference that it can introduce into the classroom.

The Ambiguity of Time

Above all, the arrival of play takes time, but in a very general sense. It doesn't require that you start by blocking out huge chunks of "playtime," so much as it requires continued patience and playing with the conditions of play over long periods of time. It requires time to continue to explore and question with your colleagues, with parents, with administrators. It requires time to play with things differently, to feel things out, and to start again. It requires time to wrestle and play with your own fears and desires, to give space to the people around you. But it also means the time to alter our perception of time itself, the ways in which education commits and conditions our experience of time in the name of progress. It takes time to realize that play is always arriving, all the time.

Questions for Discussion

- Consider the conditions for play to begin. How do we signal to each other that play is desired? What do we do to sustain it? Is it different for adults, children, or a pet? Can you recollect a time when play was instigated? Can you recollect a time when play was thwarted?

- Consider a time when play may feel difficult or impossible. What are some factors that might make this the case? What are ways you might play with those factors?

Further Reading

Coffino, Jesse Robert, and Chelsea Bailey. "The Anji Play Ecology of Early Learning." *Childhood Education Innovations* (January/February 2019).

Jones, Denisha. "Resisting Neoliberal Reforms in Early Childhood Education: Play Pedagogy as the Antidote to Germ." In *The Commodification of American Education: Persistent Threats and Paths Forward*, edited by T. Jameson Brewer and William Gregory Harman. Gorham, ME: Myers Education Press, 2021.

Moffett, Chris. "The Play of Art: Propensity and Pedagogy in Contemporary Chinese Early Childhood Education." *Studies in Art Education* 62, no. 3 (2021): 222–35.

Activity

Choose a social scenario that you can observe without being interrupted (a public space, class, recess, family gathering, and so on). Write without stopping and without judgment for five minutes, noticing any elements that encourage or discourage play, whatever they might be. Rest, and then notice if you are seeing your surroundings differently or not. Write down anything that has stayed the same or changed in your perception.

Notes

1. Brian Sutton-Smith, *The Ambiguity of Play* (Cambridge, MA: Harvard University Press, 1997).

2. Mary Louise Pratt, "Arts of the Contact Zone," *Profession* (1991): 38.

3. Pratt, "Arts of the Contact Zone," 38.

4. Valarie Mercilliott Hewett, "Examining the Reggio Emilia Approach to Early Childhood Education," *Early Childhood Education Journal* 29, no. 2 (December 1, 2001): 95–100.

5. James P. Carse, *Finite and Infinite Games* (New York: Free Press, 1986).

6. Ian Bogost, *Play Anything: The Pleasure of Limits, the Uses of Boredom, and the Secret of Games* (New York: Basic Books, 2016), xii.

9

Katzi Txumu'n

Creating a Curriculum of Mesoamerican Short Stories for Philosophical Conversations with Children and Families

Cristina Cammarano and Kimberly Arriaga-Gonzalez

This essay presents a reflection on a project of curriculum creation started in 2019, in the context of a philosophy of education undergraduate course. At the time of writing this paper, Kimberly Arriaga-Gonzalez is a community programs specialist at city-operated local community center for low-income migrant families in Salisbury, Maryland. She was an undergraduate student when the project got started. Cristina Cammarano is a philosopher of education on the faculty of a public comprehensive university. The third student researcher, Esteban Garcia-Ailon, who participated in the project, has recently graduated college and is planning to become an early childhood educator. While he is not involved in writing this paper, he contributed greatly to the project we are writing about.[1]

The project consisted in creating a curriculum of short stories for philosophical discussion with children, drawn from preconquest Mexican and Guatemalan traditions. Two students were involved in the project together with the instructor. The idea for the project came from the students, who are both of Mesoamerican migrant background, and were puzzled at the lack of culturally relevant storybooks for children in our small campus library. The two student researchers were fluent in Spanish, and they were respectively of Totonaco-Nahua[2] and Awakateko-Maya[3] descent. Both researchers had a working knowledge of their families' indigenous languages and traditions. The students either recorded or involved themselves with story creation, translated stories when necessary, and wrote a discussion guide for each story. The outcome is a collection of resources, stories, lexicon, philosophical questions and images. The first presentation of the project took place as a bilingual storytelling and philosophy discussion in a virtual setting hosted by the local library[4] for children ages five to ten. A second presentation took place in the context of the 2021 Envirokids Literacy Festival, on the theme, "Earth Action: Healing Our Home." We look forward to more engagement with the curriculum at community events.

The essay works with an understanding of curriculum as an encounter emerging from the ongoing relation between the new and the tradition,[5] mediated by stories.[6] Many children who come from diverse backgrounds exist within a balance of tradition and newness (integration in a new society). The lack of stories that would make students feel seen causes a severed relationship between student and education. The encounter of the curriculum is made possible by the teacher, but it cannot happen *only* by the teacher, as it requires meaning searching and constructing by both the students and the teachers in conversation with traditions. When the curriculum in use falls short of its promise, like it happened with us, students and teachers take on a task of curriculum creation. In our view, the ultimate value of our curriculum creation is emancipatory.[7] In our paper, we outline the emancipatory task of curriculum creation when this creation takes the form of storytelling and story writing in relation to students' own cultural background and family traditions. We argue that work of this type is especially desirable for students of marginalized backgrounds, who do not often find themselves in the curricula in schools. *Katzi Txumu'n* opens a space for dialogue and story. The name of our project combines two words, *katzi*, which means knowing in Totonaco, and *txumu'n*, meaning idea in Maya Awakateko. Engaging *Katzi Txumu'n* with philosophical reflection, the relationship is made clear between story as a functional cultural tool for individuals and community, and reflection as part of self-creation. The paper considers the purpose of the project, especially in light of the student-researchers who conducted it as an emancipatory practice of canon revision and creation—thus recognizing the student-researchers as an essential part of the meaning-making relation with the tradition.

> "The more something is shared,
> the greater its value becomes."[8]

The essay reflects on this experience in the specific local learning environment, and draws connections between creative expression, learning, teaching, and curriculum creation as an emancipatory task. After offering a description of the project, we highlight some ideal components that we can recognize in it, hoping that our readers will be inspired to entertain projects in this vein.

Description of the Project

In the summer of 2020, a student research project, connected to a philosophy of education course, focused on understanding storytelling as a tool of education. During the pandemic, many families were left without educational resources for their kids. We thought it important to provide free resources. The transition to online Zoom classes changed the dynamic in the classroom. We focused on the importance of relating to one's teachers and seeing the student within the educational environment. *Katzi Txumu'n* offers a collection of inquisitive philosophical stories that can be used as at home reading guides for children and parents. The stories focus on representing indigenous Latino stories that reflect the demographic of the Eastern Shores migrant community. The process of research, writing, inspiration, and editing ideas from our booklet took a long time. We wanted to create stories that would be thematically connected to the struggles migrant children identify with. The project aimed at assisting families at home while sharing stories of mutual respect, love for the earth, and understanding.

Reflections on the Project

Katzi Txumu'n focuses on the importance of storytelling as a project of self-actualization. To better illustrate this point, now we switch to a first-person reflection by the student-researcher who cocreated the project.

Throughout my journey as a student and a book lover I (Kimberly) realized the lack of representation in media for indigenous youth. During heritage festivals in school, I felt at a loss because I did not know how to explain myself and family to my peers. To them it was sufficient to know my family migrated here from Mexico. However, the diversity of Mexico and the beauty of my culture simply felt too small against the American stereotype of Mexican immigrants. I had many comparisons to different cultures. In America, the school curriculum covered most common mythology like Greek, Roman mythology, and biblical stories. One of my favorite books to read growing up was the Percy Jackson and the Olympians series written by Rick Riordan.[9] The world I experienced through those books felt so familiar and close to me. Mythology and stories of people in the past were a familiar storytelling method. Books and their mythological stories made an impact on how I saw myself in the world. It was a symbol of strength to me to be able to see children fight for what they believed in and stand up to the adults in their lives. I've always been able to sympathize with a troublemaker. After spending a lot of time falling in love with book series similar to the one I mentioned it became harder for me as an indigenous migrant to see myself represented in these stories. I knew the struggles of characters was something I could reflect on and understand, but it was never a direct mirror for my experience as an immigrant or a native girl.

It became difficult for me to see myself in the media or in children stories because they never properly reflected my culture or identity. American media makes indigenous people exist within a historical time frame where their pain and struggle offers no sympathy. As Thomas King mentions in *The Inconvenient Indian*, indigenous youth are constantly exposed to stereotypes of indigeneity and a historical account of conquest.[10] The way we are understood offers no insight into the vibrant communities still thriving to this day. Curriculum creation meant to open a space for that truth. The truth of community, holistic knowledge, and the beauty of thriving. It was difficult to reconcile the way indigenous people are portrayed with the ones I had of my beautiful and vibrant family. The storyteller in my family is my auntie. She would know everything and anything about what's been done and said in our family. She could tell a story and have us all enthralled by the details and people involved. My Tia Mari is someone who embraces one of the oldest traditions women keep in my family; knowledge of kin. My Dad knows all about the shrines and the places where gods still lurk. The knowledge of family offers to young people the ability to recognize their personal interfamilial difficulties and pain as symbols of persistence. The value of knowing who you are a part of and the way it affects your identity allows you to reflect on yourself and to continue involving yourself with stories like *Katzi Txumu'n*.

Interacting with these storytelling spaces you are not only a bystander, you are part of the story.

While working at the youth center there have been many opportunities to use the collection of stories in a group environment. As the community program specialist I coordinate programs for the afterschool club. The group that actively participates in discussions ranges from third to seventh grade. I find the children are excited to engage in conversation about anything. The stories have provided an interesting opportunity for the kids to be exposed to philosophy and stories from different cultural backgrounds. Also, it helps build the ability to hold a theme-heavy conversation and critical thinking skills.

Working events with children from different backgrounds, I've come to realize the benefits of sharing cultural stories that include a variety of cultures. The history of indigenous people in North and Latin America can be a difficult story about genocide and colonizer cruelty. We are in a time where voices and stories are more accessible than ever: Indigenous stories can be found throughout all parts of American media and pop culture. However, identifying and respecting the origins of traditions can leave a standing impact to children's ability to recognize and appreciate differences between groups of people. This way, stories provide an opportunity to learn about identity, cultural respect, traditions, and views on home. Our stories help build a relationship to others and help acknowledge or reach the realization that everyone's home is beautiful, significant, and precious no matter of origin or differences.

Storytelling

Storytelling covers a crucial role in the preserving and loving of indigenous identity. In "Healing through Culture," Heiltsuk educator Hilistis Pauline Waterfall tells her story of being a Heiltsuk child placed in a residential school at age twelve. She describes the interruption in the transmission of knowledge caused by residential schools and by laws that forbade traditional cultural practices. She tells of her state of cultural shock: "My life was like a piece of cork tossed into the ocean at the mercy of storms and changing tides—alone, confused, afraid, disconnected, and lost."[11] She continues, "Navigating the outside world eclipsed my Heiltsuk roots and often left me caught between the cracks of these two worlds, not truly fitting into either."[12]

After being away for eighteen years, Waterfall decided to come back home to Bella Bella. There, she felt "a stranger in [her] homeland" and "ignorant" about her own heritage.[13] She undertook a journey to recover her family's history and the traditional ceremony of potlach, which had been banned from 1883 to 1951, and practiced clandestinely in private settings. Cultural transmission from one generation to the next had been broken, and the memories were incomplete. However, Waterfall was able to conduct her inquiry by talking to elders, comparing manufacts, accounts, and mourning ceremonies which had incorporated some elements of the forbidden potlach. The actual event, a community potlach organized according to the traditional knowledge, was held in 1985, "a success (that) sparked a cultural flame."[14] Heiltsuk children practiced dances and there was a resurgence in art and sewing regalia, and annual potlach ceremonies were had in schools. She concludes, "This fragile beginning has now blossomed into a strong cultural foundation that draws from individual and collective memories."[15] Waterfall's account proves that, borrowing the title of her beautiful essay, "Healing through Culture" is possible when rooted in intergenerational storytelling and dialogue.

Q'um Q'um Xiiem, Dr. Jo-ann Archbald, (2008) writes that indigenous storytelling puts you on a memory pathway.[16] Stories are told through song, art forms and repetitions: those who listen "write them in their hearts."[17] Given the history of abuse and annihilation of indigenous people in Canada, she writes, "The storied memories of Indigenous people have been assaulted," and the "intergenerational transmission of culture and memory" has been negatively affected. "However," she notes, "as Stoclo elders remind us, these storied memories were not totally forgotten but were "put to sleep" for a while"[18] These "storied memories" are there to be awakened and sparkled up by questions, intergenerational relationships and meaningful, engaged listening. These stories heard in community, Q'um Q'um Xiiem reminds us, demonstrate "individual and collective resistance to many forms of colonizations."[19] Storytelling fulfils a vital function in indigenous pedagogy, especially in view of cultural healing. Storytelling does not happen in solitude. One is a listener before being a storyteller. It is crucial that one learns the belief system in which the story belongs: one must become a member of the community and then take responsibility as a storyteller, because the story you tell has power.[20]

STORY AND COMMUNITY

One of the most important goals of *Katzi Txumu'n* revolves around engaging family, children, and friends in conversation. Finding the correct item to engage children in conversation holds challenges. In truth, stories where children are engaged in familiar storytelling within migrant indigenous families can look so different. The movement of people who rely on community or who believe community to be important can stand out against the American nuclear family. in the United States. The particular lived experience of being a migrant child can cause identity issues while growing in the collective and in community. In these spaces we find families relying on each other. Large families all pitch in to raise and care for children. When everyone is an uncle or auntie, the word for family doesn't stretch enough to encompass the care shown to children. The value in sharing stories these similar worldviews to children of indigenous migrant backgrounds means to be part of the conversation and understanding. Particularly, creating opportunity to share time with indigenous children and engage in conversation will help build their understanding of themselves relative to peers. In this form, story becomes a gift. The engagement families receive during a story relates to them personally by defining the relationship of storyteller, story, and listener. The process of this interaction relies on gift. In *Braiding Sweetgrass*, Robin Wall Kimmerer focuses on rethinking the way we think about gifts[21] and the moral obligations all living beings have with one another (Kimmerer, 27). Storytelling follows a similar condition as the sweetgrass Kimmerer talks about in "The Gift of Strawberries" (Kimmerer, 27). When mythology mixes with cultural inheritance the essence of the story shifts and becomes a story with an obligation. The story will not necessarily take on the allegorical significance that some fables are structured by. However, Mesoamerican storytelling becomes an obligation to community and to people whose stories hold strong philosophical value.

The following story sample comes from the *Katzi Txumu'n* booklet. This story tells of the Mother of Gods, Our Grandmother. It is a story focusing on the goddess of medicine and the ways her healing manifests to people and children. Specifically, the story centers around a young indigenous girl, Hum, who encounters the goddess of healing while trying to save her mother's temescal tourist business.[22] The goddess being represented in this story is Toci, a dual yielding goddess, who could be known to be associated as Yoalticitl—the doctor of the night or Temazcalteci—grandmother of baths. Here we present a short excerpt.

> When Hum was younger she was scared of the wind. Whenever a wind blew through their house or the mountain Hum felt shakier than a leaf. In one of those nights, Doña Facunda told her the story of the first healers and the temescal. One

night a girl was lost in the mountains while foraging for herbs. The mountain was always cold in the night and the girl didn't realize it was night already. She walked miles in the dark and the freezing air made her stiff. There she met a snake, white and glorious the color of slaked lime. The curious snake asked the little girl, "Child are you lost?"

Through the chattering of her teeth she answered, "No, I think I am too cold to make it home."

"I am cold too, little one. I am on my way to the baths, if you'd like I can take you there."

Thankful for the snake's kindness the child asked, "Kind snake I am too stiff to move anywhere. Can I ask you to take me with you."

The snake was confused because it did not have any arms to carry the child, and asked, "Little one I am a snake and have no arms. We can go to the healing baths together but I will need to carry you in my mouth."

The little girl was weary of the large snake but felt the sincerity of its words. "Thank you snake for taking me to the healing baths."

The snake put the girl in its mouth and hurried up the mountain to the healing baths. The girl was still too weak to feel the warmth of the healing baths, so the snake kept her in its mouth to warm up her soul and body in the healing waters.

Doña Facunda's story echoed in the temescal they were in and all Hum remembered was the feeling of fleshy herbs being wrapped in her hand and the sharp whispers of adults.

Conclusion

When Kimberly and Esteban composed and collected their stories, I (Cristina) knew that they were taking the responsibilities of storywork very seriously. Q'um Q'um Xiiem, Dr. Jo-ann Archbald, talks about this storywork as an act of "personal liberation,"[23] coming from the ability to manipulate English to convey indigenous meaning. We did face this issue when we decided to have the curriculum present in two languages, English and Spanish, that were both native to the writers but not their indigenous languages. There is power to be harnessed in intentionally choosing the responsibility to tell a story from one's tradition in a second language.

Stories are told repeatedly so that they can be remembered. Storywork opens the possibility that we take communal responsibility for cultural knowledge: carrying out this responsibility is a form of liberation. When working on translations, we are reminded that not only the stories are translated from an indigenous language into a colonizer language: they are also transformed from their oral form to a written one. But these stories are made to be told over and again. The story listener must become engaged with the story. The story works when one listens and responds.[24] That is why we wanted to present the stories to our local community children and interact with them—it is how meaning is made anew with every telling. We think this process brings about resistance and healing, as Hilistis Pauline Waterfall writes at the end of her story of how she rebuilt the potlatch tradition in her community: "Shared inheritance and cultural history that had been denied for so long were being rewoven through the strands of recollection. Through this, my Heiltsuk child started to grow again."[25]

In conclusion, storywork creates an important relationship between the present and cultural history. The importance of these traditions traces back to community leaders and indigenous scholars who shared their stories. In order to assert identity in the continuous flow of modernity and assimilation, stories represent a fountain of holistic knowledge for us all. Authors like Robin Wall Kimmerer, Rigoberta Menchu, and Nicole Ineese-Nash comment on the way Western society differs in foundational traditions and ways of living. Indigenous pedagogy can be a way of teaching that welcoming to all types of students. What is it that children truly need to learn about the world? How do we understand what it means to grow up? Can we understand indigenous pedagogy as an alternative learning system for children who don't succeed in traditional environments? It is important to treat cultural knowledge gently and understand how precious the stories of the beginning of the earth, gods of the home, and lessons of reciprocity are for the educational community.

Questions for Discussion

- In the story, Hum felt sick and needed the snake's help.
    - ◊ What does it mean to be sick?
    - ◊ How do we know what sickness is?
    - ◊ What does healing mean?

- For many families, many children grow up with the help of everyone in their community. For example, Hum not only has her mother, but she considers her neighbor family too.

    ◊ What is a community?

    ◊ Who is part of your community?

    ◊ Can families be good?

Further Reading

Kimmerer, Robin Wall. "The Gift of Strawberries." In *Braiding Sweetgrass*. Milkweed Editions, 2015.

Burgos, Elizabeth, and Menchú, Rigoberta. "Primer viaje a la finca: Vida en la finca." In *Me llamo Rigoberta Menchú y así me nació la conciencia*. Barcelona, Spain, Círculo de Lectores, 1993.

Menchú, Rigoberta, and Dante Liano. *The Honey Jar*. Toronto, ON: Groundwood Books, 2020. Rivera Cusicanqui, Silvia. *Ch'ixinakax Utxiwa: On Decolonising Practices and Discourses*. Cambridge, UK: Polity Press, 2019.

Activity

At Home with Toci: An Activity of Story and Reflection

Toci, the goddess of doctors and the temescal. The goddess Toci protects doctors and a commonplace of healing for many Mesoamericans. The temescal functions as a sauna, where when a sick person was placed inside with herbs to help treat their sickness. For many people, each one of us has something we call a place of healing. Whether it be your mother's boiling hot chicken noodle soup or staying in bed all day to sweat out a cold. We need healing during a vulnerable time. Nobody enjoys being sick. For this activity, let's think about a place of healing for us.

Every family grows alongside spaces and persons that impact their life long-term, whether it be pets, family, teachers, writers, or places. Find those spaces belonging to you and those close to you. What stories belong to you? Where have you felt the most healing and comfort? Where do you think you can find home, tradition, and legacy?

After compiling the stories, find some time to bring everybody involved together. Open the conversation by sharing the compiled stories. Focusing on the spaces of healing and the impacts it held on personal experiences of challenges, resolutions, and impressions.

The activity focuses on narrowing down our experiences with struggle, and how they can impact familial stories by leaving strong impressions, like Toci and Hum from the story.

Notes

1. Esteban, Kimberly, and Cristina met in the context of the College Assistance Migrant Program (CAMP) at Salisbury University, where Kimberly worked as a tutor in the philosophy of education course. Our gratitude goes to the CAMP program, which made our encounter possible. The summer project was supported by Salisbury University's Office of Undergraduate Research and Creative Activities (OURCA).

2. San Jose Acateno, Puebla, Mexico.

3. Aguacatan, Guatemala.

4. Wicomico Public Library, Salisbury, Maryland.

5. Our conception is broadly informed by J. Dewey's theory in Child and Curriculum, where he outlines a conception of education as a continuum between the newness of the child and the accumulation of experience of the adult world.

6. Indigenous educator Q'um Q'um Xiiem, Dr. Jo-ann Archibald, highlights the importance of stories in indigenous pedagogy. She uses the term storyWORK to "signal that Indigenous stories are to be taken seriously and that we as storytellers and storylisteners/readers/learners can work together to learn from and with these stories" (from her website, https://indigenousstorywork.com/).

7. In this, we are inspired by Q'um Q'um Xiiem, Dr. Jo-ann Archbald, who describes the liberatory experience of storywork. For reference, see *Conversations with Jo-ann Archibald about Indigenous Storywork as Pedagogy and Methodology Where Stories Are Understood in Their Power to Transform* from the Educational Studies Symposium 2018.

8. Robin Wall Kimmerer, *Braiding Sweetgrass* (Minneapolis, MN: Milkweed Editions, 2015), 27.

9. Rick Riordan, *The Lightning Thief: Percy Jackson and the Olympians* (New York: Disney Hyperion Books, 2006).

10. Thomas King, "Too Heavy to Lift," in *The Inconvenient Indian: A Curious Account of Native People in North America* (Minneapolis: University of Minnesota Press, 2012), 53–75.

11. Hilistis Pauline Waterfall, "Healing through Culture," in *Memory* (Vancouver, BC: Peter Wall Institute for Advanced Studies, 2018), 10.

12. Waterfall, *Healing through Culture*, 10.
13. Waterfall, *Healing through Culture*, 12.
14. Waterfall, *Healing through Culture*, 15.
15. Waterfall, *Healing through Culture*, 15.
16. Jo-ann Archibald (Q'um Q'um Xiiem), *Indigenous Storywork: Educating the Heart, Mind, Body, and Spirit* (Vancouver, BC: University of British Columbia Press, 2008), 236.
17. Archibald (Q'um Q'um Xiiem), *Indigenous Storywork*, 236.
18. Archibald (Q'um Q'um Xiiem), *Indigenous Storywork*, 238.
19. Archibald (Q'um Q'um Xiiem), *Indigenous Storywork*, 240.
20. Archibald (Q'um Q'um Xiiem), *Indigenous Storywork*, 26.
21. Kimmerer defines gifts: "A gift is something for nothing," 27.
22. The temescal mentioned in the story revolves around the pre-Hispanic steambaths and sweat lodges, popular all over Mesoamerica. The baths are still in use for many indigenous peoples.
23. Archibald (Q'um Q'um Xiiem), *Indigenous Storywork*, 27.
24. Archibald (Q'um Q'um Xiiem), *Indigenous Storywork*, 33.
25. Waterfall, *Healing through Culture*, 16.

10

Taking Up Space or Opening It?

Reconsidering Space in the Social Foundations Course in Teacher Education

MEGHAN A. BRINDLEY

When entering Social Foundations of Education (SFE) courses, it is common for students to wonder why it is part of their teacher education program. From the beginning, SFE and teacher education were intended to have a symbiotic relationship.[1] Yet, many find the relationship is not as intended; rather, it is troubled. The required SFE course in teacher education programs is not an education class, but it is also not *not* an education class. The class is situated somewhere (in)between an education class and core requirements for degree-seeking students. Where teacher education and SFE meet, the contact zone, isn't clearly demarcated, not only for students, but also, at times, for faculty within the programs.

A colleague (from another university) and I were talking about the pressures put on teacher education programs. Naturally, the topic of space came up and we discussed all the components that make us feel like our "suitcase" for teacher education isn't big enough for all the mandatory items we must pack. We were joking about how it can feel like packing the contents of two large suitcases into a carry-on with something always sticking out, trying to squish it all in, the suitcase bulging, and the zipper ready to pop—only to have the Transportation Security Administration (TSA) agent ask you to open the bag when you arrive at the airport, moments after successfully stuffing everything in just right (you know, the laundry volcano ready to erupt the moment you start to open the suitcase). Things will never go back together the same way once you open it. After a much-needed laugh, my colleague said, "You know, we just aren't on the same team. As a matter of fact, your discipline [SFE] isn't even playing the same game. You just take up space when we're [teacher education] running out of room."

I am regularly reminded that the SFE course I teach is taking up space in teacher education. In teacher education programs, a lot of external pressure is exerted onto the programs to be and include many things. In our program, a lot of time is dedicated to ensuring the inclusion of all components for program accreditation and the demands of the Ohio Department of Higher Education, while also attending to the valued insights and feedback from faculty and school partners working with students. However, there is only so much space and, at some point, a component has to be removed if new components are to be included in the allotted number of required field and credit hours. One course frequently mentioned for removal is the SFE course.[2] In Ohio, my home state, the course is a requirement for teacher education programs to be accredited and cannot be removed. Yet, being required is not the same as being valued. Working in teacher education, particularly during a time of change due to accreditation requirements and increased accountability, required foundations coursework is often viewed as taking up vital space (typically in the form of credit hours).

The current contact zone for teacher education and social foundations most often occurs directly in the experiences of preservice teachers in required SFE courses. By this I mean that the place where SFE and Curriculum and Instruction (C&I) are in contact is indirect, through the enrollment of students in required SFE coursework, instead of as scholars directly engaging together in interdisciplinary or even disciplinary work. This chapter looks at the nature of the disconnect or indirect contact between teacher education and the social foundations of education, exploring the contact zone between them and the missed opportunities that arise. More specifically, the chapter looks at the idea of engaging with Matthew Clarke, professor of education, and Anne Phelan's, professor of curriculum and pedagogy, concept of negative space[3] within the space of the SFE course in teacher education.

Authentic contact between SFE and teacher education cannot be achieved through a singular voice or situatedness (that is, all affirmative or all critical). There are, of course, various challenges in creating authentic contact between the fields. It is not simply enough to state both sides, or positions of the fields. To reconceptualize the way we use the space of the SFE course in teacher education, we need to engage with negative education.[4] Negative education is *not* a reference to what is absent in education. It is premised on the juxtaposition of positivist education, in which what can be seen and proven through data, evidence, or experience is what is relied on and the a priori or knowledge that is independent from experience, data, or evidence is rejected. In negative education, the a priori is allowed space. According to Clarke and Phelan,

> the positive refers to social structures, institutions and policies—best practice or teaching standards—that have become reified, while the negative is that which unsettles and disrupts the comfortable stance of the given order of things. Negativity, as a political practice that engages with the positive to reveal the historical and contingent nature of all knowledge, thus offers new conceptual resources, such as antagonism, dissensus, fantast and impotentiality, for imaging alternative scenarios for teacher education beyond the confines of current policies.[5]

The idea of "imagining alternative scenarios"[6] is essential to the task of finding and opening up new space, particularly in a space where one perceives that there is no space left. Thus, part of the task of the SFE course becomes unpacking and reconsidering things held as truth, or reality, or "normal." This is related to the notion of including the a priori, in which we don't rely on our own observation(s) or personal experience(s), but rather the use of theories to deduce or inference to obtain knowledge/reason. For some, it is not an easy task to leave personal and observed experiences behind and engage with ideas or topics that might feel uncomfortable, but it doesn't mean the space that makes it possible to reconsider and unpack ideas should not be offered to the student. If they are unwilling/unable/etcetera to investigate their own beliefs, we can also offer them the opportunity to unpack things about the course itself: Why do you think this course is in teacher education? What is the work of this course? Why is the course required by the State of Ohio?

Navigating Space(s)

Before diving deeper into the notion of finding space, the space between SFE and teacher education needs to be identified further. For this, I will use the university in which I am currently employed, as I am unusually situated (in)between teacher education and SFE. I'm a graduate student in SFE and C&I employed at a Midwestern public university. At the time of writing, 2022, my job is equal parts foundations and teacher education, and I confront that situatedness daily. At my university, C&I is located in the School of Education and SFE in the School of Foundations, Leadership, and Administration. While both Schools are housed in the College of Education and the same campus building, in keeping with national trends the Schools have different faculty meetings, and different leadership and events, which means time spent together is rare, unless faculty create it. Sometimes standing with one foot in two disciplines feels as if I'm alone on an existential island.[7]

When I engage both disciplines at the same time, in meetings or in conversations, I am often met with silence. It is so silent, the kind of silence where crickets should start chirping. The tricky bit is, I thought that including one discipline's knowledge/authors who echo the sentiments alongside the other discipline's knowledge/authors would be affirming and relay that the other discipline cares about this too. In other words, both disciplines care about something similar, or even the same, or something that overlaps, and even if we talk/write about it in a different way, we are in a shared conversation. We're on the same side. When I first found SFE, I was overjoyed that someone was having the conversations about schools and teaching that I wanted to be having in C&I, but felt there wasn't space for. It was affirming for me that scholars in another discipline were also concerned with the things I was concerned with, and they spend a lot of time talking and writing about the things at length. It helped me feel a sense of comradery beyond my teaching colleagues into a related discipline. It felt as if those of us fighting for education and teaching grew exponentially in number when I found SFE. Yet, when I bring up one discipline in the other, the light in colleagues' eyes seems to disappear rather abruptly and leaves me wondering why (hence the existential island). After all, this space where the disciplines of C&I and SFE meet is part of the reason the SFE course was originally developed!

Historically, the SFE course was developed at Teachers College, Columbia "to provide a firm foundation on which educators . . . might rest the specialized technical equipment of their respective professional functions."[8] In other words, the first SFE course, ED 200F,[9] was designed to deal with areas of education outside the scope of teaching and to provide a common language and outlook among the preservice teachers and faculty. The foundations scholars desired for students to think about what constitutes an informed and ethical decision in their practice and to comprehend the consequences of those decisions.[10] The syllabus was determined by the current events and political climate so that the preservice teacher could gain a basic understanding of how social and individual problems of the times influence education in *their* classrooms *in the present moment*, specifically, in their classrooms as teachers.[11]

To accomplish this task, the interpretative, normative, and critical lenses through which schooling could be critiqued were developed and ED 200F is credited as the founding initiative that gave SFE its critical orientation—questioning what schools are and what they ought to be.[12] Yet, the criticality of SFE is often where the relationship between the fields falls apart. While SFE is inherently critical in nature, the goal is *not* to blame teachers, nor is it to advocate for throwing out everything established in education and teaching. The goal of SFE is to point[13] at things that impact the lives of teachers, students, and schools that are *beyond* the control of teachers, students, and schools and in the hands of government, society, and problematic structures, providing preservice teachers with the opportunity to recognize how the world impacts their future careers and students. As society and politics shift and change, so does the impact on schools and teachers, thus, the course takes a dynamic approach to looking at the current context of schools in society at that particular moment in time.

I want to acknowledge that many scholars in SFE have not taught in k–12 classrooms. Trusting that others who haven't lived the life of k–12 classrooms could understand the situatedness of teachers is tough. Yet, I want to stress: SFE scholars are capable of recognizing and conveying the fact that there is strain placed on the profession of teaching, you as the teacher, the schools in which you work, and your students. The field of SFE has critical conversations about teaching and education, but the intent is not to eclipse all that there is that is good in education and teaching. Just as William Pinar[14] asks, SFE carves out space for complicated conversations[15] and interdisciplinary thought. These complicated conversations can be both affirmative and critical in nature, not just one or the other. SFE has critical conversations about teaching and education in the hopes that future teachers will recognize that there are external pressures, aims, and soon placed on teachers' shoulders, what those are precisely, why they are there, how that impacts teaching and education, and to deliberate if those things should be there and, if they shouldn't, what should be there, if anything?

Engaging with the negative space in education means seeking out space that is opened to us by looking for ways that unsettle the "comfortable stance of the given order of things."[16] While there is much discourse on negative thinking, the key take away from Clarke and Phelan[17] is that we must recognize that the operationalized outcomes of education such as benchmarks, indicators, standards, and outcomes have *"become"* the object of education.[18] They are no longer the representation of the object of education, they *are* the object of education. In regard to the SFE course, the dialogue is no longer the object of the experience, the grades are the object of the course.

Operating (In)Between

In the space in between positive and negative thinking, the potential to think otherwise[19] or (in)between the spaces exists. While being in between connotes that something sits in the middle of two things, being (in)between acknowledges that something can be both independent and/or overlap something else at the same time. The boundaries are not absolute. There is an acknowledgment that being (in)between has a duality, a seeping into each thing's space is possible. Therefore, it is not enough to engage with negative thinking, rather, both positive and negative thinking must overlap.[20] Clarke and Phelan[21] refer to this overlapping as the imbrication of positive and negative thinking, the space in between, stating that simply looking at a mirror image of the positive is not enough. Thus, "mutual imbrication is a key point . . . neither the positive nor the negative is sufficient; new thinking and new directions . . . require their mutual interplay."[22]

This space requires engagement with the political, the unstable space of tension between the positive and negative.[23] In this way, the negative allows us to engage with the political in order to unsettle structures and knowledge and disrupt accepted policies and practices[24] that we view as problematic. If we do not engage with the space in between, we run the risk of fixating the political on the operationalized outcomes and products of "what works" and "best practice" or "evidenced-based practice,"[25] rather than on the experience of all that leads up to the product. Clarke and Phelan view "what works" and "best practice" or "evidenced-based practice" as "simplistic solutions and formulaic answers" that prevent us from "engaging with the complex problems and questions that accompany both living and teaching."[26]

Thinking in this middle ground may be uncomfortable.[27] It may ask us to question and be critical of things we love about education and teaching, but ultimately the space of being (in)between is generative in nature.[28] This means that this space is open to newness, allowing it to manifest in thought, ideas, ways of thinking, and so forth. In this middle ground is the place where we can point[29] to problems in teaching and education and say, "Look! Look at the way this impacts students, teachers, parents, communities, etcetera." When we identify and are critical of things we love, such as teaching and education, it doesn't mean we don't love them or that everything is bad and needs to be thrown out. It assists us in recognizing that what we believe is worth preserving in education and teaching and what isn't, allowing us to appreciate and affirm the good parts.

An example I can share from my own teaching in SFE pertains to what happens when students come to the course with particular ideas surrounding the notions of "best practices." My student, Reese (pseudonym), came into the class with the belief that politics is entirely separate from the life of the public school and, according to their experience of schools, politics has no space in the school. For months, the class read and we discussed the aims of public schools in light of particular topics that can trouble the ideas contained in those aims: inequalities and the notion of "equal education," culturally responsive teaching and the space in schools, should teachers share political views in classrooms, and so on. Each day, Reese would find a sticking point and stand firm. This was typically respected by the class without much pushback, but one particular day another student huffed and asked Reese, "When you go vote, where does living in a democracy begin and end? Does it start when they hand you your ballot and end when you give it back? Where does it go?" Reese looked like the Grinch the moment his heart grew three sizes. Suddenly exclaiming, after about a minute of silence, "I think I've got it! I *understand* why this class has a title called Education in a Democratic Society! Do you guys get it? At first I thought, like duh, obviously, when I saw the name of the class, but I *know* why it's called that now. Like I actually get it. The school as a school itself is political. Schools live inside the democracy! Schools don't live outside it. Democracy is *everywhere*!" I wish I could show you a picture of Reese's face in that moment, it was as if a million neurons had made new connections in Reese's brain; shock, awe, wonder, new ideas, new *space*. Reese went on and on firing off connections to our class, some students looking like they had no idea what just happened and, others, affirming and directing Reese to further connections. The connections Reese made varied from fundamental to nuanced.

In the SFE course, these complex moments where we are critical of education and teaching, a field many of us will or do devote our lives to, can feel like a betrayal. After all, we are pointing to the faults of *our* profession, but for Reese and other students, these moments are where space is found. By engaging in complicated conversations and by critiquing, affirming,[30] pointing,[31] and looking at things normatively, the potential for space to be found where there appeared not to be space is realized.

The goal of SFE is not to take up space in teacher education, it's to open it. SFE opens and holds the space for critical conversations that often there is no space for in content coursework, already busting at the seams due to the demands placed on it. While there are varying scholarly perspectives on the purpose(s) of social foundations courses in teacher education, perhaps the most concerning notion surrounding the purpose of the course is that students are often fuzzy about what it is and that they further find the course to be worthless.[32] While much attention has been paid to naming the purpose of the course,[33] the perception of the course's value to students is often still in question, particularly when it can't be immediately applied to their future teaching.[34] If the SFE course in teacher education does not *affirm* the inherent good of teaching and education,[35] students can find it difficult to participate in the critical conversations.

By opening up the space to critique the things we love, education and teaching, SFE is better positioned to help students perceive the goals of the course and understand the problematic notions surrounding and in education, *but it requires that students identify what they believe to be the problematic notions impacting education and teaching*, not adopt what I believe. Using the space of the SFE course to embrace Clarke and Phelan's[36] idea of negative education, provides students with space to unpack and reconsider their *own* beliefs, not operationalized outcomes for the course. It can also provide more space in teacher education for critical conversations about education and teaching that may be squeezed out of methods courses. Methods and content coursework is intended to teach the content and the methods. SFE courses are intended to ask if the methods, content, and aims we have for students align with and allow students access to the aims we hold as a society for education and for teaching. Important to recall here is the previously mentioned distinction of required versus valued. Foundations courses are often students' "first exposure to the field [teacher education] during their collegiate years."[37] So, instead of foundations taking up space in teacher education, what would happen if we opened it?

Questions for Discussion

- What critical conversations would you like to have about education and teaching?
- What do you want to acknowledge as inherently good about teaching and education? In other words, what do you want to preserve in education and teaching for future generations?

Further Reading

Clarke, Matthew, and Anne M. Phelan. "The Power of Negative Thinking in and for Teacher Education." *Power and Education* 7, no. 3 (2015): 257–71.

Gorlewski, Julie, and Eve Tuck, eds. *Who Decides Who Becomes a Teacher? Schools of Education as Sites of Resistance*. New York: Routledge, 2019.

Activity

At many institutions, courses and programs have become instrumentalized or operationalized in teacher education. This means that the aims, benchmarks, indicators, standards, and outcomes have *"become"* the object of education instead of the education *itself* remaining as the object of education. In other words, grades are no longer the representation of the object of education, they *are* the object of education. Using a teacher education course syllabus, university program outcomes/goals, or licensure guidance for new teachers, identify elements of operationalization. If you find these elements, rewrite them in a way that reorients the course/program/licensure to focus on education as the object of education versus the indicators/standards/outcomes.

Notes

1. Mary Rose McCarthy, "The Rise and Fall of ED200F," *Educational Studies* 39, no. 2 (2006): 134–45.

2. Joseph Watras, "Teacher Tests, Equal Opportunity, and the Foundations of Education," *Educational Studies* 39, no. 2 (2006): 124–34.

3. Matthew Clarke and Anne M. Phelan, "The Power of Negative Thinking in and for Teacher Education," *Power and Education* 7, no. 3 (2015): 257–71; Matthew Clarke and Anne M. Phelan, *Teacher Education and the Political Power of Negative Thinking* (New York: Routledge, 2017).

4. Clarke and Phelan, *Teacher Education and the Political Power*.

5. Clarke and Phelan, "The Power of Negative Thinking," 257.

6. Clarke and Phelan, "The Power of Negative Thinking," 257.

7. Kathy Hytten, "On Building Islands of Decency," *Educational Studies* 54, no. 1 (2018): 99–108.

8. Lawrence Cremin, David Shannon, and Mary Evelyn Townsend, *A History of Teachers College, Columbia University* (New York: Columbia University Press, 1954), 145, quoted in McCarthy, "The Rise and Fall of ED200F."

9. McCarthy, "The Rise and Fall of ED200F," 138.

10. Steve Tozer and R. Freeman Butts, "The Evolution of Social Foundations of Education," in *Handbook of Research in the Social Foundations of Education*, ed. Steve Tozer, Bernardo P. Gallegos, Annette M. Henry, Mary Bushnell Greiner, and Paula Groves Price (New York: Routledge, 2011), 4–14.

11. McCarthy, "The Rise and Fall of ED200F."

12. McCarthy, "The Rise and Fall of ED200F."

13. Gert J. J. Biesta, *World-Centered Education: A View for the Present* (New York: Routledge, 2021).

14. William F. Pinar, *What Is Curriculum Theory?*, 3rd ed. (New York: Routledge, 2019).

15. Rachel Wahl, "Should Teachers Advance Justice or Reduce Polarization?," *GroundWorks* (2021): 1–5.

16. Clarke and Phelan, "The Power of Negative Thinking," 268.

17. Clarke and Phelan, "The Power of Negative Thinking"; Clarke and Phelan, *Teacher Education and the Political Power*.

18. Clarke and Phelan, "The Power of Negative Thinking."

19. Clarke and Phelan, "The Power of Negative Thinking"; Clarke and Phelan, *Teacher Education and the Political Power*.

20. Clarke and Phelan, "The Power of Negative Thinking"; Clarke and Phelan, *Teacher Education and the Political Power*.

21. Clarke and Phelan, "The Power of Negative Thinking"; Clarke and Phelan, *Teacher Education and the Political Power*.

22. Clarke and Phelan, "The Power of Negative Thinking," 268.

23. Clarke and Phelan, "The Power of Negative Thinking."

24. Clarke and Phelan, *Teacher Education and the Political Power*.

25. Clarke and Phelan, *Teacher Education and the Political Power*.

26. Clarke and Phelan, *Teacher Education and the Political Power*, 16.

27. Gert J. J. Biesta, *The Rediscovery of Teaching* (New York: Routledge, 2017).

28. Clarke and Phelan, "The Power of Negative Thinking"; Clarke and Phelan, *Teacher Education and the Political Power*.

29. Biesta, *World-Centered Education*.

30. Joris Vlieghe and Piotr Zamojski, *Toward an Ontology of Teaching: Thing-centered Pedagogy, Affirmation, and Love for the World* (New York: Springer, 2019).

31. Biesta, *World-Centered Education*.

32. Nancy Beadie, "From 'Teacher as Decision Maker' to Teacher as Participant in 'Shared Decision Making': Reframing the Purpose of Social Foundations in Teacher Education," *Teachers College Record* 98 (1996): 77–103.

33. Dan W. Butin, ed., *Teaching Social Foundations of Education: Context, Theories and Issues* (Mahwah, NJ: Lawrence Erlbaum, 2005).

34. Jennifer Mueller, "Does Talking the Talk Mean Walking the Walk? A Case for Forging Closer Relationships between Teacher Education and Educational Foundations," *Educational Studies* 39, no. 2 (2006): 146–62; Lee S. Shulman, "Reconnecting Foundations to the Substance of Teacher Education," *Teachers College Record* 91, no. 3 (1990): 300–10.

35. Vlieghe and Zamojski, *Toward an Ontology of Teaching*.

36. Clarke and Phelan, "The Power of Negative Thinking"; Clarke and Phelan, *Teacher Education and the Political Power*.

37. Rachel Boyd Potter, "Artisans, Architects, and Apprentices: Valuing the Craft of Teacher Education," *Teacher Educators' Journal* 9 (2016): 10.

11

The Value of Therapized Education
Exploring the Story and Theory of Reflexive Tension

STEVEN ZHAO AND JESSE HABER

In recent years, education has seen the rise of a therapization of pedagogy and student learning. According to Kathryn Ecclestone and Dennis Hayes, this entails a growing emphasis on the emotional experiences/problems of students as targets of therapeutic support and intervention.[1] This emphasis not only seeks to pay greater attention to student emotions in education, but in its more radical forms therapization also reconceives education as defined by emotionality itself. Understandably, its increasing trends have stimulated concerns regarding its consequences and scrutiny of its frameworks. This has arguably resulted in opposing perspectives between the progressive boosters of its paradigms and the reactionary "conservatives" aiming to preserve the "traditional" ideals and standards of schooling.

In this chapter, we articulate and claim the important ideal of therapization as existing in the tension *between* the opposing perspectives. It is a tension that ought to both challenge education to recognize the inner lives of students while preserving its very ideals that ground such recognition in shared purpose and reference. We believe the value of therapization is turning education into a perpetual question to which each pedagogical moment is an opportunity to fundamentally *conceive and reconceive* the meaning of learning. We draw from Charles Taylor's discussion of authenticity in concert with lived examples of therapeutic applications as both professional practice and educational experience. First, we explore stories of therapeutic learning and conundrums in and around classrooms. Second, we provide a brief overview on therapization *in* and *as* education. Finally, we discuss the notion of "authenticity" as an important framework that illuminates therapization's value as pedagogical reflexivity.

Dispatches from the Classroom

Jesse will draw from his experience as therapist, lecturer, and student to place our philosophical investigations into an experiential framework. As such, each of the following vignettes will be told from Jesse's perspective, occupying different roles in different settings, specifically, the therapy room and classroom. In doing this, we hope to illuminate how the therapized classroom has both broadened the ways in which we conceptualize both classroom and education, while also highlighting how without the proper structures and clear philosophical goals in place, a therapized classroom can also have its drawbacks. For the sake of brevity, we will draw one example from each of the following: the counseling office, the classroom, and finally, as a student in postsecondary education. This will hopefully illuminate how a therapized classroom touches on and influences each layer of education: first, for the teachers struggling as their scope of practice has increased in primary and secondary classrooms; second, on the psyche of the students that grow up in this classroom and how they conceptualize subjectivity and education; and finally, third, on the blurred lines in the classroom created around expectations in a postsecondary graduate-level program.

Over the last decade, what is expected of educators has shifted, exemplified by new and expanded mandates for teachers.[2] One major way this shift has affected teachers pertains to the broadening of scope in relation to students' mental health. While each district may have its own way of conceptualizing this shift, the overall message is the same: we are becoming more concerned with the social and emotional health of our students. Their education must explicitly include components on mental health, social health, and a broad understanding of how mental health issues may affect our daily functioning. Teachers have now explicitly become the arbiters of this more authentic and vulnerable classroom.

The Value of Therapized Education | 185

> I have been working with this client biweekly for over a year. He teaches in public school and has been coming in for therapy in order to process some life stressors and changes in his day-to-day functioning. This week, he opens by discussing some uncertainty about a new aspect of the curriculum that he is expected to teach. As his therapist, he begins asking me questions about schizophrenia, ADHD, abusive relationships and general overviews of psychological disorders. This is an unordinary interaction and so I ask about it. He responds that as part of the new curriculum he is expected to teach his eighth and ninth graders about mental health. Over the course of a week, he is to cover topics such as social and emotional health, abuse and mental health coping strategies. As he is in therapy himself, he admits that he is well aware that this unit is beyond his scope of practice. Upon further investigation, he reveals he took a several-day training on these topics (with the option for additional training on his own time), and then was expected to be able to teach it each semester to his classes. We spend the rest of the session discussing his discomfort and, pragmatically, doing some psycho-education to help him feel more comfortable with the content he is expected to continue to teach on mental health.

This educator's story is in no way unique. This new mandate has brought a bevy of professional development opportunities. However, outside of the usual "Pro-D" days these opportunities are often beyond the normal expectations of teaching. As such, if a teacher wants to become proficient in this expanded scope, there necessarily becomes a choice about whether they will invest their own time in supplementary learning. Add to this that as the classroom becomes more therapized, a commensurate rise in school counselors has not occurred. In British Columbia, the current ratio of counselors' to students is 1 to 693.[3] One might imagine that even in more traditional modes of education, this would be insufficient to meet the needs of the student body. However, this problem is compounded when we consider that when therapy enters the classroom, the outcomes can be unforeseen—perhaps bringing to the surface psychological concerns that students may need to be tended to in a timely manner.

This shift in the teaching and learning environment *should* necessitate some input as well from the therapeutic community. Most notably, some input on the scope of practice and the ethical codes that are cornerstones of registered therapists. The conversation surrounding the best practices and procedures for counseling is much too large to tackle in a chapter of this size. However, as a means of elucidating the considerations that we think are often overlooked, it might be helpful to begin to ask a few questions that are standard in the field of counseling and therapy. Ethical considerations of the therapeutic relationship (which is what must be established if a classroom is to be therapized) necessitate some sort of code and scope. The following example is from one of the provincial counseling regulatory bodies where the authors of this chapter reside: "Counselling is a relational process based upon the ethical use of professional competencies to facilitate human thriving. A counsellor's scope of practice is that use of recognized and evolving professional competencies."[4] Here, it may be important to note that *counseling* and *therapy* will be used interchangeably. Application of these values to the classroom is an ethical necessity if one is to take the project of classroom therapization seriously. As such, reflection on it brings up ethical considerations. Some of these include, but are not limited to: How does a therapized classroom facilitate human thriving? Have our students agreed to this when they enter our classrooms? Have we as educators been adequately prepared to meet the professional competencies of the therapeutic environment? If so, what are the implications of the dual roles of therapist and educator? What therapeutic modalities are we operating from, and how are we to know we are practicing effectively, and ethically? Now that we are some years into the process of therapizing the classroom, how has this affected our students and their relationship and understanding of mental health, vulnerability, and subjectivity to education and educational outcomes?

> "I either will do well in school, or my mental health will suffer. I have to make a choice." This was not the first time encountering this sentiment in my psychology class. The statement had come from an eighteen-year-old student sitting in the front row. We were discussing the concept of intelligence, and what these students thought constituted intelligence. While there were some minor disagreements, there was an overwhelming sense that intelligence was a fluid concept, that people were "smart" in all kinds of ways, and that the difference between those who were intelligent and those who were not was more of a question of domain, than ability. The above statement came when one

student said that she could do better in school (she was an A student) but that if she did she would have to make a choice between mental health and grades. This sentiment was met with scattered nods of approval. Ultimately, she was indicating that she needed to make a choice between being an authentic, healthy version of herself and higher scholastic achievement.

What this conversation and many like it indicate is that students have begun to think in dichotomous terms between good mental health and high achievement in schooling—a dichotomy built on their experiences (and often rooted in reality) in the secondary and postsecondary school system. We believe that what has been offered to them is either a model of academic excellence that places the highest value on self-sacrifice and can-do determinism, or a model of anything-goes self-care-indulgent subjectivity in the name of "good" mental health. The pendulum swing of these extreme positions seems to lack the important middle arc. When it is suggested to students in class that getting a full night's sleep might help both their mental states and their grades, the disbelieving scoffs can be heard down the halls: it is easy for a postsecondary lecturer to make that suggestion, but then who will do the assignment that is due in the morning? It is in this thinking that we can see the lack of reflexivity, the inability to conceptualize other values and outcomes to the academic and emotional problems these students face.

We argue that what a weak *therapization* (a term we will elucidate in the following section) of the classroom has done is mishandle mental health as an integrated topic of education. At its essence, we see the classroom as becoming a more complex site of learning and personal growth *without* the commensurate training that an ethical (that is, informed and regulated) approach to therapy and the therapeutic relationship might entail. Instead of a dialectic, the heightened emotionality and centering of subjective experience have resulted in layers of confusion, both on personal and professional levels. As such, instead of thinking of oneself as adaptive—as possibly existing between the described extremes—a student may instead come away with *only* a new vocabulary. A student may emerge from these attempts at integration with the language of a new way of conceptualizing self and other, without the depth of meaning which, arguably, yields the essential components for personal growth, insight, and change. Armed with this new lexicon of therapy, students may simply use this vocabulary to justify and reinforce this dichotomous thinking—the elevation of one's subjectivity over all else or stripping the authentic self away in the service of a more conservative work ethic and achievement.

A final contribution regarding a personal experience, one that ignited the inquiry about authenticity, freedom in education, and classroom relationships follows:

> I am halfway through a graduate program in education. I entered this program already having a graduate degree, but wanting to explore education and its alternative approaches. The coursework was engaging and exciting, and one of the most liberating aspects was the freedom to write and explore areas that best related to my own interests and goals. In one particular class, an educator stipulates that they would like us to hand in our assignments in American Psychological Association (APA) format. I am used to this, as it is the standard formatting practice for my field. A few other students are less comfortable with it, and in class express their dismay about this requirement to our instructor. Roughly forty-five minutes of the class is consumed with a conversation about why the APA requirement is too much, and how previous instructors were more fluid with their expectations. The instructor is patient and kind in asserting her preference, but ultimately allows the students to make their own choice regarding what format to complete their paper in. I am surprised by this, and taken aback by the insistence on the student's way of doing their work. I am left wondering how this rigidity on the student's part is beneficial to the goals of education and in particular graduate work. I am left wondering whether the search for a therapeutic classroom has, in some ways, done a disservice to the resilience and reflexivity of my classmates.

The Weak and Strong Therapization of Education

The therapeutic concern in education is centrally about how the connections between learning and emotional experiences can be understood and reconceived. Therapeutic concern can be done through a wide variety of pedagogical approaches that connect emotions to learning. For the interest of this chapter, we will mainly discuss their broader educational goals as opposed to their specific applications. This is due to two reasons. First, the scope of this chapter is simply insufficient to comprehensively discuss all the details. Second, it is useful to propose categories of such goals as this can stimulate conversations about their implications. Broadly, we propose categories that therapization can be *strong*, where emotionality is the basis for which education ought to be changed and understood; and it can be *weak*, where emotionality supplements education by enriching and supporting learning needs. Let's first examine strong therapization in greater detail.

Strong therapization frames therapy not to support education per se but as a critical framework that reveals limitations of "traditional" schooling and possibilities for its change. Ideal learning, in this sense, is not just about being more emotionally "healthy" as much as being defined by the valuing of emotionality itself. Curriculum can be tailored to promote and affirm emotional expressions *as* the meaning of learning. For instance, expressive spaces can be given through activities such as drawing, journaling, mindfulness, and so on.[5] By doing so, expressing emotions is treated as an end in itself. For emotions are not a means to get better grades but an opportunity to affirm the inherently important experiences of students.

In more radical forms, affirming emotions can lend to problematizing schooling—particularly regarding its neglect of students' inner lives. If emotions are framed as inherently educational, then activities *for* their expression can resist schooling paradigms that deem emotions as hazardous to actual learning.[6] For these paradigms should be "dismantled" for more inclusivity of students' emotional realities for their authentic learning. As Beth Berila writes, "We have to . . . dismantle deeply held ideologies, and create alternative, more empowering, ways of relating to one another. In order to achieve this outcome, students need to . . . examine . . . at the level of our internal thoughts and feelings."[7] Here, the students are understood to be *structurally* obstructed in terms of discovering the innate learnedness of their personal emotional experiences. In other words, learning is uncovering what is already within the students. This, in return, frames standards of curriculum, performance measurements, and so forth as always carrying the risk of suppressing what is unique and personal to students.

In essence, strong therapization enables a humanistic and emancipatory rhetoric—education is promoted as an "unlearning"[8] for the "empowerment, authenticity" of the "true self."[9] This depends on a conceptual framing of emotions that shifts *away* from the individual level as a strict level of concern, such as *only* making sure that students' mental health is supported or "fixed." Rather, emotions are also approached as reflecting *structural symptoms* of "bad" schooling and the systemic means to addressing its failures by affirming its innate value. Learning problems do not reflect student problems but the schools that failed to express and affirm what students already feel and know. Our previous example regarding students emphatically resisting APA formats can be understood as one instance of this perspective. APA standards, in this sense, were framed as encroaching on the authentic expressions of inner affections of the desires, experiences, and meanings that constitute who one is. To conform to its format, then, is to abide by a false performance enforced by external norms that entail the inevitable sacrifice of one's inner and spontaneous freedom.

Weak therapization, on the other hand, recognizes that learning depends on students' mental health. This view promotes pedagogy as equipped with mental health literacy for "Effective early identification [of psychological issues], timely referral to mental health specialists . . ." and implementation of "school-based mental health programs."[10] What can be inferred from this is that standard educational goals (that is, concern for competence as demonstrable outcomes) are implicitly retained. Concerns for emotions are informed by addressing their dysfunctional risks in "harming" certain academic performances.

Recall our example about the teacher who was expected to integrate mental-health-related themes and strategies into his classroom. In his situation (as, is increasingly the case with many teachers), there exists a sharp division between the meaning of education and mental health. What this means is that emotions are *not* intrinsically educative but must be addressed separately *in addition* to classroom curriculum (as opposed to *defining* curriculum). Directly put, curriculum is not led by the inner emotions of students but can possibly be disrupted by their "dysregulated" manifestations. As a teacher, then, he must emphasize emotions not as educative goods in themselves but as potential risks to be managed and coped with. This does not necessarily mean emotional suppression, for teachers can very well promote the "healthiness" of emotional expressiveness. Instead, it means that emotionality is conceived as serving a greater end-goal rooted in scholastic and psychological norms, whereby emphases of expressiveness *might or might not* be conducive to their facilitation. In contrast to strong therapization, emotions are approached as *individual* risks and opportunities. Rather than pointing to schooling issues, they point to student problems that should be corrected by specialists or prepared teachers. Pedagogical mandates might be issued to classrooms to ensure student social-emotional regulation and available support for those who "deviate" from psychological norms. Although students can be encouraged to *express* emotions, the underlying intention is not to emotionally define schooling. Rather, expressions are the medium to assess and maintain psychological "normalcy" for scholastic performance.

Naturally, weak therapization can be criticized by strong therapization's proponents. For it neglects systemic issues by reducing learning only to the individual. As education focuses on psychological support for students, the greater problem of structural oppression simply becomes perpetuated.[11] In other words, the noble advocacy for greater in-school mental-health resources is but a paternalism that pacifies students and maintains the institutional failure to actualize their innate value. For strong therapization, instead of corrections to acceptable standards, emotions should be embraced as opportunities to disrupt them. Students should not be held accountable as failed learners, rather, schools should be accountable as failed environments for embracing emotions as genuine learning.

On the other hand, however, strong therapization can also be critiqued as riskily facilitating what Frank Furedi describes as a "diminished self."[12] Such is framing the student excessively around their emotional vulnerability, fragility, and risk factors. Students increasingly take on a self-image constituted as "suffering from low-self-esteem," or "feeling stressy" from the demands of schooling and society. As Ecclestone and Hayes remark, therapized education now "has an ethical purpose, to make people feel safe and secure, and the pursuit of knowledge does not feature in it at all. This vision . . . is an articulate celebration of the loss of the confidence in the academy."[13] For accommodating emotions as an end can be "a profoundly destructive experience" where the "love of subject is replaced by the love of individuals."[14]

What the perspectives can reveal are opposing fundamental vision(s) of education. For emotions can be framed as either correctable for *serving* educational standards or *problematizing* such standards to accommodate their expression. Scholastic and psychological "competence" are readily embraced on one side while evidenced as educational problems on the other. Essentially, such opposition is founded on disagreements about the sources of "learnedness." Strong therapization approaches learnedness as already existing *within* students that must be drawn out with accommodating environments. Learning is not acquired but discovered. Weak therapization, in contrast, understands learnedness as acquired by students with supplementing environments. Emotional support is relevant insofar as they facilitate this supplementation. Directly put, while strong therapization sees a completed student in need of subtracting external limitations to reveal learnedness, weak therapization sees an incomplete student in need of adding ingredients to finally achieve learnedness.

The problem between these perspectives, however, is not about whether they are correct or incorrect about learning. Rather, it is about each perspective fixing the other as an opposition rather than another *valuable* side to the complexity of education. We believe ideal learning involves *both* perspectives, where students are approached as simultaneously complete and incomplete. For it is this very tension that informs an important pedagogical *reflexivity* of student-teacher relationships. To further clarify this, it is important to elaborate on the reasoning underlying their opposition. This reasoning reflects a deep cultural narrative regarding what it means to being human, to which its entrenched values continue to inform such oppositions. This narrative, essentially, regards the human as defined by a conflict between the internal life of self and the external world of the public. For educators, it is useful to explore such narrative that legitimize different pedagogical philosophies. To begin, we offer a brief reflection on Charles Taylor's examination of the idea of "authenticity" of the modern sense of self.

Authentic Origins

In *Ethics of Authenticity,* Taylor describes our modern culture as imbued with an "authentic" idea of self, which is a "form of inwardness, in which we come to think of ourselves as beings with inner depths."[15] This inner self is emphasized as an intrinsically legitimate source of both original truth(s) as well as "moral importance."[16] Being "authentic" is relatively a "modern" self-understanding. This ideal came from a long history of limited "moral freedom" where "people used to see themselves as a part of a larger order"[17] that defined their lives with predestined roles affixed within societal structures. This eventually shifted toward valuing authenticity through influences of Romantic expressivism, which "greatly increases the importance of this self . . . by introducing the principle of *originality*: each of our voices has something of its own to say."[18] This inner truth is essentially discoverable in acts of expression—"We discover what we have it in us to be by becoming that mode of life, by giving expression in our speech and action to what is original in us."[19]

What authenticity brings is a conflict between the "inner" and "outer" worlds. Because the inner world is regarded as intrinsically valuable, the outer world can become villainized as snuffing the soul of honesty and originality. As Taylor argues, "It accords crucial moral importance to a kind of contact with myself, with my own inner nature, which it sees as in danger of being lost, partly through the pressures towards outward conformity,"[20] such that it can ultimately force "on us the idea that authenticity will have to struggle against some externally imposed rules."[21] The inner and outer conflict does not mean a permanent irreconcilability, however. Rather, it serves to emphasize that their conflict is importantly enabled, if not then reinforced, by authenticity.

Taylor's crucial thesis is addressing the problematic debate between what he regards as the "knockers" and "boosters" of authenticity. For knockers, the culture of authenticity is criticized as a decadent state of indulgent narcissism and "moral laxity."[22] For boosters, authenticity represents the "rise of a spontaneous, gentle, loving . . . culture,"[23] where protecting the self rescues our spirit from a disenchanting world. For Taylor, both are problematic because each is only concerned about whether authenticity should be justified as a value to begin with. Instead, it is better that the debates be "about it, defining its proper meaning,"[24] rather than its justification. We should clarify how authenticity can be meaningful and not how it should or should not exist. Taylor proposes this because he argues that authenticity avails a meaningful life precisely through a tension between *both* inner originality and outer principle.

On the one hand, we need to preserve personal integrity as it alludes to the valuable truths of our lived experience, while on the other, the dignifying meaning of our experiences importantly depends on its connection to things that surpass our personal interests (that is, serving a greater community or purpose). Being authentic is meaningful because it reflects one's agency regarding one's commitments as personally justified as a transcending concern. One is no longer imposed into obligatory service but is reflexively appraising the degree to which one's service is justified as a "good" *choice*. This avails the freedom to challenge both inner self-understandings and the outer world. For the desire for authenticity compels an examination of the compatibility between the self and the outer world of commitments—for instance, through explorations such as "Is this what I believe in?" "Am I the right person for this?" or "Does it feel right to do this?" As Taylor asserts, "If authenticity is being true to ourselves . . . then perhaps we can only achieve it integrally if we recognize that this sentiment connects us to a wider whole."[25]

It is important to note that both sides of authenticity are valid in their mutual criticism. If authenticity neglects transcendent commitments, it becomes the empty egotism that knockers criticize. For Taylor, "I can define my identity only against the background of things that matter. But to bracket out . . . everything but what I find in myself, would be to eliminate all candidates for what matters."[26] Yet, self-denial is similarly questionable, for outer orders fail to matter and evolve without the reflexive dignity of our choice to commit to them *honestly and critically*. Importantly, therapization continues the problematic debates of authenticity. Like knockers, proponents of weak therapization continue the warning against eroding educational ideals. Strong therapization is criticized to replay the coddled egotism of authenticity, as intellectual commitments are frivolously chucked for self-indulgent expressions. On the other hand, the "boosters" of strong therapization render the outer educational world accountable and therefore, warrant its structural changes. For the inner lives of students are conceptually "protected" as inherently valuable and the reason with which educational ideals ought to be challenged to be ever accountable.

Through this consideration, we are given a basic framework that illuminates the problems and opportunities within the pedagogical conundrums that our students and teachers increasingly face. What our two previous examples (the students' resistance to APA and the teacher's role in mental-health lessons) demonstrate is the fact that the difficulty of their situations precisely indicates the problem of the divided approaches in therapizing education. For one, students' inner lives mark authentic truths that ought not to be managed by scholastic norms (of APA). Yet, for the other, teachers can approach the very same inner lives as objects of management to ensure adequate conformity to such norms. Both approaches are problematic because neither acknowledges the pedagogical value of the other. The former fails to grasp the necessity of norms just as the latter overlooks the intrinsic significance of inner lives, thereby confining pedagogy with a stubborn hold on a mere partial reality of education. In other words, the true pedagogical problem in students resisting APA formats, for instance, is not about the obstacles against authentic expression but the complex reality that such resistance reveals about education and therefore, what it means *as a learning opportunity*. With this in mind, let's explore this further as what we would like to refer to as the ideal of "reflexive tension."

Therapization as Reflexive Tension

What strong and weak therapization represent are a partial validity of each other. Accommodating emotions can indeed compel structural changes while riskily enabling empty egotism, whereas "regulating" emotions can preserve important educational ideals while reinforcing their oppressive risks. However, like the authenticity debate, the essential value of therapization becomes lost through a caricatured regard between opposing perspectives. To "rescue" the therapizing value, we ought to understand the inner lives of students and the outer order of schooling as *mutually constituted*. Learnedness is *both* discovered from respecting students' completed inner self and formed by externally supplementing the self, who remains humbly incomplete without greater concerns and ideals. This dual consideration introduces a valuable reflexive tension that negotiates an educative "balance" between inner will and outer commitments. Education's increasing openness to the inner life, therefore, is an injection of important complexities into the classroom and pedagogical relationships that render them always fundamentally questionable and changeable.

When the classroom holds both emotional experience and intellectual discipline as the meaning of learning, student grievances, for instance, are no longer simply concluded as correctable behaviors or celebrated authenticity. Rather, the educator is positioned to wrestle with its expression as both a legitimate sign of structural harm that ought to be challenged and a personal disconnection from educational ideals that ought to be mended. This presents an ambiguous tension that compels important reflections on what students and educators *truly* need and what education ought to mean in relation. Essentially, therapization's importance lies in revealing the intrinsic complexity of the educational enterprise, sustaining the question of what schooling and learning ought to be throughout moments of teacher-student encounters. For each moment presents the opportunity to critically think about, reconceive, and preserve the "authentic" meaning of learning and education for the teachers and students in question. The "problem" of APA resistance, for instance, does not indicate the priority to protect either student expression *or* institutional traditions per se. Instead, such a problem can and ought to be an educative opportunity to openly think about what scholastic norms (such as the APA) even mean *in relation to* student learning. Ultimately, we believe therapization's true value speaks to a reflexivity that must reconcile students' inner and outer worlds. Norms do not have to be rejected nor embraced but can be held as the complex reality of our learning and teaching and through this, discover moments of educative opportunities conducive to the formative developments of both learners and the institutions of learning. In concluding our chapter, we offer some questions and an activity to readers in the spirit of holding *education as an active question*: Can student-teacher relationships be curated to not only tolerate ambiguity but thoughtfully cocreate its opportunities? If so, how? In closing, one final vignette to demonstrate how this reflexive tension might be found within a slightly different setting: clinical education for practicing mental health clinicians.

> We are in our third session covering the topic of Exposure Therapy. It has, in some ways, been a challenging topic, since the theory and practice include encouraging clients to seek out their fear-inducing stimulus. The challenge comes in two varieties: the first is that many practitioners in the room are uncomfortable with asking their clients to seek out distress, the second is that they themselves have reactive responses to some of the content. When I (Jesse) talk about the irrationality of fear of spiders, one participant reminds me that it is possible for poisonous spiders to migrate to our northern landscape (even if it is very unlikely), justifying her distress in a spider's presence. In this setting, we are able to stop the lesson and discuss how that reactivity is further perpetuating a cycle of fear and anxiety rather than dispelling reactive emotional behaviors. This sparks a conversation where other clinicians are able to chime in, share experiences of overcoming fear and relating to one another's distress. We end the session with a better understanding of ourselves and how we are in the world and in our bodies. The anxious response to spiders of the initial clinician does not magically go away, but together, we supported one another while simultaneously challenging the maladaptive, automatic, and distressing responses.

Questions for Discussion

- Are there ever dilemmas in your teaching practice between caring for the well-being of your students and committing to the integrity of the curriculum? If so, how have you addressed them and, more importantly, why did you address them in the way(s) that you did? Were the reasons related to school policy, the students' circumstances, your personal intuition, and so on?

- What do you think are the implications of emphasizing the student over the curriculum and vice versa? If it is possible to pedagogically balance between the student and the curriculum, what would this look like both in your practice and in educational theory?

Further Reading

Palmer, P. J. *The Courage to Teach: Exploring the Inner Landscape of a Teacher's Life* (20th Anniversary Edition). San Francisco, CA: Jossey-Bass, 2017.

Taylor, C. *The Ethics of Authenticity*. Cambridge, MA: Harvard University Press, 2018.

Activity

Teaching is rife with spaces of pedagogical discomfort and ambiguity. This activity is aimed at developing your own reflexive practice. To begin, recall one such instance of discomfort or ambiguity. Gently breathe and begin to write out your feelings, nonjudgmentally, about the instance. When you are finished, set aside your writing, consciously slowly inhale and exhale three to four times. When you are ready, reread what you have written and sit with these two questions: Where do these feelings come from? What can I learn from seeing and being empathetic to this part of myself?

Notes

1. Kathryn Ecclestone and Dennis Hayes. *The Dangerous Rise of Therapeutic Education* (Chicago, IL: University of Chicago Press, 2019), ix–xv.

2. BC Curriculum, "Core Competencies," accessed February 20, 2022, https://curriculum.gov.bc.ca/competencies.

3. BCPSEA, "Provincial Collective Agreement," accessed 2022, https://bcpsea.bc.ca/wp-content/uploads/2021/06/00-Provincial-Collective-Agreement-2019-2022-May-2021.pdf, 27.

4. BCACC, "Code of Ethical Conduct and Standards of Ethical Practice," accessed February 20, 2022, https://bcacc.ca/code-of-ethical-conduct-and-standards-of-clinical-practice.

5. Guy Claxton, *Building Learning Power* (Bristol, UK: TLO, 2002); Mary Tew and Jason Park "Emotional Rollercoaster: Calming Nerves at Times of Transition." *Curriculum Briefing* 5, no. 3 (2007): 21.

6. Beth Berila, *Integrating Mindfulness into Anti-Oppression Pedagogy: Social Justice in Higher Education* (New York: Routledge, 2016), 25–30.

7. Berila, *Integrating Mindfulness*, 26.

8. Berila, *Integrating Mindfulness*, 28.

9. Kathryn Ecclestone and Dennis Hayes, *The Dangerous Rise of Therapeutic Education* (Chicago, IL: University of Chicago Press, 2019), 136.

10. David Armstrong and Gill Armstrong. *Educational Trends Exposed: How to Be a Critical Consumer* (New York: Routledge, 2021), 95.

11. Michalinos Zembylas, "The Therapisation of Social Justice as an Emotional Regime: Implications for Critical Education." *Journal of Professional Capital and Community* 1, no. 4 (2016): 286–88.

12. Frank Furedia, *Therapy Culture: Creating Vulnerability in an Uncertain Age* (London: Routledge, 2004), 110.

13. Ecclestone and Hayes, *Dangerous Rise*, 96.

14. Ecclestone and Hayes, *Dangerous Rise*, 101.

15. Charles Taylor, *The Ethics of Authenticity* (Cambridge: Harvard University Press, 1992), 26.

16. Taylor, *Ethics of Authenticity*, 29.

17. Taylor, *Ethics of Authenticity*, 3.

18. Taylor, *Ethics of Authenticity*, 29.

19. Taylor, *Ethics of Authenticity*, 61.

20. Taylor, *Ethics of Authenticity*, 29.

21. Taylor, *Ethics of Authenticity*, 63.

22. Taylor, *Ethics of Authenticity*, 75.

23. Taylor, *Ethics of Authenticity*, 79.

24. Taylor, *Ethics of Authenticity*, 73.

25. Taylor, *Ethics of Authenticity*, 91.

26. Taylor, *Ethics of Authenticity*, 40.

12

Old Wisdom for Contemporary Problems

A Civic Republican Approach to Dis/ability in Education

KEVIN MURRAY AND JESSICA D. MURRAY

In this chapter, we aim to contribute to the tradition of practically and educationally useful philosophy.[1] We draw on an old—extending back at least to republican Rome, established in the late sixth century BCE—but recently revived and reworked tradition in political philosophy to grapple with an important concept and the thorny normative questions confronting educators and educational policy makers that follow in its wake. The old tradition is civic republicanism, about which we will say more below, and which is sometimes also called the neo-Roman tradition.[2] The important concept is *dis/ability*,[3] which is a contested and consequential concept, especially as it interacts with educational work, and we will have more to say about it below. We hope, above all, to provide a sketch of a normative compass that can help to orient educators and policy makers as they work through the normative questions that emerge from disability in education.[4]

We intend this normative compass to be particularly useful in what Mary Pratt calls "contact zones . . . social spaces where cultures meet, clash, and grapple with each other, often in contexts of highly asymmetrical relations of power."[5] It emerges from contact zones: we are an educational practitioner in public p–12 schooling and a practitioner and researcher in higher education working together to bring an ancient philosophical tradition into contact with contemporary educational problems. And it is meant to help navigate the many overlapping contact zones related to disability in education, where students and parents and teachers, citizens and school board members and other elected officials, and the disabled and the nondisabled come together to construct educational environments and experiences.

In particular, we will argue that one of the main commitments of civic republicanism—that freedom should be understood as nondomination—can, and should, serve as the main value calibrating the normative compass for educational work focused on disability. The benefit of freedom, rather than some other moral or political value, animating such a compass is that some conception of freedom is already widely accepted across the range of political views. It is a solid and strategic point from which to embark.[6] We turn next to describing disability and civic republicanism, with special attention to getting clear about freedom as nondomination.

Disability

The normative compass we sketch cannot function without some conception of disability to orient it. How disability and its educational consequences should be understood is a knotty problem, and one that seems unlikely to be resolved, at least to the satisfaction of the public in general. Drawing on education research, critical disability studies, and the emerging field known as "DisCrit,"[7] we hold that disability is best understood as a social, rather than individual or medical, phenomenon.[8]

What does it mean to say that disability is a social, or socially constructed, phenomenon? Above all, it means that disability should be understood as a feature of educational and broader social and economic environments, rather than as a feature of particular students or individuals.[9] Individuals do differ widely in their attributes, capacities, needs, and aspirations. But disability does not inhere in individuals or their differences. Instead, it results from the interaction between individuals and the educational, social, and economic environments they navigate. Particular individuals are "disabled"—claimed by the category of disability—by the organization of the school or broader social or economic structure. Any such environment will feature categories of ability and disability, fashioned in the image of its norms, values, expectations, demands, and practices, that will claim and disable some set of individuals. The striking title of Ray McDermott's chapter on developing a social conception of disability—"The

Acquisition of a Child by a Learning Disability"—neatly captures the view: disability resides in the school and exists before any particular student enters the educational environment, waiting to capture and disable students whose individual differences do not align tightly with that environment.[10] On this view, disability is seen as "a better display board for the weaknesses of a cultural system than it is an account of real persons."[11] It follows that educational work focused on understanding and addressing disability and its consequences should attend carefully to the educational environment and its structure, expectations, and demands, rather than focusing only on the student deemed disabled. To limit educational attention to the individual student is to misunderstand disability and to position the student as the problem to be "fixed," while taking for granted the broader educational context where disability resides.

An example may serve to illuminate the notion that disability is a social phenomenon. Consider a young student who has been diagnosed with attention-deficit/hyperactivity disorder (ADHD) and who is about to enter middle school, where she will face a growing demand to focus quietly for long periods of time and to demonstrate her knowledge of a given topic through timed assessments. Suppose that she frequently experiences difficulty with sustained sitting and silence and that she does not perform especially well on timed assessments. Where is the disability located, and how should it be addressed? Those who take disability to be a thoroughly medical or individual phenomenon would suggest that the disability is in the student, a result of the functioning of her body and mind, and that the student should be treated medically and educationally—say, with medication and learning support—so that she can meet the demands of the educational environment. The basic problem to be resolved is the student rather than the educational context. Those who take disability to be a social phenomenon would provide an alternative analysis. On their view, it is true that the student does differ from other students in her attributes and experiences, and it is likewise true that medical and educational intervention may benefit the student. But disability is not seen as a feature of the student. Instead, it is seen as a feature of the educational environment, spawned by the behavior it demands from students and the measures used to determine educational success. The environment, and in particular the demand to focus silently for extended periods and to demonstrate knowledge through timed assessments, creates a category of disability that exists prior to the student and that captures and disables her as she enters the educational environment. Again, while medication and learning support may benefit the student, our attention is drawn to the environment so that it can be modified to make categories of disability disappear. In this case, different teaching and assessment strategies may be adopted that do not cause the student's learning differences to constrain her.[12]

The socially constructed category of disability creates a distinction between "disabled" and "nondisabled" and frames those deemed disabled as inferior and those deemed nondisabled as superior. In schools, students marked as disabled are often taken to be abnormal, a problem to be resolved through educational and other work.[13] When we fail to see the social nature of disability, we are limited to "fixing" the student claimed by disability, rather than examining and transforming the environment that disables her. This framing of ability and disability results in profound discrepancies in outcomes for people with and without disabilities in academic achievement, discipline and legal referrals, and employment and educational opportunities.[14]

Civic Republicanism

The normative compass must also include a clear understanding of civic republicanism and, in particular, its conception of freedom as nondomination. The civic republican tradition in political thought and practice is ancient, with its roots in the Roman Republic founded after the expulsion in 509 BCE of the final king of Rome, Lucius Tarquinius Superbus.[15] Republicanism was shattered after the fall of the Roman Republic—often dated to 27 BCE, when the Roman Senate granted Octavian the titles *princeps* and *augustus*, effectively establishing the Roman Empire[16]—but later reappeared and played a major political and intellectual role in in the medieval independent cities of northern Italy, the English republic of 1649 to 1660, and the American War of Independence.[17] The tradition has been recovered and reworked during the past three or four decades, with particular attention devoted to remedying the thoroughly unacceptable features accumulated over its long history, including tight economic, sexual, and racial restrictions on republican citizenship. What has emerged is a political position that is decidedly progressive, thoroughly democratic, and fiercely opposed to domination, subjection, and involuntary dependence. In this chapter, we draw mainly on the philosopher Phillip Pettit's and the historian Quentin Skinner's development of civic republicanism, but many scholars have contributed to the endeavor to reclaim and update the tradition.[18]

Three main commitments are typically taken as characteristic of civic republicanism: the view that freedom should be understood as nondomination, an emphasis on the vital importance of the mixed constitution, and deep sense that citizens must "keep the republic to its proper business" by playing an actively contestatory role in governance.[19] Freedom as nondomination is the central and most distinctive feature of civic republicanism, and we describe it further below. The mixed constitution ensures that power is never concentrated in a single person or group, but rather shared among and only ever entrusted to multiple bodies. The contestatory citizenry is meant to be "committed to interrogating all elements of government and imposing itself in the determination of law and policy," in this way guarding against corruption and other abuses of power.[20] Drawing on Adam Ferguson, an eighteenth-century Scottish thinker, Pettit calls this contestatory disposition "the 'refractory and turbulent zeal' of any people fortunate enough to live under a government they could shape. He [Ferguson] thought such zeal was required to ensure the eternal vigilance that . . . was reckoned to be the price of liberty."[21]

Both of these republican commitments point to the origin and meaning of the term "republic" itself, which comes from the Latin *res publica*, and which can be roughly translated as "the public affair" or "the thing of the people." As the name suggests, from its Roman beginning through to its modern revival, the tradition has been ferociously anti-absolutist and anti-autocratic, taking governance to be the affair of citizens in general.

For civic republicans, the mixed constitution and the contestatory citizenry are taken to be necessary for achieving and safeguarding freedom as nondomination. Without them, and the work they do "organizing a government that would promote the equal freedom of citizens without itself becoming a master in their lives,"[22] republican freedom cannot be established, let alone defended against the many inegalitarian and authoritarian threats that cut against it.[23]

What is freedom as nondomination, or republican freedom?[24] Following most civic republican writers, we describe republican freedom by first describing what republican freedom is not, namely, the liberal conception of freedom as noninterference, which emerged in the seventeenth and eighteenth centuries, and which challenged and eventually eclipsed republican freedom.[25] Pettit and Skinner contrast freedom as nondomination with this liberal view of freedom as noninterference, which they take to be thoroughly deficient.[26] On their interpretation, freedom as noninterference wrongly takes freedom to be a property of choices, rather than a property of persons. An individual is taken to be free in virtue of their ability to make this or that choice without actively being prevented from doing so.[27] The main civic republican argument against freedom as noninterference is that it fails to recognize that a person may not be interfered with in this or that choice and may yet be thoroughly unfree. This is just the case, for example, for slaves "whose choices never happen to conflict with the will of their master."[28] These slaves may be "able to act without the least interference," but "nevertheless remain wholly bereft of their liberty. They remain subject to the will of their master, unable to act according to their own independent will at any time."[29] The worker in an authoritarian and nonunionized workplace may enjoy the goodwill of a benevolent boss, and consequently exert some level of control over his work without active interference, but he remains all the time in thrall to the boss's arbitrary power, without recourse to protective laws or regulations.

The watchful intolerance of potential, in addition to actual, interference is the central feature of freedom as nondomination. Freedom as nondomination corrects the deficient liberal conception of freedom by identifying not actual interference but rather the very existence of the power to arbitrarily interfere as lethal to freedom, even when it is not exercised. The slave will not be free when the master possesses the power to interfere because they will be dependent on the master, unable to interact with them—to look them in the eyes and to talk straight with them without deference or fear—on terms of equality.[30] The worker will not be free when she must depend on the kindness of the boss in order to avoid damaging interference in all aspects of her work life. On the republican view, the slave and the worker are unfree—dominated, forced into relationships of dependence and subservience—by virtue of the presence of the dominating power to interfere, no matter whether it is used. To be properly free is to be in the position of nondomination, that is, "the position of the independent person who has no master or *dominus* in their life" and who thereby has the capacity to make their "choices without any need to seek another's permission."[31]

For civic republicans, it is a protective shield of law, policy, and norms that secures freedom as nondomination for citizens and guarantees the equal status of the *liber*, the free person, vigorously defended against the dominating power of a master. These laws and norms "incorporate you in a protective and empowering force field and establish you in the enjoyment of your freedom."[32] The worker is guarded against domination—against her boss's power of arbitrary inference and the relationship of dependence and subservience it imposes on her—by a legal structure that, for example, safeguards the right of workers to organize and form unions and to appeal to an independent body when terminated from their employment. When we are nestled within the proper laws and norms, we need not speak in "the mealymouthed tones of the servant" in order to avoid interference, and no citizen will have "reason to speak in the presumptuous tones of the master."[33] We are able to "walk tall and assume the status of an equal with the most powerful in the land," with no "reason for fear or deference of the kind that a power of interference might inspire."[34]

Disability and Nondomination

With an understanding of disability, civic republicanism, and freedom as nondomination in hand, we turn now to sketching the normative compass, calibrated by republican freedom, that can be useful in orienting educators and educational policy makers in their educational work focused on disability. Where does the compass point?[35] What direction does it suggest educators and policy makers should travel? A complete description is beyond the space available to us in this chapter, but below we propose one civic republican educational principle to animate the compass, aimed in particular at guiding policy.

In general, the republican compass demands that educational institutions have systemic methods of protecting students marked as disabled from domination and subservience and, in particular, that educational systems secure for disabled students full access to education, no matter their specific teacher or school. While federal policy has driven significant progress for students with disabilities,[36] their access to education often relies, in practice, on the benevolence of individual educators or administrators, a dynamic made evident through variations in outcomes for students with disabilities across teachers.[37] Freedom as nondomination exposes the problematic nature of this model, and enhances our ability to see how structures—protective shields against domination—can help to ensure that students with disabilities receive the educational opportunities and experiences they deserve.

Policy and Nondomination

The policy principle maintains that the policy structure governing educational work on disability should form a defensive shield—"a protective and empowering force field"[38]—against domination, arbitrary power, and involuntary dependence for students marked as disabled, and that those students and their families should be actively included in the development and implementation of such a policy structure. Students and their families should be included in deliberation about the policy structure in order to ensure that the policy structure itself does not come to function as a source of domination and arbitrary power. To illuminate this principle, we consider educational policy focused on behavior and discipline in schools, how it fails to satisfy the policy principle, and how it might do so.

Current discipline models typically exclude and dominate students, with a disproportionate impact on students with disabilities. These exclusionary practices stem from zero-tolerance policies, which originally rose in popularity in United States schools after the school shooting at Colorado's Columbine High School in 1999.[39] However, these policies are ineffective as behavior deterrents, have not made schools safer, and have not improved student behavior.[40] Despite this evidence, these policies have become a standard response to even minor behaviors.[41] Twenty percent of all public middle and high school students have been suspended at least once.[42]

Research demonstrates that these exclusionary punishments are arbitrarily applied and at the discretion of the administrator based on teacher and administrator perception of the student.[43] While administrators are tasked with carrying out specific discipline models, within such models they use personal discretion, resulting in many instances of students being suspended and excluded from school based on behavior unrelated to bullying, harassment, discrimination, or violence and tobacco, drugs, or alcohol, even when nonexclusionary consequences are an option within the school's discipline model.[44] In Indiana, 95 percent of exclusionary consequences resulted from nonviolent and nonthreatening behaviors such as truancy, dress code violations, and tardiness, while only 5 percent resulted from drug-, alcohol-, tobacco-, or weapon-related behaviors.[45] Administrator and teacher perception of a student's "disobedience" or "disrespect" are the reasons for the vast majority of suspensions,[46] which puts students with disabilities at a higher risk of being suspended because they are more likely to be perceived as a threat than nondisabled students.[47]

Despite some progress in including students with disabilities in schools, exclusionary discipline models continue to dominate and push out learners labeled as disabled at disproportionately high rates, with rates of suspension for these students being three times the rate of their nondisabled peers.[48] Students in special education represent only 12 percent of youth enrolled in public schools, yet are 75 percent of those who are physically restrained in school[49] account for 25 to 26 percent of suspensions and expulsions[50] and are 25 percent of those involved with law enforcement.[51]

Given these conditions, the policy principle and the civic republican compass assert that educational policy should serve as a protective shield against domination for students with disabilities and include them in decision-making processes. The republican compass is particularly sensitive to the relations of involuntary dependence and subservience created when students with disabilities are not wrapped in such a protective shield against domination and the arbitrary power to discipline and punish. There are significant policy implications of republican freedom, specifically around behavior support systems. The normative compass points to the use of restorative justice and tenets of democratic teaching at the policy level to protect students from arbitrary interference and domination in the realm of school discipline and to help them to become contestatory citizens, able to advocate, organize, and resist for their own freedom.

Tenets of democratic teaching, such as a commitment to equal opportunity and shared decision-making power,[52] can be used within a behavioral support model to protect students.[53] Restorative practices, which hold that true justice means repairing the harm, the relationships, and the community rather than imposing blame and punishment, empowers youth to take responsibility for their actions and remedy the harm they created.[54] Instead of blaming and pushing out "offenders," democratic teaching combined with restorative practices view all learners as equal. They allow students with disabilities to stand "eye-to-eye" with fellow students, teachers, and administrators because they allow all to share responsibility for the community through making collaborative and meaningful decisions for that community. Incorporating restorative practices as well as democratic teaching into behavior policy in schools provides a shield to students with disabilities against domination by traditional exclusionary practices.

Conclusion

We have sketched a normative compass, animated by a social conception of disability and by the civic republican view of freedom as nondomination, that can orient educators and educational policy makers in their work focused on disability. As developed in this chapter, the compass remains partial at best. We have described the general direction the compass points—toward the development of a protective shield against domination and involuntary dependence for students with disabilities—and we have drawn out some of the compass's implications for policy related to disability, in particular behavior and discipline policy. A more complete republican compass would be useful in guiding educators and policy makers across the full spectrum of educational work focused on disability.

Questions for Discussion

- How might educators and philosophers who endorse the liberal conception of freedom as noninterference respond to the republican conception of freedom as nondomination? How might they respond to the republican "normative compass" for grappling with questions of ability and disability in education sketched in this chapter?

- The republican normative compass developed in this chapter is partial, focused mainly on educational policy and disability. What might civic republican thought, and especially its conception of freedom as nondomination, have to say about pedagogy—about how the teacher arranges her classroom, the classroom community, learning activities, assignments, and assessments? What pedagogical approaches and strategies might best form a "defensive shield" against domination for students with disabilities?

Further Reading

Pettit, P. *Just Freedom: A Moral Compass for a Complex World.* W. W. Norton, 2014.
O'Shea, T. "Disability and Domination: Lessons from Republican Political Philosophy." *Journal of Applied Philosophy* 35, no. 1 (2018): 133–48.

Activity

One learning activity that can help students to explore the social model of disability and republican freedom takes the form of a card game.

Students will break into small groups of four and sit so that they can play a card game (at a table, pushing their desks together, and so on). Approximately three small groups—twelve students—are required for the activity to work well. Each small group will need its own standard deck of playing cards.

Each small group will be given a set of instructions for the game, which resembles the popular game Hearts, but where students are seeking to win cards rather than to avoid them. *The central trick is that each set of instructions will differ from the others, such that each group is playing a slightly different version of the game.* For example, in one group, the highest card will win the hand, and hearts will be the "trump" suit. In another group, the lowest card will win the hand, and spades will be the "trump" suit. *That each group has a different set of instructions must be kept secret from the students.*

Students are given their instructions, and then allowed to play a practice round in their small groups to ensure that they understand the game and their version of its rules. Again, the differing rules must be kept secret. Questions students have about the version of the game at their table should be answered while standing at the group's table, rather than answered loudly for all to hear.

After students play a practice round and feel that they understand the game well enough to play, take the instructions sheet away from each group. This is vital for the activity and stops students from consulting the instructions at any point during the activity.

When all groups are ready and no longer have their instructions, play can begin. *Importantly, students are not allowed to talk—or to use sign language, or to write—at any point until the activity has finished. They are allowed to use gestures, but they cannot speak, sign, or write.* You may need to circulate to ensure that this rule is being followed.

Once each group finishes the first round of play (after all cards have been played and won by players), the group will determine who won the fewest cards during the round. That person in each small group—the "losers" of the round—will move from their current group to a new group. *Silence must be maintained during this process.*

A new round will begin once students have settled into their new groups, and the same process will continue (play the round, determine the "loser," and have that student move to a new table) until at least five rounds have been played—preferably more rounds if time allows. Some students will likely begin to understand the trick of the game—the differing instructions for each group—but they should remain silent until the activity has finished.

Once five or more rounds have been played, the activity finishes, and the class will engage in large group discussion. Students will likely be animated after finishing the activity and discovering—or finally be able to talk about—the differing rules, and they might fruitfully carry the discussion and connect to the relevant concepts and themes without needing much guidance.

In case more structured discussion is needed, consider the following questions:

1. What happened when a new player came to a group? How did the players already in the group interact with the new player? Did they help? Guide? Harm? Take advantage? Look down on? Why did they react how they did? What did the new player do? How did the new player feel?

2. Who tended to win? Who tended to lose? Why was this the case?

3. Who had power in this activity? Who was subjected to that power? How was power used? Were any players exposed to domination?

4. What was disability in this activity? Where was it? Who was disabled? How and by what were they disabled? Why were some disabled but not others?

5. Were players free in this activity? In the liberal sense of freedom as noninterference? In the republican sense of freedom as nondomination? Who was free, if anyone? Who was unfree, if anyone?

6. How might freedom on the republican view—nondomination—be secured to players in this activity? What structures, rules, policies, and norms would secure freedom for them?

Notes

1. For a classic example of this philosophical tradition, see Amy Gutmann, *Democratic Education* (Princeton, NJ: Princeton University Press, 1987). For a more recent example, see Jennifer Morton, *Moving Up without Losing Your Way: The Ethical Costs of Upward Mobility* (Princeton, NJ: Princeton University Press, 2019).
2. See Quentin Skinner, *Liberty Before Liberalism* (New York: Cambridge University Press, 1998). See also Quentin Skinner, *Hobbes and Republican Liberty* (New York: Cambridge University Press, 2008).
3. We borrow the formulation "dis/ability" from the field of critical disability studies, where it is often used to call into question and to challenge standard conceptions of the word and the suspect meanings attached to it. For simplicity, we revert to "disability" for the remainder of the chapter.
4. We borrow the notion of a normative or moral compass from Philip Pettit, *Just Freedom: A Moral Compass for a Complex World* (New York: W. W. Norton, 2014).
5. Mary Pratt, "Arts of the Contact Zone," *Profession* (1991): 34.
6. For more on the value of beginning with an already broadly accepted view, see John Rawls, *Political Liberalism* (New York: Columbia University Press, 1993), 139. There Rawls develops the notion of "overlapping consensus," where citizens affirm the foundational values that "govern the basic framework of social life—the very groundwork of our existence—and specify the fundamental terms of political and social cooperation" through their differing individual political views. In this case, the groundwork value "freedom" can be affirmed, for example, by the social democrat as well as the libertarian for reasons that are internal to their competing political commitments.
7. DisCrit is the coming together of critical disability studies and critical race theory. See, for example, David Connor, Beth Ferri, and Subini Annama, eds., *DisCrit: Disability Studies and Critical Race Theory in Education* (New York: Teachers College Press, 2016).
8. This view of disability is typically called the "social model of disability" and is contrasted with the "medical model of disability."
9. See Ray McDermott, "The Acquisition of a Child by a Learning Disability," in *Understanding Practice: Perspectives on Activity and Context*, eds. Seth Chaiklin and Jean Lave (New York: Cambridge University Press, 1993). See also Ray McDermott and Hervé Varenne, "Culture as Disability," *Anthropology & Education Quarterly* 26, no. 3 (1995).
10. Ray McDermott, "Acquisition of a Child."
11. McDermott and Varenne, "Culture as Disability," 327.
12. It is important to recognize that the modifications to the educational environment called for by the social conception of disability require considerable time, labor, resources, and autonomy, which many educators and their schools

and districts do not now possess. More fundamentally, it may well be the case that modifying the environment to diminish or disappear one category of disability (for example, ADHD) will enhance or strengthen another (for example, social anxiety disorder) or that environmental modifications are unable to make certain kinds or degrees of disability vanish (for example, a particularly severe intellectual disability), at least with current technology. Despite these limitations, we maintain that the social conception of disability remains the proper general view for guiding educational thought and practice.

13. See Connor, David, Beth Ferri, and Subini Annama, eds., *DisCrit*. See also Katie Ellis et al., eds., *Manifestos for the Future of Critical Disability Studies* (New York: Routledge, 2020).

14. See U.S. Bureau of Labor Statistics, *Persons with a Disability: Labor Force Characteristics News Release* (2021). See also U.S. Department of Education Office for Civil Rights, *2015–2016 Civil Rights Data Collection: School Climate and Safety*, 2018.

15. For a recent account of the overthrow of the Roman monarchy and the founding of the Roman republic, see Mary Beard, *SPQR: A History of Ancient Rome* (New York: Liveright, 2015).

16. For a recent account of the fall of the Roman Republic, see Edward Watts, *Mortal Republic: How Rome Fell into Tyranny* (New York: Basic Books, 2018).

17. For a historical overview, see Pettit, *Just Freedom*. See also Philip Pettit, *Republicanism: A Theory of Freedom and Government* (Oxford, UK: Clarendon Press, 1997).

18. For example, see Cecile Laborde and John Maynor, eds, *Republicanism and Political Theory* (Hoboken, NJ: Blackwell, 2009). See also Lena Halldenius, *Mary Wollstonecraft and Feminist Republicanism: Independence, Rights, and the Experience of Unfreedom* (New York: Routledge, 2015).

19. Philip Pettit, *On the People's Terms: A Republican Theory and Model of Democracy* (Cambridge, UK: Cambridge University Press, 2012), 5.

20. Pettit, *On the People's Terms*, 12.

21. Pettit, *Just Freedom*, 132.

22. Pettit, *On the People's Terms*, 5–6.

23. We use the terms *freedom as non-domination* and *republican freedom* interchangeably here and elsewhere in the chapter.

24. There is rich and lengthy philosophical literature on freedom, which we cannot detail in this chapter. For the paper that is typically taken to set the stage for philosophical discussion of freedom, see Isaiah Berlin, "Two Concepts of Liberty," in *Liberty*, ed. Henry Hardy (New York: Oxford University Press, 2002). Berlin marks a distinction between "negative freedom," freedom from constraint and interference, and "positive freedom," freedom to realize self-mastery or self-perfection in light of some vision of what human beings should be. Quentin Skinner calls republican freedom a "third concept of liberty." It is distinct from

negative freedom because it recognizes not only actual but potential arbitrary inference as lethal to freedom, and it is distinct from positive freedom because civic republicans do not maintain that some particular vision of human perfection or mastery is required for freedom. See Quentin Skinner, "A Third Concept of Liberty," *London Review of Books* 24, no. 7 (2002).

25. See Pettit, *On the People's Terms*, 5–6.
26. See Pettit, *Just Freedom*.
27. See Pettit, *On the People's Terms*, 9.
28. Skinner, *Hobbes and Republican Liberty*, xi.
29. Skinner, *Hobbes and Republican Liberty*, xi.
30. Pettit, *Just Freedom*, xxvi.
31. Pettit, *Just Freedom*, 3.
32. Pettit, *Just Freedom*, 25.
33. Pettit, *Just Freedom*, xxvii.
34. Pettit, *Just Freedom*, xxvi.
35. Little work has been done on the relationship between disability and civic republican thought. Among the few papers on the topic are: Jurgen De Wispelaere and David Casassas, "A Life of One's Own: Republican Freedom and Disability," *Disability and Society* 29, no. 3 (2014). Tom, O'Shea, "Disability and Domination: Lessons from Republican Political Philosophy," *Journal of Applied Philosophy* 35, no. 1 (2018).
36. Jane West and Peggy Schaefer Whitby, "Federal Policy and the Education of Students with Disabilities: Progress and the Path Forward," *Focus on Exceptional Children* 41, no. 3 (2008).
37. Allison Gilmour, "Teacher Certification Area and the Academic Outcomes of Students with Learning Disabilities or Emotional/Behavioral Disorders," *Journal of Special Education* 54, no. 1 (2020). See also Roddy Theobald et al., "High School English Language Arts Teachers and Postsecondary Outcomes for Students with and without Disabilities," *Journal of Disability Policy Studies* 31, no. 4 (2021).
38. Pettit, *Just Freedom*, 25.
39. See Mara Schiff, "Can Restorative Justice Disrupt the 'School-to-Prison Pipeline?'" *Contemporary Justice Review* 21, no. 2 (2018).
40. See American Psychological Association Zero Tolerance Task Force, "Are Zero Tolerance Policies Effective in Schools? An Evidentiary Review and Recommendations," *American Psychologist* 63 (2008). See also James Pyne, "Suspended Attitudes: Exclusion and Emotional Disengagement from School," *Sociology of Education* 92, no. 1 (2019).
41. See Mara Schiff, "Can Restorative Justice Disrupt?"
42. National Center for Education Statistics, *Digest of Education Statistics* (Washington, DC: U.S. Department of Education, 2016).
43. Jacob Williams et al., "The Enemy among Us: Do School Administrators Perceive Students with Disabilities as a Threat?" *NASSP Bulletin* 97, no. 2 (2013).

44. See Tony Fabelo et al., *Breaking Schools' Rules: A Statewide Study of How School Discipline Relates to Students' Success and Juvenile Justice Involvement* (New York: Council of State Governments Justice Center, 2011). See also Russell Skiba, *Zero Tolerance, Zero Evidence: An Analysis of School Disciplinary Practice (Policy Research Report No. SRS2)* (Bloomington, IN: Indiana University, 2000).

45. Karega Rausch and Russell Skiba, *Discipline, Disability, and Race: Disproportionality in Indiana Schools* (Bloomington, IN: Center for Evaluation and Educational Policy, 2006).

46. Russell Skiba et al., "Race Is Not Neutral: A National Investigation of African American and Latino Disproportionality in School Discipline," *School Psychology Review* 40, no. 1 (2011).

47. Jacob Williams et al., "Avoiding the Threat: An Exploratory Study into a Theoretical Understanding of the De Facto Segregation of Students with Disabilities," *NASSP Bulletin* 99, no. 3 (2015).

48. See U.S. Department of Education Office for Civil Rights, *2015–2016 Civil Rights Data Collection: School Climate and Safety*. See also U.S. Department of Education Office for Civil Rights, *Civil Rights Data Collection Data Snapshot: School Discipline* (2014).

49. U.S. Department of Education Office for Civil Rights, *Civil Rights Data Collection Data Snapshot: School Discipline*.

50. U.S. Department of Education Office for Civil Rights, *2015–2016 Civil Rights Data Collection: School Climate and Safety*.

51. Sheldon Horowitz, Julie Rawe, and Meghan Whittaker, *The State of Learning Disabilities: Understanding the 1 in 5* (Washington, DC: National Center for Learning Disabilities, 2017).

52. For an example of democratic teaching in action, see Meira Levinson, *No Citizen Left Behind* (Cambridge, MA: Harvard University Press, 2012).

53. See Deneca Winfrey Avant, "Unwrapping Tradition: Shifting from Traditional Leadership to Transformative Action," in *Transformative Leadership: A Reader*, ed. Carolyn Shields (Peter Lang, 2011). See also Paul Carr, "Transforming Educational Leadership without Social Justice?" *Transformative Leadership: A Reader*, ed. Carolyn Shields (New York: Peter Lang, 2011).

54. Mara Schiff, "Can Restorative Justice Disrupt?"

13

A Humanistic Baseline in the Rural School

Sarah Freye and Dini Metro-Roland

A Rural Baseline

It's an hour-long drive to the high school where I teach.[1] I leave before the sun rises, a thermos of coffee to keep me awake through the miles of endless cornfields. There are other schools closer to where I live: urban and suburban districts that would cut my commute in half. But there is something about the rural school that has captured me—a unique space where students grow up in a seemingly isolating landscape, a sense of camaraderie between teachers and families that is absent in other towns. The field of rural education is criticized for relying too heavily on anecdotal evidence, but in the rural space the practitioner is often the only researcher. As the first few students begin to trickle into my room, I become both teacher and researcher, for the rural school serves as contact zone between teacher and academic. As teacher, I will do my best to engage them in this week's reading, and encourage them to try out something new in their writing. But as a researcher, I want more for my students, more for the rural school that has such possibilities for authentic learning. I note the barriers, inadequacies, and inequalities that prevent my students from flourishing.

And where better to look for a guide to research and praxis than political philosophy? In a lecture delivered at Stanford University as a part of the Tanner Lecture Series, Danielle Allen puts forth what she calls the "humanistic baseline," a way to view equitable education.[2] Allen observes that policy makers often overlook the intrinsic purpose of education, and instead focus on the economic competitiveness and political stability of the state. Because policy makers are concerned with education on a grand scale, it's not surprising that success is reduced to something measurable, that is, standardized test scores and graduation rates. Conversely, practitioners are more interested in "micro-level" issues, such as social, emotional, and intellectual growth of individual students who they see every day. The latter are "eudaemonic" interests—intangible aspects of a young person's development, and difficult to measure. Too often, schools place a neoliberal utilitarian emphasis on vocational education, and "equality" becomes synonymous with "finding a job." But in Allen's view these macro-level goals do not encompass enough of the things that provide true flourishing because her humanistic baseline covers more than just a student's ability to compete in the global workforce.[3] Allen posits that through education schools and practitioners need the following:

1. To prepare ourselves for breadwinning work
2. To prepare ourselves for civic and political engagement
3. To prepare ourselves for creative self-expression and world making
4. And to prepare ourselves for rewarding relationships in spaces of intimacy and leisure[4]

While the first may be present in state assessments, the last three are more eudaemonic; nonutilitarian items that prove difficult to track and assess. But these parts of the humanistic baseline are arguably the most important for equitable education because they could and should support the true flourishing of young people in the country. In my educational institution in rural Southwest Michigan, there is some evidence of the four elements of Allen's humanistic baseline in action. But I believe the rural school has the potential to incorporate these aspects of the baseline, with more complexities and intension, serve as a basis for educational policy change and improvement.

Breadwinning Work

During my daily planning period, the door to my office is always ajar; outside sit two girls with their Chromebooks, chatting in Spanish and working on a virtual health science course. A student stops by to present me with a new doorstop he crafted in his building trades class, my last name painstakingly etched into the reclaimed wood.

These interactions are a reminder of how robustly the district invests in career and technical education (CTE), which is ideal for the students who will ultimately join their parents in factories, farms, or specialized labor positions, like plumbing or construction. Here is Allen's first piece of the humanistic baseline; preparing rural students for rural breadwinning work. Students must be prepared for what Allen deems "economic self-sufficiency" in order to access other notions of fulfillment. In this high school, there is a full-time career coach who develops community partnerships, bringing local workers into high school classrooms for lectures and demonstrations. There is a bussing system for students to leave campus for various vocational training, and upperclassmen are encouraged to intern in the town for school credit. The district's goal is that even disadvantaged students can receive a diploma and thus obtain breadwinning work. These programs are aligned with the state's provisions for "college and career readiness," yet in the rural school, there is an emphasis on "career."

These programs are aligned with the state's provisions for "college and career readiness," yet in the rural school, there is an emphasis on *career*. Postsecondary enrollment at our school is below the state average, and we produce very few first-generation college students. Any students who are college bound are counseled by educated parents, or are lucky enough to have a teacher who will work with them after school or during lunch to help fill out applications and write recommendation letters. Students can learn the basic necessities for breadwinning work, but what of the other elements of a humanistic baseline? What of, as Allen puts it, education *as* education?[5]

Civic Engagement

Our English Department is experimenting with a new curriculum. The last bell has rung for the day, and my colleagues and I squeeze into our students' desks to discuss how they are responding to the most recent unit. As we group into pairs and plan the next few weeks, I recognize how different this collaboration is compared to the uniform plans I have taught at other schools. But here, I am only limited by what is affordable. I have the freedom to choose which books, films, and articles my students consume. And with some thrifty practices, my students get to read new articles and diverse stories as part of the curriculum. I can focus on choice, and bring their voices into my classroom. I even receive a small stipend to spend on my classroom library, and there are no barriers for the diverse books I fill my shelves with. While standardized curriculums have been the mainstays of urban and suburban school management, in a small town like mine schools still have the freedom and choice to circumvent these industrialized practices.[6]

Teacher autonomy could be a key element for preparing students for civic and political engagement—the second step in Allen's framework. The teacher is the link between individual students and their learning. However, standardized curriculums erase the emphasis on individualized learning and instead define the successful outcomes of a group. A standard approach to teaching civic engagement (that is, the history of our country, or the importance of voting) does not "consider the issue of civic engagement from the perspective of each student rather than the social system."[7] The teacher could, however, choose to circumvent the social system, and use their classroom to address the micro-level elements of how to be a citizen, and doing so with colleagues is all the more powerful. Allen references linguistic capacities as the mainstay in successful civic engagement:[8] how children learn to express themselves through language is therefore a critical piece of the eudaemonic curriculum, and, to my delight as an English teacher, a place where students have the opportunity to truly flourish. Moreover, these micro-level aspects of education emphasize giving a voice to all students, which allows an equitable participation in society.

Of course, giving teachers autonomy doesn't mean that they will align with the humanistic baseline. Without adequate support, teachers may be unmotivated to enrich their curricula with authentic engagement. For instance, at my school there is hardly any incentive for teachers to pursue graduate degrees, and little exists in the way of innovative professional development. And while the principal goes out of his way to empower teachers in the building to use their own expertise when it comes to assessments, there is more pressure at the district level to conform to stifling standardization practice. Indeed, already the elementary schools teach using purchased scripts and prescribed lessons. It is cost effective to purchase a curriculum that boasts to provide "data-driven" results, and this again aligns with macro-level policies. In a rural school, this piece of the humanistic baseline can be strengthened by continuing to allow teachers to utilize what they believe to be the right method for the individual students they have. Keeping these practices attentive to the individual needs of the students (at a microlevel) allows for growth.

Creative Self-Expression and World Making

My fourth-hour class is English 11, but the title is misleading, as most of the students in the class are not in eleventh grade. Teagan is a tenth grader who loves to read. Antonio is a senior giving the class a second try. Maya is a special education student, and James is taking the class pass/fail. There are twenty-eight students in this class, and each unique personality is celebrated as I blindly lead them through the trials of the English language.

I believe that the blended levels of my rural school contribute to my student's access to what Allen calls "world making," which I interpret as creating a harmonious and stimulating community. Unlike the traditional ability-tracking structure of courses, students of all levels take the same core classes—mostly due to size constraints and staffing. There is, therefore, a need for differentiation, which benefits all students. It is an advantage to give an assignment that challenges all of my students, and also to celebrate when even my struggling students succeed. Students who would normally be tracked together for poor behavior or low skills instead contribute to a diverse community within the classroom. I find that classes develop true collaborative personalities, and students work together to succeed in their learning. I admit that it is harder to differentiate lessons and manage behavior for students with special needs when they share the same room with English language learners and advanced placement learners. However, that is an opportunity for students (and instructors) to negotiate an authentic reflection of their own community, in which people bring different assets and different needs.

The biggest stressor in this environment is class size, not demographics. During the pandemic, when class sizes were halved, it was easier to differentiate between students, and achievement gaps were minimal. And while our sizes are still smaller compared to an urban school, an untracked classroom becomes harder to manage. Teachers must be given the space and time to focus on the relationships we build with students through the lens of their learning, rather than form relationships based on their progress. According to Allen, a teacher's ability to flourish is an important indicator of student success, and students are more likely to be on track when both are future oriented.[9] Untracked classes are a true commitment to diversity, because so often the same students spend all of their classes together. In the rural space, communities must coexist; the same is expected in the rural classroom. Because rural schools track less, there is more opportunity for both lesson differentiation and interaction between students of different academic, class, and cultural backgrounds. Students are actively engaged in their own world-making, thus achieving a part of the humanistic baseline. However, a critical part of a community is the strength of diversity, and breaking down barriers of inequality, which is a struggle for all schools.

Rewarding Relationships

It is a month into the semester, and I have a new student in my fourth-hour class. He slouches to a seat in the back, and I double check with the teacher across the hall. "Sorry," she tells me, as she pulls her door shut, "I have too many of them in this hour. He'll do better with you." I am angry, and not just because my caseload has grown. I am angry because "them" refers to Hispanic in a derogatory fashion. I am used to students switching into my class. Counselors and administrators often recommend a student to my room because they will "do better." I am angry because it is not a compliment to my teaching, but rather a condemnation of another teacher's bias. I head back to my room to welcome Alex to our class.

The last pieces of Allen's framework focus on the nature of relationships. A real danger to eudaemonic flourishing lies in marginalizing the needs of our diverse voices. There can be no true world-making if the students in a community do not see themselves as capable of self-expression, for the relationship component of Allen's baseline lies in how humans struggle "in conditions of pluralistic diversity, to come to collective decisions about our polity's course of action."[10] My students, ever active on social media, maintain public lists of which staff members are allies and who should instead be avoided; they do not need to witness firsthand harassment to know which classrooms welcome members of minority groups. While publicly I condemn these profiles, privately I notice the same patterns of ignorance and hate. There is a worrying deficiency of culturally responsive teaching in our district, and this creates a barrier to students' flourishment. Like many rural areas, the population is diversifying at a rapid rate. Almost 30 percent of students in my district identify as

Hispanic, and those families also often identify with the broader conservatism of the area. And though many of our families primarily speak Spanish, resources for English language learners in my district are woefully limited. There is little push in support for language learners, especially for older students who rely on their bilingual classmates to help them with coursework. Hispanic males are far less likely to graduate than their white counterparts, and there is hardly any representation of Hispanic culture in the curriculum.

So I am not surprised that Alex chose a seat in the back. I do my best to uplift Hispanic voices, and ensure that my students know their heritage is embraced as part of our learning, but I, too, am ignorant of their culture. Like many of my colleagues, I don't speak Spanish. It seems like an immensely wasted opportunity to embrace the community's diversity as a strength while underserving students with so much potential. Imagine if there were a bilingual elementary school, or we invested in students of color who could in turn become future educators and staff? A teacher shortage is a threat to sustaining progress at a macrolevel. The solution is to encourage local recruitment and retention. But ultimately, until students see themselves in their educators, they will continue to feel marginalized, which will in turn affect their abilities to flourish.

Conclusion

It is opening night, and the stage is awash in energy. The students have spent endless hours rehearsing their lines, memorizing dance routines, collecting props, painting the set, and timing the lights. A freshman usher leads a group of stern-looking nuns to their seats in the front row, another makes room for a wheelchair in the squashed aisles of the multipurpose room. I send them backstage for the start of the show, and take my place at the back of the room. When the curtain opens, eudaemonia enters downstage right: here is world making made literal, the thrum of engagement evident in the relationships onstage and off. In this moment, Allen's ideals come to life as students navigate the space using what they have learned.

Rural schools in the United States do not get the scholarly attention that suburban and urban schools do—but their unique qualities (both strengths and weaknesses) deserve more attention from educational scholars. Limited resources, and even more limited attention, lend themselves to the obscurity of rural academia thriving and challenges. It is easy to urbanize the space and apply the same stifling standardization policies without proper care for the distinctive environment that is a rural school. The insular nature of a rural district positions it as uniquely situated to achieve a humanistic baseline where urban or suburban schools cannot. There is opportunity for humanistic flourishing that thrives in diverse classrooms, relative teacher autonomy, and a strong community spirit in the smallness, isolation, and lack of attention. The groundwork for the intersection of utilitarian and eudaemonic practices has been laid, and an investment into rural education could change the course of thoughtful civic engagement in disenfranchised areas of the country. But we must examine the national, state, and local policies that diminish flourishing. Too often, an effort to "close the gap" between rural and nonrural schools becomes a hasty implementation of privatization. Advocacy groups like the National Rural Education Association consistently recommend and celebrate adoption of for-profit standardized curriculums, destroying the freedom that strengthens rural classrooms.[11] Districts should instead invest in bilingual spaces, young teachers, and accessible technology. Rural schools can succeed in cultivating Allen's humanistic baseline, as they already have the potential to flourish.

Questions for Discussion

- How can establishing baselines for flourishing contribute to a more equitable education system?

- What aspects of a rural school are overlooked or misconstrued in educational policy and administration?

- What advantages in teaching do smaller, rural schools have over their urban or suburban counterparts?

Further Reading

Allen, Danielle, *Education and Equality: The Tanner Lectures on Human Values* (Stanford, CA: Stanford University Press, 2014), 1–59.

Activity

I have imagined how philosophy can be realized in a physical space: the characters already existed, I had only to add what I thought could improve my teaching. How can we build the elements of the humanistic baseline into existing spaces? Consider what makes your classroom space unique. For each step of the humanistic baseline, list what you do in your teaching practice that might fit within this framework.

1. To prepare ourselves for breadwinning work,
   - How do you help students navigate life after high school?
   - What kinds of conversations do you have about college or careers?
   - When do students get to meet or observe career professionals or college professors and students?
2. To prepare ourselves for civic and political engagement,
   - What literacy practices do you include in weekly lessons?
   - How do you include local, national, and international perspectives in your classroom?
   - What local policies impact your classroom?
3. To prepare ourselves for creative self-expression and world making,
   - How are students placed in classes, and how might these structures change?
   - When can students be creative in your class?
   - How much agency do students have in their learning?
4. And to prepare ourselves for rewarding relationships in spaces of intimacy and leisure,
   - How do you include diverse voices in your classroom?
   - Who authors your classroom texts?
   - How do you make sure students feel worthy of education?

Notes

1. This and all other student names are pseudonyms.
2. Danielle Allen, *Education and Equality: The Tanner Lectures on Human Values* (Stanford, CA: Stanford University, 2014), 5.
3. Allen, *Education and Equality*, 10.
4. Allen, *Education and Equality*.
5. Allen, *Education and Equality*, 14.
6. Michael Corbett and Dianne Gereluk, eds. *Rural Teacher Education: Connecting Land and People* (Singapore: Springer Nature, 2020), 310.
7. Allen, *Education and Equality*, 28.
8. Allen, *Education and Equality*, 32.
9. Allen, *Education and Equality*, 47.
10. Allen, *Education and Equality*, 15.
11. Cory Epler and Leigh Weisskirk, "Rural Districts Should Use Stimulus Funds to Invest in High-Quality Curriculum," in *National Rural Education Association*, 2021, https://www.nrea.net/Blog_Post?blogid=718346.

14

Alone in the Presence of Others

Autos, *Schole*, and the Flourishing of Children in Nature-based Schools

GLENN M. HUDAK AND WILLIAM FULBRECHT

This is a first-time collaboration between Glenn Hudak, professor emeritus in philosophy of education at the University of North Carolina at Greensboro, and Bill Fulbrecht, who is currently coordinator of Forest and Shore School Early Childhood Outdoor Programs at the Brooklyn New School, P.S. 146, in Brooklyn, New York. Together they represent two sides of the same coin, so to speak, as they both share concerns about helping children flourish and a love for the natural environment, yet they come at these considerations from very distinct institutional positions and modes of articulation. As a consequence, this paper is formatted as a conversation between an academic and a practitioner, affording both the opportunity to speak from their individual perspectives.

The goal of this project is to articulate a preference for nature-based education by asking, "How might we think about educational settings that emphasize *minimal contact*, where minimal contact is viewed as the pedagogical preference?" They believe that both Jan Masschelein and Maarten Simons formulation of *schole* and nature-based education speak to this preference, in that both essentially transform the contact zone into what Glenn refers to as a site for *autos*.[1] However, in the last analysis, nature-based education is preferred because, as Glenn suggests, *autos* in nature transforms *contact zones* into autistic *networks,* whereas Bill stresses from his experience working with children outdoors the notion that "nature's diversity and abundance promotes cooperation and teamwork." What follows is their conversation and observations.

∽

BILL: Glenn, you and I have known each other for quite a long time and our lives have intersected in many ways over the years. Most recently we have shared our thoughts and observations around the question of how children learn—not necessarily concerning the best ways to teach—but simply, what our experience with children has taught us about how children teach themselves. You introduced me to the notion of *autos.* Could you explain a little about what *autos* is?

GLENN: Grounded on my experiences with my son, who identifies as autistic, and with my reading of British psychoanalyst, D. W. Winnicott (1958/1996) and on French pioneer on autism, Fernand Deligny (2015), the term *autos,* from the Classical Greek root of the word *autism,* seemed to emerge for me as the conceptual personae of my thinking about autistic spaces. *Autos* in turn, is a mode of self-affirmation in the sense of being with oneself in the presence of others without defensiveness such that one can relax in the world among friends. From here I started to think of the possibility of *autos* as an ontological possibility—the ontological condition necessary to coexist in the same space, to breathe a common air, while perhaps experiencing different points of view, so to speak, with another. All this without fear, without defensiveness, without asymmetrical relations of power distorting this moment of peace and relaxation in the world. As a philosopher of education then, I sought to learn *with* autism as a way of being-in-the-world. I recall my encounters with my son and in my encounters with nature, as moments of *autos.*

BILL: I love the notion that *autos* can be a condition where the power dynamics of a typical classroom can be relaxed, perhaps even eliminated. When I was a classroom teacher I always struggled with that lopsided dynamic. What I learned about young children was that they seemed to thrive most when left alone to make their own discoveries. I have witnessed children of all developmental stages enter a state of what you call *autos* when they discover something that truly captures their curiosity, and I have come to believe that this state of consciousness is fundamental to the process of learning and the development of true *self-regulation.* I would describe *autos* as the state of mind where a child's engagement with the object of their attention becomes so strong as to break down the boundaries between self and "other"—the child literally *becomes* the experience they are having. The experience could be almost anything, from the sensation of spinning around to watching the behavior of ants on an anthill. These experiences are often quite intense. Initially stored in the child's sensory memory, they form the basis for future understandings of abstract concepts. It is one reason early childhood experts promote sensory play in the classroom.

GLENN: Yes, and the notion of *self-regulation* is echoed in Winnicott's thinking around the notion of maturity. What strikes me is his thinking around *maturity* as he defines as the capacity to be alone in the presence of another, without defense, as friends. That is to say, the encounter between two people where each can *stand* (tolerate) being *with* the other, in a relaxed manner. Indeed, for Winnicott, emotional maturity is essentially one's capacity to be alone where, "the basis of the capacity to be alone is a paradox; it is the experience of being alone while someone else is present."[2] As a developmental capacity, here maturity is linked with one's ability to feel relaxed and at home in the world rather than isolated or disconnected. Indeed, for Winnicott, "when one is alone in the sense that I am using the term, and only when alone, the infant is able to do the equivalent of what in an adult would be called relaxing."[3]

This emerging capacity to be emotionally mature—to be alone in the presence of another—enables the child, or adult, to relax and hence engage in play, alone. For the child, this would be like building a sandcastle on the beach while her parents looked on. Here the child engages in imaginative play, paradoxically alone in her imagination, while her parent reads a novel in a chair next to her. For adults, Winnicott likens the capacity to be alone with the capacity for intimacy between consenting adult partners. He states that, "Being able to enjoy being alone along with another person who is also alone is in itself an experience of health . . . [that is, to] enjoy sharing solitude."[4] Hence mature sharing has double locations: a shared world, and a shared place of solitude, that is, *autos*.

BILL: I like that phrase: "to feel relaxed and at home in the world rather than isolated or disconnected." This is something teachers look for in young children as an indication of their ability to function in a school setting or *contact zone*.

GLENN: Exactly. This sense of feeing at home, of being present, reminds me of the difficulty of being relaxed with another when there's little, or no conversation between two people. I recall the times when my son and I would drive from North Carolina to New York, a trip of about 750 miles. During these drives we frequently experienced long periods of silence in the car. To break the silence, I sometimes asked him what he was thinking—small things, like what he wanted to listen to on the radio, or if he was hungry. His responses were always very brief. At first, I was worried, thinking that perhaps my son was upset or mad for whatever reason, but then I would ask him how he was feeling and he would always give the same reply: "I'm okay." While *he* may have been okay, *I* was uncomfortable and feeling vaguely distraught. Was I doing something wrong as a parent? Here I worried, wondering how to work with his autism.

To this end I came upon the work of Fernand Deligny, who really opened my eyes in that he too wondered about how to be with autistic youth in his charge. His story starts in the late 1960s when Deligny established an experimental center in the mountains of rural France, a "raft in the mountains," as he called it, a haven to work with autistic children who had no place to live—having been either abandoned by their parents or unable to be wards of the state. From the get-go Deligny, like myself, didn't want to impose his worldview onto the children. He, like me, had a sense of what the children needed, such as food, shelter, etcetera. The rub was how to interact with the child (who didn't want to speak) without forcing them to respond (where a forced response from the child would be tantamount to a form of violence toward them). His solution was to observe them, "indirectly, by way of their journeys, instead of imposing on them an intersubjective face-to-face encounter."[5] That is, instead of encounters with the children, he experimented with map making—drawing maps that traced the children's routes through the camp, thereby tracing the child's daily journey. As Deligny observed these "wander lines" over time, he notes, "One day to my bewilderment, I realized that the *wander lines* never went out of a sort of circle."[6] While these wander lines through the living area appeared random to Deligny at first, they nonetheless revealed specific patterns over time. Indeed, what was revealed to Deligny were the children's daily habits as they wandered through the camp. Keeping with his intent to discern observations rather than make theoretical conclusions about the children, I feel that he tacitly sought the radical undoing of power imposed by institutions in the very act of refusing to name what is happening in them. Deligny made a conscious, "decision to leave the door [so to speak] that was just passed through wide open, [hence] not reducing it to progress, healing, or an 'exit from autism' . . . [this] enables him to leave the matter unresolved."[7] Deligny, like myself, wants to keep the door of the encounter open, unresolved, not only to engage with the children he worked with, or in my case with my son, but also to refrain from theorizing in order to avoid further violence on the children (and my son).

BILL: Quite an idea—that theorizing is a form of violence! But I do see his point—it is quite easy for teachers to rely on their personal assumptions when thinking about how to approach an individual child, rather than waiting for the child to reveal themself to the teacher. I find it fascinating that Deligny had the restraint to observe rather than intervene or jump to conclusions, given the year (early 1960s) and his particular circumstances. It's also significant that his observations took place outdoors, where the children had the freedom to move about at will. This could never have happened in a traditional classroom setting.

GLENN: I agree. Deligny eventually came to liken the informal networks formed by the children's wanderings to a spider weaving a web (*The Arachnean*), where within this informal web the children could find "serenity, a kind of happiness, autonomy, a cruising speed through sentient life that would be difficult to find in the institutions."[8] Here, Deligny's efforts were neither focused on theorizing the autistic child, nor were they about the child becoming an institutional subject. Rather, he sought without seeking, so to speak, to decouple the child's identity from any institutional labels, thereby freeing them from being seen as pathological children in need of some cure. Ultimately his efforts have a political value in the very act of freeing the autistic child from the burden of oppressive labels such that one can be copresent with them, rather than trying to cure them. To this end, I find Deligny's efforts to invent novel noneducational ways of being with autistic children valuable.

The issue for Deligny, and me, is not one of the educational, but what lies outside the "official" parameters of education that are also important. As such, his intent as I interpret it, revolves around the "noneducational." In other words, to liberate the autistic child's attention *away from* the traditional—the things on the classroom table (things the teacher may place in front of the student for study)—and *toward* living in their everyday world, the mundane that falls below the educational radar (such as the children "roaming" around the compound). Deligny does this because he is aware that he "speaks a language that is perhaps not that of the children, hence he struggles to allow the child to exist in their own singular way without their existence reduced to a psychological or educational insight."[9] Instead of "psychological or educational insights," there are nonintentional "dances" between children and adults vital to the formation of the Arachnean—a network that appears to have no larger pedagogical purpose other than its formation—in short, the "noneducational moment." In revealing the noneducational, Deligny's efforts tacitly aim at dissolving any contact zone to allow for the network to form instead. Here, what Deligny learns are not "facts/ideas" about autism, but rather, the "way" of the network as a moment of living with autism.

BILL: I can understand how this must have helped you in your relationship with your son—to be comfortable just "being" together.

GLENN: It did help me, in that the concern is not so much to understand my son, per se, but rather to be present and allow him to lead in our dance together, as it were. This begins by noticing his everyday habits and working with them, not so much to build a network, but instead, as Deligny puts it, to maintain the web of connection—of presence between us. As such, the contact zone of asymmetrical power relations dissolves in the very unintentional maintenance of a web of "being alone in the presence of another without defense," that is, *autos*.

BILL: Deligny's work also applies to the work we do with young children in the forest. Our role as teachers is much like his. I think of the forest in the same way—as a place where children can be "alone together"—a place where they can choose to explore nature on their own, or with others, or simply be side-by-side without an overshadowing expectation from the adults.

GLENN: Can you give an example?

BILL: In 2015, I had the opportunity to begin a modified version of the European model of forest schools[10] at a progressive public school in New York City. That year the prekindergarten teachers and I began taking the classes to a nearby park for weekly "forest days." In this section of the park, the designers had managed to closely reproduce the ecology of a natural forest and had incorporated several tree trunks from trees that had fallen during a recent storm. The only clearly human-made feature of the play-space was an old-fashioned hand pump that emptied water into a log trough. By our third or fourth trip to the forest, the teachers and I began to appreciate the effect the natural environment had on the children's activity.

One day, as the children spread out to explore the space, Louis (not his actual name), a four-year-old boy, became attracted to the pump.

Louis was a child whose teacher had expressed some reservations about bringing him to an open space, as he regularly ran out of the classroom several times a day, requiring the aide assigned to his care to chase after him. He was prone to knocking down other children's block structures and had a lot of difficulty sitting still on the meeting rug for story time. His language skills were underdeveloped, and he experienced frequent meltdowns resulting in full-blown tantrums. His ability to *self-regulate* had been brought into question. But here, on this day, he was completely absorbed in the workings of the water pump. Although several children drifted in and out of his immediate space, he paid no attention to them. He was clearly "in the zone"—a state of *autos*, of being alone in the presence of others.

Not wanting to disturb him, I stood several yards away to observe. I quietly took out my phone and began to record the event on video. In his hands were several leaves, and he was placing them in the water trough, watching intently as they floated toward the end and spilled over onto the pebbles below. He then returned to the hand pump and pumped more water, this time placing a different type of material in the stream. I watched as he first placed a stick, an acorn, a pebble, and a feather in the stream—each time running alongside as all were washed down in the rush of water. At one point, he became focused on the pump itself. Finding a long twig nearby, he began pushing it upward into the spout and watching as the water was diverted while he pumped. Noticing that the twig was forked, he next began "walking" it down the trough as if it were a little person, saying softly to himself, "Run! Run!" He stayed with this activity for a good twenty minutes, until he was interrupted by the teacher's call to lunch. At this point I stopped the video and put my phone away.

Later that day, as the teachers and I reviewed the video, his teacher looked up and with tears of joy exclaimed, "I'm so happy to see this!" Seeing Louis in this new context changed the way everyone perceived him. We were now able to see his strengths and his intense curiosity. Over the next few weeks, we watched as the other children began to warm to Louis, seeking him out to include in their play.

In our discussions about what we were witnessing, we realized that, in the forest, the potential for exploration and discovery was ever-present and the materials were infinite, and we were brought to the question of *competition*. In the classroom, Louis had to compete for everything—favorite blocks and toys, attention from the teachers, time with special friends, the space to move around—but here, in the forest, there was little need for competition. If a child wanted a stick, there were sticks everywhere. If a child wished to be alone, there was room to be alone. If a child wished to play with others, there were many others to play with. Further, we had left it up to each child to find something of interest—something personal—that they could explore or engage with, and this opened up a new dynamic between students and teachers. Freed of the necessity to dictate what should happen in the learning environment, we allowed ourselves to engage in exploring the forest *with* the children. Instead of answering questions the children might have about nature, we had to join the children in their wonder. We soon found we had questions of our own, and this drew us more deeply into investigations with the children. As colearners, we now shared power with them—leading us on a journey of discovery together. This sense of equality spilled over into the school classroom and the teachers felt the experience of coming together in the forest helped solidify the classroom community.

As we thought about Louis and his exploration of the pump, we could clearly see that he had been practicing true *self-regulation*, in that he had sustained a prolonged interest in a self-determined activity, and this led us to the conclusion that what we had actually been expecting of Louis in the classroom was *compliance*—the ability to bend to the will of another. At the end of the day, it was *Louis* who had taught *us* a valuable lesson.

If we accept that Louis was in a state of *autos* while exploring the pump, what role did this play in his *learning*? I have to believe that Louis's experiences at the pump were becoming integral to *who* he is—that the sensation of rushing water carrying boats made of leaves was forming a basis for his later understanding of concepts he was likely to encounter in high school physics class and beyond.

So, Glenn, if Deligny's observations can be considered a kind of nonpedagogy that is aligned with what we practice in the forest, would you say it was *preferable* to a more traditional approach?

GLENN: For me, the best way to draw out my preference for nature-based education is to compare it to the "perfect school," in Masschelein and Simons's terms: *schole*. Here I see *schole* as embodying *autos* as a place to be alone in the presence of another, without defense, as a friend. In their notion of *schole*, the school is "literally a place of *schole* [the classical Greek root for school], that is the space of free time. What we have in mind is the school as a place and time of profanation, a place/time where words are not a part of shared language, where things are not (one's) property and to be used according to guidelines, where acts and movements are not habits, where thinking is not yet (a system) of thought, and where students are not conceived of as 'not yet potentially able.'"[11]

Clearly then, *schole* affords the student a possibility to flourish via free exploration as *autos*. However, what distinguishes the *schole* from nature-based education is *not* an issue over *autos*, as both embody *autos*. Rather, the point of difference revolves around the formation of Deligny's Arachnean network. Why? As Masschelein and Simons point out, "The teacher is an e-ducator, that is, someone who puts something on the table . . . and so transforming the world into 'things for free use.'"[12] As I alluded to earlier, Deligny wants to avoid putting anything on the table for the autistic children he is working with. He is not concerned with the teacher putting things "on the table" for free use by the children, who are then led out from their everyday life to experience the world anew via things represented on the table.

Why, again? Because the table functions as the pedagogical device for bringing the students and teacher together. And while there is a space of *autos* where, either alone or together, collectively they can interact without the need to be defensive, the table here is a pedagogical device, a technology that directs bodies in a certain way and toward a certain direction, that is, focusing on the objects placed on the table. The table gathers one's attention. It allows children to focus on their thoughts, to ponder and contemplate, to inspect the objects—in short, to face the object presented. But most importantly, as the object grabs the child's attention, the table fades into the background, and as unobtrusive, the table becomes the *where* in the child's works, the site of study—the site of education—where the world unfolds. Indeed, facing the table is educational.

The network, as I argued earlier, is noneducational for Deligny. It is not a conscious design, nor is it a pedagogical device like the table. French philosopher, Anne Sauvagnargues, sees Deligny's network as embodying a sort of "ecological competence . . . in this sense, the network always involves a milieu [as it is always situational and engages with its environs]. . . . The second main characteristic of the network is that it is never an order of consciousness, will, calculation. . . . This is why it is difficult to theorize this reserve. . . . The network is frail. . . . It is provisional . . . a network that is completed becomes institutional and dies."[13] The key takeaway here is that the network for Deligny is *never finished*, it is frail, it is experimental and most of all it is *not human centered*. It is more than a work in progress, as it is a living milieu itself, like a spider's web!

As I see it the nature-based education you describe, Bill, leans in many ways toward the noneducational in that the network that is formed is not the perfect school, nor does it intend to be.

BILL: I wonder what it means, then, for the *contact zone* (in our case the natural environment) to be a zone of minimal contact? To be *noneducational*? This may seem to be quite a contradiction when the contact zone in question is a traditional school building, but if we accept your notion of *autos* as being crucial to the process of *learning*, things become clearer for me. In a zone of minimal contact—that is, where children have a large measure of autonomy in their choice of activities and movement—children have many opportunities to experience the state of *autos*. In order to create such a zone, we must flip our conventional notion of "school" on its head and prioritize *lived experience* over the absorption of information through the various mediums of text, video, and lectures. Books and lectures have their place, of course, but when students also have a broad base of lived experience, abstract concepts will be easier to comprehend.

In so far as the indoor classroom goes, I like Masschelein and Simons's metaphor of *the table* as a device for focusing children's attention. As an example, I think back to the use of clay in my kindergarten classroom. When a group of children are seated together around a mound of clay there is room for both collaboration and independent activity. It is a small contact zone in which children can be "alone in the presence of others without defensiveness." But, as Sauvagnargues points out, any network that is formed during the children's imaginative play at the table is frail and must end with the school bell. This may be a step closer to "perfection" in the traditional classroom, but here we must look at the physical environment itself to understand the distinct advantages of taking children outdoors for free exploration and discovery.

When we are indoors, we are surrounded by four walls. The space is decidedly finite, and we are confined within it. The materials, too, are finite and are dictated largely by the teacher's choices and the demands of the curriculum. While some materials such as clay or blocks may facilitate imaginative play more readily than others, we must always come back to the finite reality of the classroom.

Outside in nature, the parameters are different. Nature's diversity and abundance promotes cooperation and teamwork. Absent physical walls, the space becomes potentially infinite. So too are the natural materials that fill the space. The children not only form networks with one another, they also have the opportunity to form a bond with the networks of nature under their feet. I would argue that this is the greatest benefit from brining children outdoors and into the forest, because when children are in nature the emphasis is on their *experiences*. They are living their lives, gathering the memories that will be necessary for them to realize their place in the world and their understanding of it. The *network* here is not a mere human construct—it is the world itself.

Questions for Discussion

- What is your personal definition of *autos*?
- Under what circumstances do you experience *autos*?
- How do you feel when you are in a state of *autos*?

Further Reading/Videos

https://bnsforestandshore.blogspot.com.
https://naaee.org.
https://naturalstart.org.
Sobel, David. *Nature Preschools and Forest Kindergartens: The Handbook for Outdoor Learning*. St. Paul, MN: Redleaf Press, 2016.
Louv, Richard. *Last Child in the Woods*. Chapel Hill, NC: Algonquin Books, 2005.
The Rise of Forest Schools, TV Ontario, May 21, 2018, https://www.youtube.com/watch?v=g3QwHJmUvBg.
"Forest Schools: Lessons in Outdoor Education," *CBS Sunday Morning*, March 14, 2021. https://www.youtube.com/watch?v=0QbkKqqLhls.

Activity

HOW DO YOU CULTIVATE *AUTOS* WITH YOUR STUDENTS?

Autos, the capacity to be alone in the presence of another, without defensiveness, just doesn't happen all at once. It occurs over time as your body needs to adjust to its environment to really feel comfortable with others, especially with strangers (and in strange surroundings).

Plan several trips to a local park where students can be with others in nature.

- When students return to their classroom, inquire about any difficulties they feel in "just sitting" in the park (remember, *autos* is an embodied sense, feeling).
- Have them draw or write about those moments when they "forgot" themselves while just wandering in the park.
- Follow this up with inquiry about their time in the school building: have they ever felt this way in class (that is, have they felt *autos* in school?) When? Where in school? What was going on?

Autos is not an intellectual activity, rather it is about feelings, more specifically the embodied feeling of being at home with others.

Notes

1. See, Glenn M. Hudak, "On the Allure of Bridges vs. Diving for Pearls: A Phenomenological Inquiry into Autism & Ontological Inclusion," *Philosophy of Education* 76, no. 3 (2020).

2. D. W. Winnicott, "The Capacity to Be Alone," *The Maturational Processes and the Facilitating Environment* (Madison, CT: International Universities,[1958] 1996), 30.

3. Winnicott, "Capacity to Be Alone," 34.

4. Winnicott, "Capacity to Be Alone," 31.

5. Fernand Deligny, *The Arachnean and Other Texts* (Minneapolis: University of Minnesota Press, 2015), 13.

6. Sandra Alverez De Toledo (ed.), *Maps and Wander Lines: Fernand Deligny 1969–1979* (Paris: L'Arachneen, 2013), 7.

7. Alverez De Toledo, *Maps and Wander Lines*, 408.

8. Alverez De Toledo, *Maps and Wander Lines*, 408.

9. Alverez De Toledo, *Maps and Wander Lines*, 407.

10. "Forest School Foundation" (contains video and research articles/resources) https://www.theforestschoolfoundation.org/research-resources.

11. Jan Masschelein and Maarten Simons, "Schools as Architecture for Newcomers and Strangers," *Teachers College Record* 112, no. 2 (February 2010): 544.

12. Masschelein and Simons, "Schools as Architecture," 547.

13. Anne Sauvagnargues, "Deligny: Wander Lines," in *Artmachines* (Edinburgh, UK: Edinburgh University Press, 2016), 164.

15

Okinawa's Lesson for Peace and Democracy
Indigenous Values, Political Tension, Military Contact Zones, and the International Women's Club

Kanako W. Ide[1]

> We live in the same world; that aspect of nature is common to all.
> —John Dewey, *Art as Experience*

The purpose of this essay is to explore the moral aspects of the philanthropical, feminine, and publicly open contact zones where locals and American military associates intersect through cultural activities on the Okinawa Islands, Japan. It will also examine whether these spaces have any educational meaning, paying specific attention to the ideas of *yuimahru*, an indigenous Okinawan moral value that teaches the practice of mutual aid.[2]

The essay does not disregard the intensity of political debate regarding the justification of the existence of American military stations in Okinawa, which has continued for almost eighty years. At the same time, the essay does not seek to engage in the dichotomy of either justifying or protesting. Rather, it begins with the assumption that, whether good or bad, just or unjust, some local Okinawans and some American military associates have experienced a type of friendship in these contact zones. Regardless of the political power balance and difficult debates involved, some locals in Okinawa have found creative ways to deal with what might otherwise be an unsustainable situation. This essay intends to present the moral value of *yuimahru* as a supporting factor.

Historically and continuously, native islanders of Okinawa/Ryukyu have been compromised by the influence of visitors from various directions—from China, main island Japan, the Philippines, and the United States, for example—both welcome and unwelcome. Some visits are short-term, but some visitors migrate to the islands permanently. In terms of Okinawa's contact zones,[3] in the last seventy-nine years, American military personnel and their associates have comprised one of the most distinctive categories of newcomer, drastically influencing the islanders at all levels.

Here is a short history of Okinawa. The United States began occupying the islands after the Battle of Okinawa in 1945, establishing the government of the Ryukyu Islands, which remained in place until its reversion to a prefecture of Japan in 1972. To this day, however, all US military forces continue to have stations in the Okinawa Islands. About 15 percent of the island territories are used as American military facilities, and there are about 50,000 military associates living in Okinawa.[4] This is a remarkably high population for such a condensed space, compared to any other American military station in the world.

In order to discuss the contact zone more fully and with a sense of friendship and the Okinawa/Ryukyu indigenous moral value, *yuimahru*, the chapter focuses on the specific case of the Okinawa International Women's Club (OIWC). OIWC was originally established to provide cultural and social spaces, shared by some local women and some American military wives, as part of a stream of cultural policies implemented to emphasize democratic rule during America's Okinawan occupation in the 1950s. However, OIWC remains active to this day, and importantly, uses the word *friendship* to describe the contact zones it fosters. How has this women's group been able to sustain practices of reciprocity for over sixty years in the midst of political tensions stemming from the American military presence in Okinawa? Which moral values are learned by the members through the group's activities? Why has it been possible to establish such a unique contact zone only in Okinawa, despite the American military's deployment across so many territories in the world?

Okinawa International Women's Club

OIWC is a nonprofit women's social club, proposed in 1953 and established in 1954 by Hideko Higa, wife of the chief executive of the Ryukyu Islands (of the United States). The current mission statement of the group is "to provide opportunity for International Friendship through social contacts and to further intellectual, cultural and welfare interests in the community."[5] OIWC has been understood as a women's group that promotes cultural exchanges between foreigners (mostly American military spouses and associates) and local Okinawans, and donates the funds generated by its various joyful fundraising activities mainly to off-base society.

OIWC was initially founded to create an upper-class cultural community shared by Japanese and Americans, and to fulfill an aspect of cultural policy. With 25 percent Ryukyuan/Okinawan/Japanese and 75 percent American members initially, the power balance was clear, with one of the group's "life guide" pamphlets stating that membership "offers American ladies the opportunity to meet Okinawan ladies whose husbands are business and professional men."[6] OIWC members were socially presumed to be either "housewives" or "leisured women," and so most OIWC activities were scheduled on weekdays, with the monthly luncheon held at resort hotels or officers' clubs on base. Mire Koikari described such a contact zone with a reflection of the contemporary social ideology as "the 'domesticaton' of cold war military occupation in Okinawa [which] contribut[ed] to US hegemony-building in a deeply gendered and gendering manner."[7]

Since the organization of various women's groups was part of the initial US agenda to rule the Ryukyu Islands smoothly, the reversion in 1972 led to some of them being closed. OIWC, however, transformed in order to adapt to postreversion society, and for over half a century has undergone a unique development, to this day bringing off-base society into contact with on-base communities through cultural, educational, and social welfare activities.

One of the biggest transformations for OIWC in postreversion Okinawan society was a shift away from its originally unequal balance of nationalities, toward an emphasis on equality and openness as central values. According to its current statement of membership, "Women of any nationality residing in Okinawa Prefecture who are interested in the purpose of this Club will be eligible [for] membership."[8] Today, of approximately 400 members,[9] half are classified as Japanese/Okinawan and the other half as foreign/American. The organizing policy of the board also emphasizes equality,[10] comprising 50 percent international and 50 percent local members, with a new president selected every year from alternating sides. The monthly luncheon, which is the biggest monthly OIWC main event,[11] has an entertaining theme and is hosted by the Japanese and then the foreign side, alternating each month, and the location of the luncheon party switches on- and off-base as well. In addition, OIWC organizes various events for smaller groups.[12] Each group organizes one event per month, alternating hosts from the foreign and Japanese sides. All OIWC events are always done bilingually, and using both currencies, JPY for Japanese events and USD for American events.

While the achievements of the contact zone in terms of equality and openness are remarkable, OIWC has not fully leveled its original power imbalance. For instance, membership recruitment is still different for the foreign and Japanese sides. On the foreign side (American military spouses for the most part), recruitment is in August, the beginning month of OIWC's yearly calendar (the group follows the American school calendar; the Japanese calendar starts in April), which aligns with military moves from one duty station to another, and members are usually from relatively younger generations, around twenty to forty years old. Since they are usually stationed for two to three years in Okinawa, their average membership lasts for a couple of years. On the other hand, Japanese/Okinawan members remain in Okinawa for most of their lives, some remaining with the OIWC for sixty years. The fact that Japanese memberships are more stable than those on the foreign side is reflected in the rule that those desiring Japanese membership require two references from current members. Although the American side's members are open-rank women in the military community, the Japanese side's members are more carefully selected. This indicates that while, for the American side, recruiting members from the spouses of officers and enlisted personnel is a way to maintain numbers, for the Japanese side, it is about maintaining OIWC's overall social status. At the same time, as a result of over sixty years of constant relocation on the American side, the generation gap between Okinawan/Japanese members and American members is significant, with some of the youngest US members just out of college, and the oldest Japanese members aged eighty to ninety years old.

Sixty years of social change poses some other challenges to both the Japanese and the American sides in terms of equality and openness. OIWC is facing a transformation in social assumptions about gender. For example, the requirement of new Japanese members to have a certain social status, as well as leisure time to participate in activities, has caused it to fall behind the times—many members cannot join OIWC events because, in addition to being the spouse of a professional, they are also professionals in their own right, working during the daytime. Also, as social norms transform, so do aspects of military professionalism and culture, leading, for example, to more male American military househusbands. There is also increasing racial, sexual, and national (European, Filipina, and Taiwanese) diversity in the membership community, all of which raises sensitive issues. It is important to remember that OIWC's active mission is to provide a contact zone for "international friendship," which it continues to do, even while holding these social contradictions and issues.

Four Interpretations of Friendship in the Contact Zone

There are four ways in which contemporary Okinawa studies understands the contact zone between locals and American military associates in Okinawa: as unjust, just, a-just/a-unjust, or comprehensive. The image of women plays a different role in each of these approaches. Each position evaluates OIWC's contact zones and friendship differently.

The first and second interpretations are mainstream and relate to social justice and political issues that stem from the existence of American military bases in Okinawa. They centralize social justice issues but are usually divided into two opposite positions, anti- or pro-US base. In anti-US base positions, the contact zone is viewed as a place in which to articulate social injustice. In pro-US base positions, it is a place of social and cultural development. The third interpretation avoids or minimizes political debate, instead treating the family units formed by American military associates and local islanders as contact zones. The fourth interpretation is more comprehensive. According to Etsujiro Miyagi, who classifies the US policies employed by the US occupation along the lines of cultural policy, the military stations have led to an increase in both humanity and inhumanity.[13] Miyagi analyzes this as having had two main effects: justifying the sovereign act with absolute power, and contributing to social improvement.

Each position views the image of women in Okinawa differently. In the "unjust" perspective, local women are seen as victims and American military men as wrongdoers. For instance, Michael S. Molasky discusses the American military's presence on the island as an injustice, presenting a collection of various literatures centralizing the contact zone as a place of sexual exploitation between local female islanders and male American military associates.[14] In the "just" viewpoint, which emphasizes the public aspect, American military/professional women are viewed as contributors to the island's development. Arguing from the pro-US base position, Ryunosuke Megumi[15] presents the contact zones as providing educational opportunities for islanders, describing a space in which American female military associates, as professionals, teach and help local Okinawans, particularly emphasizing the role of these women in improving local knowledge about hygiene and nursing. In the "a-just/a-unjust" position, the contact zone is understood as family, inhabited by couples comprised of partners from different sides. Kaori Miyanishi describes the daily life struggles of international married couples (American husbands/fathers/ newcomers and Japanese wives/mothers/native islanders) in maintaining their relationship.[16] In the comprehensive viewpoint, Koikari describes how both American and Okinawan wives helped to teach each other better housekeeping and mothering skills in a space of public exchange intended for improving private life, thus advancing the argument beyond Megumi's simpler, politically subjective, pro-US base position, emphasizing that "Okinawan women were neither simply 'victims' nor 'resisters.'"[17]

The "just" viewpoint seeks to understand the friendship of OIWC by following the original intention of the cultural policy. From this standpoint, the resonance of friendship is taken literally. Moreover, OIWC's friendship looks like a kind of role model. Turning "friendship" into a symbology identified with the United States is a way of appealing to the success of US diplomacy and its deployment of military forces. It understands these forces as having been deployed in order to support Japan and Okinawa, to help democratize, develop, and protect them—that is what constitutes it as "friendship." On the other hand, from the "unjust" viewpoint, OIWC's "friendship" looks like just another piece of propaganda. This viewpoint claims that the resonance of "friendship" has to be carefully examined in the context of political debate over the US military bases, because it has been so often used as a conventional phrase to justify and advertise the American military's stationing in Japan/Okinawa/Ryukyu. Tatsuhiro Ohshiro sharply points out how impossible it is to achieve a literal "international friendship" between ruler and oppressed.[18] Unlike the perspectives addressed above, the topics of friendship and the OIWC are out of the framework for the "a-just/a-unjust" viewpoint, because neither one takes family life into account.

In the comprehensive viewpoint, there are two sides to OIWC's friendship. On the one hand, it reflects a justification of the original cultural policy that led to its creation. On the other hand, it goes beyond that. The interest of this essay is to extract the elements of OIWC's friendship that have overcome political issues. However, the focus here is on the educational meanings of the contact zone created by OIWC as a public space for public good between local Okinawans and American military associates.

Again, the "friendship" proposed by OIWC is not irrelevant to these political usages of the resonance of friendship. Their long-term social services more or less have taken the role of a fortress, defending the occupation with a moral vindication that America is here for protecting, rescuing, and democratizing Ryukyu/Okinawa. However, the forms of "friendship" proposed by OIWC remain distinctive in character, and at the same time, are not withdrawn from aspects of political ideology, for the following reasons.

First, OIWC's friendship is not designed to be shown off as a justification of political ideology. To those tough political questions of whether the US military presence is just or unjust, OIWC's response is basically mute. This does not mean that OIWC is unaware of the contradictions, but rather that it seems to place more value on maintaining its unique group practices. Minimizing political arguments (even if total ignorance is impossible), OIWC quietly continues its social services and cultural activities. Its quietness in fact protects its social engagements, and helps it to maintain a healthy spirit for group activities. As a result of focusing on practice itself, rather than the display of it, their contact zones are miraculously apolitical spaces in which people can nurture friendship, even in the midst of political conflict. The members of OIWC, on both sides, testify that engaging in OIWC activities is spiritually rewarding, cultivates their joy, and makes their life in Okinawa meaningful.[19] It indicates two things. First, that this nonmarket economy-driven practice for public good cultivates members' personal lives, as well as the OIWC community, as a contact zone. Second, as a result of engaging in practices for public good, members learn to feel attachment to the Okinawa Islands and come to love Okinawa. These understated but public, active but quiet, rewarding but nonprofitable actions are some of the factors of the apolitical, nonmarketized, feminine, and publicly open contact zones that this essay aims to capture.

Indigenous Moral Values and Democracy

There is one last question to address. Although American military stations are located all over the world, clubs and activities like OIWC exist and remain only in Okinawa. Why is this? As Miyagi and Koikai explain, it was the uniquely characteristic cultural policies installed during the period of Okinawa's occupation that created conditions for the development of OIWC. Another possible reason is the density of the American military population on a small island. However, these factors are still too weak to fully answer the question. How are OIWC members able to engage in such time- and energy-consuming labors without a salary or a common religious faith? In other words, what is the common faith linking these people over time and across political differences? There must be some unavoidable social value deeply rooted in the nature of Okinawa itself.

This essay presumes that the social nature of people on the Okinawa/Ryukyu islands is to educate everybody fairly and equally, regardless of their heritage or nationality, when they practice something to support others. It is proposed here that this is due to the influence of *yuimahru*, the Okinawa/Ryukyu indigenous moral value, and that this is what fundamentally sustains the contact zones of OIWC.

Yuimahru is a folkloric expression from the Okinawa/Ryukyu area, meaning "reciprocity," and could be considered as a traditional gift theory and gift economy. "*Yui*" means providing/receiving labor without any duty/demand of reciprocity; "*mahru*" means circulation. *Yuimahru* originated in the seventeenth and eighteenth centuries as a practical necessity,[20] but it is understood in Okinawa today as the social norm, and teaches that the way to fulfill social obligation is to share the burden of community social welfare, as "action ethic[s]."[21] According to George H. Kerr, the spirit of *yuimahru* is deeply embedded in the core of Okinawan/Ryukyuan identity because of the ongoing sense and quality of mutual support in its communities,[22] the mutual financial support systems created among migrated Okinawan/Ryukyuans in foreign countries such as Hawaii and Brazil in the early twentieth century, and the islands' remarkable mutual assistance between families, relatives, friends, and community members.[23]

However, there is almost no further academic research focusing on *yuimahru*, as though it were a blind spot in Okinawa studies. This may be because it is for contemporary local Okinawans too much of a daily practice, too much like common sense to be brought into the academic discussion. However, Tetsuo Najita, an American historian, captures *yuimahru* as a part of *mujinkoh*, meaning "cooperative unlimited compassion" and "indicat[ing] mutual aid,"[24] and discusses it as a more comprehensive social norm in the history of ordinary Japanese economy. Najita states that "The phrase 'mutual aid' . . . remains a powerful imperative underlying the moral consciousness of the populace,"[25] because it is a bushcraft: "nature must serve as the first principle of all knowledge . . . that is, the natural universe is absolute and infinite, with neither a beginning nor an ending. Because this absolute principle must serve as the basis of objective knowledge, geographies and cultural communities acquire meaning in relation to it. Being absolute and infinite, however, nature is never totally knowable, and human knowledge also is always limited and relative."[26] The moral value of reciprocity represented by *yuimahru* is powerful in Okinawa because its historical and cultural context is rooted to the island's very nature.[27] Najita also states that, despite being a Buddhist term, the agreement of mutual aid "was not about praying to gods and bodhisattvas for salvation but about humans taking action to save themselves."[28] People need to have practical preparations and solutions for unavoidable but difficult-to-predict disasters. The practical solution in Okinawa is *yuimahru*. This practice of reciprocity is a wisdom in everyday life for powerless people, helping them to minimize the damage caused either by natural disasters such as typhoons, or human disasters such as excessive taxation. For powerless people, *yuimahru* has been learned as an effective method for solving actual problems, rather than confronting powerful authorities, which tends not to yield the same results. In this sense, in *yuimahru*, nature, morality, economics, and wisdom are inseparable.[29]

On the other hand, according to Najita, this indigenous moral value was misunderstood as "inappropriate for a modern democratic economy"[30] by the allied occupation of America. As a result, the practices associated with mutual aid were politically discouraged in post–World War II Japanese society as well as Okinawa. He claims: "Many persuasive voices in Japan did not subscribe unequivocally to this Jeffersonian concept of democracy. Economic individualism may well have been a valuable principle, but the vast majority of Japanese continued to believe in the deeply entrenched ideal of cooperative democracy, and the establishment of mutually supportive human relations based on the value of equality was vital to their society."[31] Najita's argument is even more provocative than Koikari's and Miyagi's comprehensive viewpoints, because he is denying the affirmative aspect of cultural policy that intended to implant "the moral value of democracy" in Okinawan society. For Najita, "democracy was an important value that actually was not foreign to Japan."[32] He means that, since mutual aid can be identifiable as a moral value in democratic society, Okinawa was already established as a type of democratic society, without American teaching. Najita's interpretation can be even more provocative: if the American allied occupation overlooked the indigenous moral value of "democracy" embedded in the local nature, then we must ask whether their idea of democracy was actually "democracy" at all.

Thus, Najita's idea opens alternative interpretations for understanding the contact zones created by OIWC. It could be said that these spaces, in fact, are providing an educational space for learning and practicing *yuimahru* and for nurturing and sustaining this indigenous moral value, even though the original cultural policy that created OIWC was about denying indigenous moral values. In addition, since *yuimahru* is the moral value embedded in the nature of the island, it does make sense that OIWC's reciprocal activities work only on Okinawa's islands. As a result of engaging in social services, members naturally acquire and maintain friendly connections with each other, sharing the spirit of *yuimahru* through all being located on the island. Since OIWC's activities can be identifiable as *yuimahru*, those gift receivers of OIWC's social welfare can "appropriately" accept their generosity. OIWC is not providing a learning process of "Jeffersonian" democracy for local Okinawans, rather the group is providing to its members a learning opportunity in how to be a good Okinawan. Thus, OIWC is proof that the social norm imbedded in the islands' nature is actually more influential than the social norm that is artificially installed with the intention of imbedding political power.

Conclusion

This essay aimed to capture a unique phenomenon of the Okinawa Islands; some local women and some American military spouses/associates sharing a contact zone in which they actively practice and learn *yuimahru*, bound by friendship, regardless of the ongoing political debate over the existence of American military facilities on the islands. These uniquely philanthropical, feminine, and publicly open contact zones created by OIWC demonstrate the powerful influences of the indigenous moral value of *yuimahru* extended to all of Okinawa's inhabitants. Moreover, this community, seemingly sustained by the ethics of *yuimahru*, offers a precious moral lesson to those outside of Okinawa, that it is *not impossible* to maintain and develop friendship, even in the face of intense political debate. These contact zones offer alternative strengths in maintaining a space of peace.[33]

Questions for Discussion

- How can we, in such a diverse contemporary society, create educational contact zones in which people can naturally learn and practice reciprocity?

- Consider some other moral values, besides *yuimahru*, that you either observe in society or think could be of benefit to society?

Further Reading

Najita, Tetsuo. *Ordinary Economies in Japan: A Historical Perspective, 1750–1950*. Berkeley: University of California Press, 2009.

Activity

To keep thinking about the moral practice of reciprocity and how it lives in different cultures, let's watch the film *Pay It Forward*, https://www.imdb.com/title/tt0223897/.

- As you watch, make a note of examples of reciprocity.

- Consider paying it forward—doing something for someone (often a stranger) so that they will in turn to something kind for another?

- Now think culturally, what are some of the ways that reciprocity is manifested in the United States context of the film. Can you think of other examples of reciprocity in other contexts such as how might it manifest differently in regards to race, gender, class, ethnicity, and particular generations.

Notes

1. The chapter was supported by JSPS KAKENHI grant numbers 17K04583 and 21K02180.

2. Mary Louise Pratt, *Imperial Eyes: Travel Writing and Transculturation* (London: Routledge, 1992); and "Arts of the Contact Zone," *Profession* (1991): 33–40.

3. Pratt, *Imperial Eyes*, 7; and "Arts of the Contact Zone," 34.

4. "U.S. military base in Okinawa as seen by numbers," Okinawa Prefecture, accessed June 27, 2021, https://www.pref.okinawa.jp/site/chijiko/kichitai/tyosa/documents/p32.pdf and https://www.pref.okinawa.lg.jp/site/chijiko/kichitai/documents/h28toukei02.pdf.

5. Okinawa International Women's Club (OIWC), "Constitution and By-Laws of the Okinawa International Women's Club," Essay II, June 2020, https://oiwc.weebly.com/uploads/2/1/6/5/21657192/oiwc_constitution_and_bylaws_2020_-_june_2020.pdf.

6. "Okinawa International Women's Club," in *Welcome Okusan: Annual Publication of Isle Tell*, vol. XIII, no. 12 (pamphlet, Okinawa, 1970), 70.

7. Mire Koikari, *Cold War Encounters in US-Occupied Okinawa: Women, Militarized Domesticity, and Transnationalism in East Asia* (New York: Cambridge University Press, 2015), 19.

8. OIWC, "Constitution and By-Laws," Essay III.

9. Accurate membership numbers are 160 foreign and 206 Japanese, as of March 2020 (Enid Randall, phone interview by the author, April 2020).

10. OIWC, "Constitution and By-Laws." The elected officers are: one president, selected from alternating sides each year, two vice presidents, two secretaries, and two treasurers (one of each from each side). There are thirteen committees: Membership, Welfare, Culture Group, Programs, Publicity, Historian, Newsletter, Social, Reservation, Hospitality, Tours, Ways and Means, and Cooking. Including advisory position members, over forty people serve as OIWC board members. OIWC, "2019–2020 OIWC Board Elected Officers," accessed June 27, 2021, https://oiwc.weebly.com/board.html?fbclid=IwAR0KvTYhGJ_V4ucMANMu8BsfBoRebtUC0-j3Bec9bfkOLSn2EJSiyoV1PCw.

11. The first event of the year is a welcome tea party in late August. From September to June, each luncheon has an entertaining theme accompanied by

a dress code such as Kentucky Derby hats or kimonos. Of the ten yearly luncheons, three (December, March, and June) are particularly important for OIWC. While the luncheons are not connected to the group's fundraising, the December luncheon is accompanied by the Christmas bazaar, OIWC's biggest fundraising event, and the March luncheon is accompanied by the Spring bazaar, which is the second-biggest. The June luncheon functions as the year-end party, and in addition to announcing the new president and board members for next year, it is important because OIWC members present donations received during their yearly activities. For instance, in 2018, eleven social welfare groups, such as shelters (for animals, children, mothers, and the disabled), orphanages, and nursing homes, received their requested items (such as air conditioners, electric appliances and devices, musical instruments, and furniture) as donations from OIWC. Today, the average OIWC annual donation is around two million yen.

12. Each member belongs to one of ten cultural groups: Eisa, Bingata, Ikebana, Washi, Sango, Ryukyu, Unai, Neko, Fukurou, and Hoshi. The Hoshi group was newly created for those who work full time and are unable to meet during the daytime. Each group usually has about twenty-five members. The "Sakura" cultural group existed until 2017 to 2018 (Enid Randall, phone interview by the author, April 2020).

13. Etsujiro Miyagi, *Okinawa Senryo No 27 Nenkan: America Gunsei to Bunka No Henyo* [Okinawa Occupation for twenty-seven years: American Military Administration and the Transformations of Culture] (Tokyo, Japan: Iwanami Shoten, 1992), 47–50.

14. Michael S. Molasky, *The American Occupation of Japan and Okinawa: Literature and Memory* (London: Routledge, 1999).

15. Ryunosuke Megumi, *Okinawa Wo Yutakani Sitano Wa America Toiu Shinjitsu* [A Truth America Developed Okinawa] (Tokyo, Japan: Takarajima Sha, 2013).

16. Kaori Miyanishi, *Okinawa Gunjinzuma no Kenkyu* [A Research on Military Spouses in Okinawa] (Kyoto, Japan: Kyoto University Press, 2012).

17. Mire Koikari, *Cold War Encounters in US-Occupied Okinawa: Women, Militarized Domesticity, and Transnationalism in East Asia* (New York: Cambridge University Press, 2015), 16.

18. Tatsuhiro Ohshiro, *Cocktail Party* (Tokyo, Japan: Iwanami, 2011).

19. Interviews by the author in Naha, Okinawa, Japan, with: Kyoko Kanno, Erasmia Iliaki-Smith, and Enid Randall, January 24, 2018, at an OIWC cooking event.

20. Usaku Sakai, ed., *Ryukyu Retto Minzoku Goi* [Folkloric Vocabulary of the Ryukyu Islands] (Tokyo, Japan: Daiichi Shobo, 2002), 50. *Yuimahru* was originally a way of making tax payments. In the seventeenth and eighteenth centuries, each village in Okinawa/Ryukyu was identified as a unit of tax. In order to fulfill the duty, Okinawans in the village covered each other. *Yuimahru* is also practiced

among neighbors when they have scheduled reroofing or have to rebuild their houses after typhoons.

21. Tetsuo Najita, *Ordinary Economies in Japan: A Historical Perspective, 1750–1950* (Berkeley: University of California Press, 2009), 3.

22. George H. Kerr, *Okinawa: Shimanchu No Rekishi* [The History of an Island People] (Tokyo, Japan: Bensei Shuppan, 2014), 228–29.

23. Najita, *Ordinary Economies*, 96.

24. Najita, *Ordinary Economies*, 92.

25. Najita, *Ordinary Economies*, 235.

26. Najita, *Ordinary Economies*, 3.

27. Najita, *Ordinary Economies*, 177.

28. Najita, *Ordinary Economies*, 92.

29. Najita, *Ordinary Economies*, 141.

30. Najita, *Ordinary Economies*, 176.

31. Najita, *Ordinary Economies*, 214.

32. Najita, *Ordinary Economies*, 217.

33. The author has relied on the tremendous generosity of OIWC members. I want to thank Enid Randall, Erasmia Iliaki-Smith, Kyoko Kanno, Maria Rock, Emiri Miyauchi, Hatsuko Fujisawa, Asako N. Alarcon, Lori Hensic, Jonna McGraw, Taiko Terukina, and Nobuko Uchiyama.

Coda

Creating an Equitable and Fruitful Contact Zone of Philosophers and Teachers

CARA E. FURMAN, VIKRAMADITYA (VIK) JOSHI,
MEGHAN A. BRINDLEY, STEPHANIE A. BURDICK-SHEPHERD,
JOY DANGORA ERICKSON, HILLARY POST, MICHELLE JOHNSON,
HOLLY A. F. LASH, KYLEIGH P. ROUSSEAU, AND LINDSEY YOUNG

This book began with a commitment to bringing philosophers and teachers (broadly defined) together as peers. From the inception of this project, we trusted that if we came together in a "contact zone" in a manner that intentionally mitigated potentially hurtful power dynamics associated with such spaces,[1] something fruitful and mutually beneficial would emerge. In other words, if philosophers and teachers were to share space and work as peers, they could support each other's tasks and make something new. As voiced by kindergarten teacher, Hillary, in the opening of the introduction, "This was exactly what" many of us "needed." What made it work so well?

Simply sharing space is not enough. "Contact zone" is largely descriptive. Take the rocky intertidal zone of the Pacific Northwest. It is a vibrant, exciting, ecosystem in which a diversity of creatures thrive located between land and sea and shifting with the tides. It is not an ethical space and what occurs isn't always positive or fruitful for all involved. As Mary Louise Pratt writes, contact zones are "social spaces where cultures meet, clash, and grapple with each other, often in contexts of highly asymmetrical relations of power, such as colonialism, slavery, or their aftermaths as they are lived out in many parts of the world today."[2]

As highlighted in the introduction, such relationships of dominance tend to mark the contact zone between the philosopher and the teacher. Philosophers frequently offer tips or suggestions for how teachers ought to think philosophically. Rarely is the teacher asked, "What are the ethical questions that you're asking right now in your teaching?" or "How can I, as a philosopher, think about those questions with you?" Teachers too can be dismissive of the knowledge a philosopher might bring—rejecting, for example, the questions they pose or the frames they offer as too far from reality to be valuable.[3]

In this chapter we turn to the nuts and bolts of an equitable and fruitful contact zone. What did it mean for authors to occupy this contact zone and create work that dually enriched philosophy and practice? Where the story of this book began at a preconference at the Philosophy of Education Society's yearly meeting,[4] we conclude with a panel organized by Vik Joshi the following year in which we explored the nature, ethics, promises, and challenges of engaging in philosopher-teacher writings. In this essay, I (Cara) begin by sharing how the initial preconference was constructed to support fruitful and nonhierarchical engagements. We then offer perspectives on partnerships from participants. We conclude with a few themes and general tips that emerged across the narratives.

Preconference: Setting the Tone

Cara E. Furman

Hannah Arendt uses the metaphor of the table to describe a context—what she refers to, from ancient Greek, as a *polis*, in which a group of people come together around a shared enterprise. As with a table around which people gather, in a polis people have something in common between them and their own individual spaces.[5] To begin, I want to highlight the shared enterprise itself, or table. For the preconference, participants were invited to come together as philosophers and teachers to cowrite an essay that pushed past asymmetrical power balances. Having a product in mind, however nebulous, kept us gathered at a shared table and also helped ground the joining together through the goal of future publication. Workshop groups were then developed around a common theme I heard in each essay to draw participants around a shared subtopic to think together. In the Introduction, we reference Nicholas Burbules and Kathleen Knight Abowitz's call for philosophers and educators to reshape a table in order to better situate together.[6] In the remainder of this chapter, we will describe what such a table can be and how it feels to sit together in this way.

Access

A key element of the preconference was ensuring that all parties were able to attend. Academic conferences typically cost considerable money. While academics come to a conference for the intellectual and community experience, they also directly and materially benefit from the opportunity and many have some form of financial assistance from their university to support attendance. Where a few teachers had employers who supported conference attendance, most could only get funding for preapproved professional development with more "practical" foci.

For teachers to join the preconference we needed to either subsidize their attendance with a grant, offer discounted conference fees, or allow participants to join without physically attending. Video conferencing ultimately allowed us to welcome all participants, with those identifying as philosophers and teachers choosing the modality that best fit with their circumstances. Teachers who traveled were also able to attend the preconference free of charge thanks to the Artistic Excellence Programming Grant from San Jose State University's College of Humanities and the Arts.

Protocols for Communication

Due to the potential for power imbalances, as organizer I put together protocols to structure how participants participated. Group norms were established both for asynchronous communication as well as in the synchronous workshops so that all participants had entries into the conversation and felt their work was welcome. For example, participants were directly told not to line edit each other's work without permission to mitigate against some feeling like the students of other participants.

The protocol below was distributed ahead of time, and groups were strongly urged to use it (even if it felt awkward) with the advice that a protocol would improve access and strengthen the conversation among those who didn't know each other. Each group also had a predesignated chair who facilitated the activation of the protocol and kept time.

- Authors present for three to five minutes on major themes and questions they have for readers.
- Each reader offers one to two pieces of warm feedback (elements of the piece that intrigue you, that you feel really work, that drew you in).

- Each reader offers one to two suggestions or questions to consider for revision with an eye toward a public audience.
- Authors and readers engage in more informal follow-up conversation with a chance for authors to ask more questions and get the last word.

In sum, participants were guided to notice what others were doing, focus on the positive, and then ease into any critical feedback. This structure built trust, offered guidance to participants with varied experiences of giving and getting feedback, and focused conversation around the authors' intentions instead of the reader's agenda.

Community Building

Though the writing partners knew each other prior to committing to the workshop, they didn't necessarily know each other as philosopher-teachers or writing collaborators. Additionally, while some people came to the conference knowing many others (and often quite well), others came not knowing anyone. Prior to the conference, I created a virtual page using a program called Padlet, where participants were invited to a "virtual social hour" and prompted as follows:

> Please introduce yourself to the group sharing
>
> 1. Your name and affiliation
> 2. A picture of one of the items in your workspace you treasure
> 3. A favorite book

At the end of the conference both the zoom participants and the in-person participants participated in a guided reflection on the day. To facilitate conversation, these discussions occurred separately with one group on Zoom and the other meeting in-person. It was from these reflections that I (and I think participants) began to see the value of the project and how important it was to not only bring together philosophers and teachers in a contact zone but also to be mindful of the construction of the zone itself. I now turn to the voices of the participants.

Have I told you the one about a philosopher and a teacher meeting in a bar?

Stephanie A. Burdick-Shepherd

Let's set the scene. It is the early fall 2020, prevaccine. In Wisconsin, the state where I teach and live, schools are closed but bars have reopened. In fact, bars are now self-serve, drive-thru, walk-in pick-up and drink on the patio kinds of places. My social media feed is filled with hatred, disgust, and parents "screaming" at one another. I have my undergraduate students in a philosophy of childhood course learning virtually with a class of second graders once a week; their teacher is a former student, Michelle. We see second graders doing cartwheels or cooking ramen soup in the background. I have students in my class that refuse to turn on their video feeds. But we also see smiles—my students notice that young children ask good questions. Michelle recognizes that her young students are learning about each other. We are both very tired, but we also recognize that we are learning new things about technology, about teaching, and ourselves. Most importantly, we have a text chain with one another that traces our worries, fears, and allows us the ability to share the brief moments of hope and joy. The year marches forward; we each get our first vaccines. And then I receive an email from Cara Furman with a call for papers on work being done in the "contact zone" between teachers and philosophers. I immediately text Michelle.

> (Stephanie) "It is perfect.... We can discuss multiple topics but the entire year last year was a contact zone of resistance of possibility, of critique and examination, of mourning, of loss."

> (Michelle) "Oh my goodness even the discussion we had about time with the kids!!!"

We agree that we need to write together, that we just might have something to say about this difficult year. And then we ask: where can we meet? We decide that between my children, our partners, and possible different kinds of exposures and risk factors that we should meet outside. And so, we meet at a local bar. We end up talking a summer night away, as folks drag race down the avenue with notes of car exhaust adding local flavor to our cocktails.

Michelle and I continued for the rest of that year *and the next* to grapple with finding space and time to work. Somehow on our screens and on brick patios, we build an essay about the experiences we went through as educators thrown into crisis teaching.

Do not worry, my purpose today is not to embed us in the argument about whether bars should have been reopened before schools. Rather, I want to suggest that the experience of writing with an educator, during extremely difficult times, and reflecting back on this process, allows me the space to ask a philosophical question: What if a hidden component of the relationship between philosophy and pedagogy is friendliness? This is an important question and one that I had previously considered only as a personal question, unique to my own experience of doing philosophy. But as we wrote and talked together I realized that the relationship between friendship and the doing of philosophy should be taken much more seriously. In terms of this book, when I look at the relationship between philosophy and pedagogy through the lens of friendship, I think we are forced to consider the methodological question: What kinds of things might we do differently/better/more of when we look at interdisciplinary work from the construct of friendship?

The time today is too short for this whole question so I look only at the following question: *How can one be a good philosophical friend to a k–12 educator?* Our experiences in these difficult democratic times showed me that being a philosophical friend to those who work with k–12 students is about making space and time outside of the contact zone[7] that is k–12 teaching, in order to be a philosophical witness to the work of teaching and learning.

Hansen writes of this orientation,

> Witnessing calls on the inquirer to work on her- or himself, to cultivate her or his aesthetic, moral, and reflective capacities as fully as possible in order to act in recognition of the dignity of the person in the role of teacher. This recognition means something richer, more far-reaching, and more demanding than approving or disapproving of the teacher's work, as such. It means responding to the teacher's presence holistically: not by passing judgment according to a preset calculus, but by reaching a considered judgment through mindfulness of the relation between persons and education itself. To acknowledge

the dignity of teachers supports them in fulfilling their own core task, recognizing and acting on the dignity of the persons in the role of student.[8]

Educators who work on justice, or who challenge the status quo, or who wonder about the purpose of teaching are often doing this part of their work outside the rules and assigned professional duties. Like many educators, in universities and in school districts, the world of virtual learning was creating a host of challenges, and administrators struggled with finding ways to meet the needs (and desires) of students and families. Michelle and I each struggled with aspects of our institutional authorities. But Michelle was in a position that was quite different from mine. While I was issued guidelines, Michelle was issued strict rules about online work, time spent in instruction, and curriculum focus. We hear this in her description of our Wednesday afternoons.

> Each week of teaching I found myself battling an ever-increasing weight of frustration, rage even, toward the education system I was trapped in. I knew what my students needed, I knew what I needed, and it was not creating five-minute-lesson videos to be followed by a worksheet. . . . I broke the rules when I planned our Wednesday meetings, I aligned them with no standard and gave no assessments. Yet I considered it, and still do, the most valuable class I taught throughout the week, because our focus was seeing each other.

When my students and I visited Michelle's virtual classroom, we were witness to an educator actively challenging the boundaries of her profession, and yet we could not discuss this in the room itself. This would have been to voice that "teachers break rules." How could I actively support Michelle, knowing that she was jeopardizing and risking her livelihood? How could I ask her to write about these moments, to share this with the public? I could do nothing but listen and so in the darkness of a chilly fall evening, under a space heater, Michelle and I discussed what it meant to challenge authority, to speak against systems as an educator during the pandemic.

On the surface, I simply sat with her and gave her a space (and time) to share her deepest fears about the work she was doing. But I am convinced that sitting with educators and providing witness to the work they do to cultivate themselves and their students as learning persons has deep implications for the work of philosophers.

As I bore witness to Michelle, I was also invited to consider my own position of privileged freedom—freedom to create pedagogy, to foster new ways of learning with my students without a fear of rebuke or censor. I was also asked to consider my role in Michelle's life, as someone able to listen to the work of an educator carefully without passing judgment. And I consider this orientation, in some ways, the orientation of a friend.

To be able to bear witness in this way, with this orientation, means that one takes action to forge both space and time for the educator's testimony. How can those of us who work with educators make these kinds of spaces? Is it possible to work to make these spaces without hiding them in the shadows or in the strange spaces that pandemic crisis lends to collaborators, like Wisconsin bars?

I turn now to what it meant for me to recognize that most of our work as coauthors was in fact, a particular witness to the always present tension between despair and hope that educators live in daily. As I bore witness to Michelle, she also provided the same orientation for me as I learned that to be a philosopher meant not always being in the mode of critique but being that of a listening mirror, developing new modes of what it meant to be and do philosophy, I let go of citations and I released the need to move toward an argument.

In some sense, the work of witnessing testimony seems foreign to both the philosopher and the pedagogue. The work of the philosopher is to think through what has been said. The work of the pedagogue is to practice—to actively engage the world of the real. But if I analyze that very long text string Michelle and I built over the years between 2020 and 2021, and the chapter that resulted from it, I see over and over again that what we started from and what we continued to circle back to was that in order to argue our position we first needed to see one another, fully present, standing, as is it were, naked in all our rage and our strange hope.

I give you another passage from our text string.

(Michelle): "Is it okay if I leave it until next year to make changes? I want to fix these up but there is so much also to do."

(Stephanie): "Yes, you do not have to change the world all at the same time. The arch of progress is long and full of bends."

(Michelle): "SO many bends . . . I've learned so much this year I feel like I'm back to knowing nothing at all. But I think that's the truest sign of learning. When you realize how little you actually know."

(Stephanie): "#sayssocrates"

Concluding as Noble Friends

Our phone calls and texts oriented toward witnessing instead of judging or analysis flattened the hierarchy of power of our first relationship that of teacher and student, and the status-riddled context of a philosopher working with an educator. The locked-down moments of the pandemic forced us into a relationship that though not built around finding a good place to eat on a Friday night was a friendship, an educative one, built around providing witness to the work we were doing as teachers. Importantly, we recognized that we needed to create spaces where there was no space and make time where there was no time in order to do this. But perhaps this is what friends always do, make things like hope and spaces to breathe appear. In Aristotle's words, we were uncovering the good life together.

Michelle and I wrote our final version of the chapter still masked in shared common spaces, tiptoeing around the new culture of politeness as we relearned to eat and drink and meet again with our friends and colleagues. Though we both agree that we are not yet out of crisis, we continue our work together, trying to figure this world out as teachers and learners and, yes, noble friends.[9]

As I look back on our many texts and the chapter we wrote I see so much of how we gave each other permission to make mistakes, to pause, to sit down, to name a difficult emotion, to give in to the crisis—in short, to give witness to each other as teacher-persons.

As I consider the importance of this component of our research to what we created, I would caution scholars to consider what it means to walk into a classroom or a school building without this orientation. It seems to me that if we want to truly understand education, whether to critique, improve, or question it, we must learn to see and listen to the people in those spaces as we would our closest of friends.

On Recognizing the Value of Friendship and the Intellectual Life of the Teacher

Hillary Post

In the most isolating days of the pandemic, the thing I missed most was connection with colleagues. Holly and Lindsey were among those colleagues, and our day-to-day exchanges (prepandemic) filled a couple of specific needs. One was friendship; I knew they were unequivocally there to support me as a teacher and as a human. The other was the opportunity to connect intellectually. We worked together in a school that nurtured teachers' deep thinking about children, teaching, and learning.

Cara has been my dear friend, colleague, and mentor since the first day I stepped foot in my graduate program. At an earlier time, the order of that list would have read mentor, colleague, and dear friend. But these days, I intentionally put "dear friend" first when I describe Cara. What began a decade ago as a strong teacher-student relationship has evolved into a true friendship based on trust, shared values, and a commitment to our teaching communities.

Cara invited Lindsey, Holly, and me to join her in the contact zone. This invitation was, unknowingly at the time, just what I needed. It was the late fall of 2021, which meant there were some more attempts at normalcy in a school setting, but my mind was still in survival mode. I worried about my ability to be insightful when my stance was getting through each day.

In our initial conversations about this project, I was struck by our ability to do philosophy in hard times. Cara guided us with the frame of "staying with the trouble." This philosophical lens became a tool for seeing and valuing the work we were doing as teachers. We shared our stories. We rippled off each other's themes. We thought together. We validated one another as thought partners. Eventually, we solidified an interconnected plan for our stories.

I felt invigorated by our shared intellectual endeavor, and seen as a capable thinker at the table. In this way, the contact zone was an opportunity to nurture the intellectual life of a teacher. Unfortunately, this is so often overlooked, and professional development with technical applications is favored. The particular contact zone I experienced with Cara, Holly, and Lindsey reminded me of what it feels like to be engaged intellectually with philosophically inclined colleagues. Not only did I think deeply about my teaching practice, but I also came up with tangible shifts to better support my students. To this end, I would advocate for more enduring contact zones for teachers and philosophers to think together as friends.

Co-construction and Accountability among Moral and Social Equals: Five Principles to Support Scholar-Practitioner Partnerships

JOY DANGORA ERICKSON

According to bell hooks,[10] it is imperative that "critical thinkers" who share the goal of transforming teaching to truly cultivate freedom, come together and "collaborate" in border-crossing discussions that create "space for intervention." It is for this reason that hooks engaged in a series of dialogues with a range of scholars whose social identities differed from her own, including white male philosopher Ron Scapp. hooks selected Scapp in part because she was troubled by accusations that white males engaging with her work were doing so merely as acts of appropriation. hooks argued that the interactions of critical thinkers within and across differences are crucial for transforming teaching practices and worldviews and, in turn, the existing systems of domination that have historically influenced what is taught and how it is taught. hooks's good remarks about the need for diverse critical thinkers to work together to create interventions rooted in transformative pedagogies directly apply to scholar-teacher collaborations, including the one I maintain with my good friend and coauthor Kyleigh Rousseau.

Though many in this community would likely agree that scholar-teacher partnerships are important for supporting students' holistic development in the classroom, there are some who maintain that teachers should function more as technicians; they should be handed research that has been interpreted for them—in the form of scripted curricula, for example—and deliver it with fidelity. This is arguably the case in many schools—it is not uncommon for state and/or district leadership to require teachers to deliver programs with fidelity. Like others,[11] I believe wholeheartedly that teaching is both an art and a science. As a scholar I view one of my major responsibilities to be supporting educators in keeping up on evolving scientific findings. However, I look to teachers to keep me updated on how the science is being interpreted and implemented in the classroom and the degree to which teachers and students perceive it to be working well. It is for this reason (and many others) that I truly value the teachers in my orbit, both as friends and research collaborators.

Though Kyleigh's administrators expressed enthusiasm that Kyleigh was working with an "early education expert" at the beginning of our partnership, the false belief that I was all-knowing was never one Kyleigh herself held. From the moment I asked her to collaborate with me on our first civic-minded antibias project, Kyleigh was keenly aware of and confident in what she brought to the partnership. Having served young children so well at home and abroad that she had been asked to coach teachers in both settings, she knew that she was a valuable collaborator—her awareness of her self-worth was and remains extremely refreshing. In fact, it was Kyleigh who suggested at the start of our first project that we list our areas of expertise before going any further; she said this would help her identify when it was more efficient to flag me (for example, in a Google comment) to support a point, find a resource, or formulate an argument in our joint writing than to use time and energy hunting for the information on her own. The simple step of identifying and respecting each other's funds of knowledge[12] and experience up front, not only saved us much time and stress in designing, employing, and reflecting on our projects, it also cultivated a deep sense of appreciation for the other's areas of expertise.[13] It is for this reason that in our postproject reflections we have repeatedly positioned the following as our first, or North Star principle for working together.

IDENTIFY AND HONOR WHAT EACH PERSON BRINGS TO THE WORK

Similar to hooks and Scapp, Kyleigh and I meet in person and/or on Zoom at the start of each project to talk and map out what we know about the research topic and question(s) and how our personal and professional experiences relate to the project. We also identify overlapping core values and goals that may be important for the project. We find common ground and recognize and appreciate where we diverge. For example, I haven't worked in a kindergarten classroom as a lead teacher for over seven years—Kyleigh's knowledge about the realities of teaching public kindergarten in today's political climate far exceeds my own right now, and if properly appreciated can only enhance our work together. Organically evolving from this first principle of honoring what we individually bring to the work came our second principle:

AGREE UP AND DESCRIBE EACH PERSON'S RESPONSIBILITIES TO THE PROJECT FROM THE OUTSET AND MONITOR PROGRESS

Again, it was Kyleigh who requested that we clearly outline each other's roles for our first project, which involved creating and implementing a series of civic-minded, antibias, early childhood curriculum maps. Being a kindergarten teacher, Kyleigh had become all too familiar with how her time became quickly consumed by school problems. I experience a similar phenomenon in my line of work. Using our collective knowledge about each other's strengths and weaknesses we decide early on in the project who will be responsible for leading the major components—for example, I am often charged with proposing a research question(s) and selecting suitable framings. Together we finalize the framing and select related research methods. Kyleigh routinely plays a key role in deciding how to implement approaches and activities in the classroom. After developing an initial research plan, we check in periodically to see if the plan is meeting our individual and collective needs and goals. We have found that scheduling a Zoom or in-person check-in meeting every two to four weeks positions us well to meet deadlines and problem solve at a pace that does not burn us out. We both feel strongly that these meetings are more rejuvenating than burdensome. In addition to keeping us productive and relieving project-related anxiety, we gain a sense of connection and find ourselves feeling heard and supported in our efforts to offer students a more transformative and socially just educational experience.

We are also in agreement that modern technology is an invaluable resource. Our joint projects have been possible because of the computers and Wi-Fi that have reliably permitted us to connect with one another despite residing in different states. It is from our gratitude for modern technology that our third principle was born.

MAKE INTENTIONAL USE OF TECHNOLOGY TO THOUGHTFULLY ENGAGE AND IMPROVE THE WORK

In our work we employ a multitude of Google tools to support our writing and keep us on track. For example, we utilize a shared Google calendar to remember and track our goals. In addition to check-in meeting dates with important details (for example, Zoom or physical meeting point), the shared calendar includes individual due dates (for example, full theoretical framing due, journal entries due), and collective due dates (for example, proposal due, first draft of chapter due). Another tool we take full advantage of is Google Docs. The afforded capabilities of commenting and suggesting edits allow us to appreciate and critique each other's work in a constructive and collegial manner. This is particularly important to us; as I am sure is the case for many others, we have received insensitive and unhelpful criticism upon sharing our writing in the past that we do not wish to revisit/be triggered by. We even appreciate that the track changes suggestions color in Google's is green—we find it to be far less stress inducing than the red that has been customary for so long in other applications. Intentional use of Google Calendar and Google Docs in combination with our computers and reliable Wi-Fi have made working together on our civic education projects a pleasure.

In addition to utilizing technology to support our organized engagement with the work a fourth commitment that we posit keeps things moving is responding to the other soon after we receive a request.

Set Parameters for Responding to Project-Related Queries

Of course, we recognize and appreciate that we each have a complex and holistic identity made up of numerous facets that extend beyond the professional pieces—and that each of these facets contributes to the whole person. However, we also recognize that to maintain a sense of confidence and accomplishment in our professional lives, including our joint scholarly projects, we require prompt feedback and support on/in our work. Because we know our joint projects best, it makes good sense for us to be the primary point person for each other. It is for this reason that at the outset of our first project we outlined several parameters for responding to work-related queries—we have and will continue to revisit these parameters at the beginning of each additional project to make sure they will continue to meet our needs. Specifically, we have agreed to respond to emails, texts, and other forms of communication within seventy-two hours if at all possible. And we have agreed that if we find ourselves at an impasse—in need of a quicker response—we will communicate the situation to the other person via a text message or phone call and make an effort to connect sooner. Our availability commitments have reliably helped us avoid wondering whether and when the other (very busy) person will respond—we have become accustomed to affording each other three days' time or explaining why we desire an earlier response.

In addition to project related support, we have found that we need and want to support each other outside of the project. Like so many educators we find ourselves leading extremely stressful lives. Our final principle is rooted in our mutual respect for one another and our commitment to sustaining our good relationship.

Carve out time and space to connect on a personal level—as friends who care

Though we (1) met at an academic institution that we elected to attend due to our common commitment to improving early childhood education and (2) continue to honor this commitment through our joint scholar-practitioner work, it was the goodness that we saw in the other person that committed us to friendship, and perhaps even more importantly, to caring for the other personally and professionally. Here, our view of care is grounded in Noddings's relational conceptualization of caring[14]—each of us recognizes how the other cares for us inside and outside of work. It is this ethic of care that allows us to be completely honest with each other about our strengths and limitations specific to our scholarly projects. And knowing that the other person cares helps to be honest and vulnerable—we both feel equally comfortable requesting and appreciating critique and help. Maintaining our caring relationship is an integral to creating our best work together.

In closing, according to hooks, "The classroom, with all its limitations, remains a location of possibility. In that field of possibility we have the opportunity to labor for freedom, to demand of ourselves and our comrades, an openness of mind and heart that allows us to face reality even as we collectively imagine ways to move beyond boundaries, to transgress. This is education as the practice of freedom."[15] Her words make it quite clear that to employ truly transformative pedagogies, each of us must first acknowledge the unjust world we live in. Upon which we must work to improve it together. Strong scholar-practitioner partnerships built on mutual trust, respect, and admiration promote the cultivation of an education for freedom. It is my sincere hope that the principles shared here—those

Kyleigh and I rely so heavily on in our work—might also support you in your own efforts to break down artificial scholar-practitioner boundaries for the sake of transformative pedagogies and for your own well-being.

Collaboration Is a Poetic Exercise

Vik Joshi

In *Arts of the Contact Zone*, Mary Louise Pratt offers an image of a teacher-student interaction that has informed my thoughts on philosopher-teacher collaborations. She presents a fourth-grade student who was given a writing assignment that took the form of answering a series of questions. Once the questions were answered, there is a paragraph written, and then the student has fulfilled the aim of the activity. From the perspective of the teacher, we would focus on preparing the assignment with the learning objective in mind, handing the assignment to the students and explaining how it is to be done, and then finishing by giving a due date for the assignment. As Pratt notes, these teacher-pupil interactions are typically "described almost entirely from the point of view of the teacher and teaching, not from the point of view of pupils and pupiling (the word doesn't even exist, though the thing [pupiling] certainly does)."[16]

Drawing an analogy between the teacher and pupil, the early stages of the collaboration between me (as philosopher) and Melissa (as teacher) involved an inequitable focus on the perspective of the philosopher. I framed the activity with an outline for an article, texts to read to prepare our interpretations, and dates to check in on our progress with each other. This was project management masquerading as collaboration. I knew Melissa was in her first year of teaching and spent evenings and early mornings preparing lesson plans for each day; from this information, I presumed the need for me to impose immediate structure and a course of action to complete the coauthored project. As Pratt highlighted with descriptions of teacher-student interactions emerging predominantly from the perspective of the teacher, the initial asymmetry of our collaborative process was a result of my presumptions. *Presumptions stifle learning. Questions protect the process.*

The shift from the first attempt at coauthorship involved an important activity in which we asked ourselves three important questions: (1) What is my role in this process? (2) What are the activities that I will engage in to participate in this collaboration? and (3) How will we build ways to dialogue and learn alongside each other that honors our voices as philosopher-teachers?

To understand the role of philosopher-teachers engaged in a collaboration is to inhabit both roles in thought and practice. For example, Melissa created a video walkthrough of her classroom with a voice-over narration to describe the various choices she made to create her classroom environment. Following this, I posed questions in a series of interviews, during which Melissa drew on not only her practice but also the books we read together to respond to each question. It became clear that a significant outcome of dialogue and communication was the *discovery of a process as poetic* for us as philosopher-teachers. How is a collaborative process poetic? Consider a poem. It has a structure (for example, sonnets, haikus, and ghazals), but the ways of reading and interpreting a poem are many. Similarly, there is a structure to collaboration (that is, building plans, setting up activities and timelines) but, as this chapter spotlights, how we interpret the process of collaboration varies. *Collaboration, in many ways, is a poetic exercise.*

In the spirit of Pratt's thought, our dialogues involved critiques of our common curriculum of readings; inquiries that built on, within, and beyond Melissa's reflections on her teaching experiences; and revisions as we read through the entire draft together, sentence by sentence. Pratt reminds us that to teach with dominance, which is no teaching at all, is to eliminate humor, resistance, and critique. The specter of effectiveness will flatten the texture of what Audre Lorde calls the "fund of necessary polarities between which our creativity can spark like a dialectic."[17] To write our coauthored chapter, we engaged in several creative acts—a video walkthrough of a classroom, lists of questions to guide interviews, writing prompts for each other to spur thought, and critical commentaries on each other's thinking. This is what hooks means by *engaged pedagogy*.[18] As emphasized in the introduction to this book, there is no blueprint or formula for a philosopher-teacher collaboration, so engaged practices must be "changed, reinvented, and reconceptualized" for every single collaborative endeavor of this kind.[19] We truly are, as Pratt shared, looking for the pedagogical arts of the contact zone not only in our teaching but also in our scholarly collaborations.

I will conclude my commentary, drawing on Pratt's characteristics of these pedagogical arts of the contact zone, to offer a range of features that Melissa and I will continue to explore as we continue our collaboration.

1. *Exercises in storytelling*: Storytelling protected our collaborative process. This is not only a matter of all collaborators sharing their stories, but engaging in a discussion of practices to support storytelling practices. For example, to support the storytelling, I offered a range of questions on Melissa's classroom experiences with an emphasis on both the practical and the affective nature of engaging with her students. This included questions about the nature of the pedagogy and how it was carried out, but also Melissa's experience of the activity, the reactions of her students, and the feelings she was left with after her students left for their next class at the end of the activity. A question is not only an invitation but, in our collaboration, Melissa shared a key insight with me: the nature of the questions helped her reimagine what kind of reflections can contribute to scholarship. The epistemic horizon was redefined for us as we challenged the invisible boundaries imposed by social-scientific research procedures and a rational discipline that has historically viewed storytelling and narration as intellectually deficient and subject to the inclinations within the self. Storytelling enables the centering of the persons who are in the experience—the teachers, students, and staff.

2. *The redemption of the oral*: Building on storytelling, our article, like much of this chapter, preserved Melissa's spoken word and integrated sections of her speech, her narration into the writing itself. We often presume that writing, not narration, is the medium of scholarship and learning. This is not a surprise, considering that our education system prioritizes the written, not the spoken, word. To redeem the oral is to reclaim the legitimacy of narration as a source of knowledge and wisdom through the sharing of stories. We will continue to explore the potential and power of the oral tradition in our forthcoming collaborative work.

3. *Ground rules for communication across lines of difference and hierarchy that go beyond politeness but maintain mutual respect*: Although we did not establish rules during our collaboration, the idea of mutually agreed on commitments and shared values to offer a foundation for the process of collaboration are vital lessons that we draw from Pratt. The notion of preserving mutual respect as we venture into a contact zone that transgresses "restrictive politeness"—that is, politeness that sacrifices forms of vernacular, or ways of authentic expression that go beyond the etiquette of hegemony—is a worthy aim for philosopher-teacher collaborations, and one that we hope to develop both in language and practices to frame methods that achieve this aim.

Like Pratt, I would like to end with an acknowledgment of hope that I see and feel as part of this project. It is heartening to feel inspired by, and imbibe lessons from, my thoughtful and kind peers pertaining to the pedagogical arts of the contact zone. Thank you all for your *engaged* ways of being, in hooks's sense of the word, and for this opportunity to build together.

So, *they* say 1 + 1 = 2

Meghan A. Brindley

The Philosophy of Education Society (PES) preconference was a unique experience for me, as I wrote *both* as a philosopher and as an educator. As a person participating in two distinct fields, I typically shift between them as I engage with colleagues. The preconference was one of the first times I participated in something as an educator *and* philosopher in the same time and space. Trying to think as both philosopher and educator has not only impacted the way I think when writing and teaching, but also affected my awareness as the boundaries of educator and philosopher vanish. By engaging in this experience, it has blurred lines between these categories in some ways, and, in others, made them more visible.

When I first heard about the preconference, the thought that I could write both as an educator and as a philosopher of education was so appealing that I applied to participate as a single "pair" of thinkers. In some ways I was going to become a philosopher-teacher or a teacher-philosopher, and the thought that I could fill two roles as one person and use both professional lexicons was freeing. When we met at the preconference I discovered there was a distinct portion of my writing that was written as a philosopher of education and then another that was written as a teacher educator coming from a background in p–12 education. The interesting thing about this was that I thought I had written an integrated piece, where I switched back and forth between the professional lexicons of philosophy of education and teacher education. Yet here we were sitting in my small group and every single person there could pinpoint the place in my writing where I switched from philosophy to education. My impression that I had successfully integrated my two professional lexicons and ways of writing, which often feel like separate parts of my brain, into one was a fallacy.

The thing that I was forced to acknowledge is that even when I thought I was using and accessing both professional lexicons and approaches to my topic of choice, I was still partitioning them off in my writing, favoring the philosophical over the teacher, perhaps unconsciously as we were engaging at a philosophy preconference. I found myself wondering if I would do the opposite, favor the teacher portion if I were at the National Association for the Education of Young Children's conference. And so, with the encouragement of my group, I set out to quite frankly do something I had been told not to do by professionals and scholars throughout my career: to integrate the two lexicons/ways of writing of my scholarship into one. For some, the switch from or integration of different professional lexicons may seem trivial, but for me, there have been many times when I've been asked to take out this piece of my writing (that is, the philosophical- or the teacher-oriented piece) and replace it with more philosophical or practical or some other type of content here (that is, quantitative, technical, etcetera). I realized during the preconference that no one had ever actually acknowledged that I frequently engage with multiple disciplines and, therefore, with multiple writing styles, methods, ways of knowing, and bodies of literature. My scholarship is a frequent changing of the guards regarding the ways I engage with what I am writing, and, for the first time, a space existed where I was supposed to engage multiple ways of thinking at the same time and in the same writing space.

Early in my career in public education, I wrote things that blurred boundaries between the fields I was engaged in, but there was no space for them. I was discouraged from writing in this manner by my mentor in the district, and contacts I had from graduate school were no longer willing to engage with the way I wanted to think about education for professional writing purposes. For a long time, I gave up the hope that I would find a space where I could write this way. I spent hours writing things the way I wanted to and then editing out the pieces "this wasn't the space for," according to whomever I was writing the piece for. Even when writing for this panel, I worried, can I write this and say this out loud to a room full or philosophers of education? Maybe it isn't philosophical enough or I won't sound enough like a teacher or maybe I need to use references that let people in the room know that I know what I'm talking about. And then one day when I was walking in the woods, I realized that I didn't need to fill my space on this panel with defending my knowledge bases to claim that I am both philosopher and teacher, because that's what this space is for. This space is for teachers *and* philosophers, and I am already a philosopher and teacher. So, *I* say, yes, sometimes $1 + 1 = 2$ and sometimes $1 + 1 = 1$ and even $1 + 1 + 1 + 1 + 1 + 1 + 1 \ldots = 1$.

Closing Thoughts

Each author of this chapter has laid out a vision and tips for coming together as philosopher and teacher. Just as each chapter in this book is written in the authors' voice and style, we have shared each narrative in full to highlight that there is no one way forward. As such, we close with a brief synthesis that we hope will support others in this work and urge readers to find their own ways.

1. Partnerships should be based in equity. What is offered may not be the same but all voices are integral.
2. Friendships support and are cultivated in this work and should involve reciprocal care, the capacity to listen, and give feedback from that place of listening.
3. Protocols that delineate roles and are mutually derived can be helpful.
4. Frequent check-ins and revision based on check-ins keeps relationships working productively.
5. Work should be mutually beneficial. All participants should grow through the engagement.

Finally, in closing, as we make new zones for more equitable contact, I (Cara) urge that we intentionally and proactively build space. The preconference began with then president of the Philosophy of Education Society, Professor Ron Glass, reaching out to me (a far more junior scholar) with an interest in having a preconference on public philosophy. We met, talked, and then he gave me room to grow something. If you are in a position of power, I would strongly encourage you to purposely open up new spaces and know that it might be a little bit messy. See what happens, experiment, and enter in as somebody who can guide and support a little bit, but let other people have their dream space.

If you find you are not in the position to offer space, you might think and think often about what kinds of spaces you want to build and how you might build them. This will help you be ready when someone says, "Hey, I've got this room, want to use it?" to jump in and say, "Absolutely and here is how I will."

We have the power to shape and reshape contact zones, to do this work together, and, in doing so, to create more room for such work to occur.

Notes

1. Mary Louise Pratt, "Arts of the Contact Zone," *Profession*, 1991, 33–40.
2. Pratt, "Arts of the Contact Zone," 34.
3. bell hooks, *Teaching to Transgress: Education as the Practice of Freedom* (New York: Routledge, 1994); Robin D. G. Kelley, *Freedom Dreams: The Black Radical Imagination* (Boston, MA: Beacon Press, 2002).
4. Thank you to PES president Ronald Glass for proposing a public-facing preconference and his ongoing support and advice. Many thanks for the ongoing support and enthusiasm of program chairs Susan Verducci Sandford, Tomas de Rezende Rocha, and Jason Wozniak.
5. Hannah Arendt, *The Human Condition*, 2nd ed. (Chicago, IL: University of Chicago Press, 1998).
6. Nicholas C. Burbules and Kathleen Knight Abowitz, "A Situated Philosophy of Education," *Philosophy and Education* 24, no. 2 (2008): 268–76.
7. Mary Louise Pratt, "Arts of the Contact Zone," *Profession* (1991): 33–40.
8. Hansen, David, "Bearing Witness to the Fusion of Person and Role in Teaching," *Journal of Aesthetic Education* 52, no. 4 (Winter 2018): 45.
9. Aristotle. "Nicomachean Ethics," *The Complete Works of Aristotle: Revised Oxford Translation*, ed: J. Barnes (Princeton, NJ: Princeton University Press, 1998),

1172a. Thus, according to Aristotle, the friendship of bad men turns out to be an evil thing (for because of their instability they unite in bad pursuits; further, they become evil by becoming like each other). While the friends of good men is good, being augmented by their companionship; and they are thought to become better too by their activities and by improving each other—for from each other they take the mould of the characteristics they approve—whence the saying "Noble deeds from noble men."

10. bell hooks, *Teaching to Transgress: Education as the Practice of Freedom* (New York: Routledge, 1994), 129.

11. Sara Powell, *Your Introduction to Education: Explorations in Teaching* (Hoboken, NJ: Pearson, 2018).

12. Luis C. Moll et al. "Funds of Knowledge for Teaching: Using a Qualitative Approach to Connect Homes and Classrooms." *Theory into Practice* 31, no. 2 (1992): 132–41.

13. My coauthor, Kyleigh Rousseau, brought a wealth of knowledge specific to antibias education in early childhood settings to our project. She had learned about and effectively employed an antibias approach to preschool education during her years spent working at an international preschool in Thailand. It is for this reason that I first reached out to her for help on a series of antibias curriculum maps I was cocreating with another early childhood teacher.

14. Nell Noddings, *Caring: A Feminine Approach to Ethics and Moral Education*, 2nd ed. (Berkeley: University of California Press, 2003).

15. hooks, *Teaching to Transgress*, 207.

16. Pratt, "Arts of the Contact Zone," 38.

17. Audre Lorde, *Sister Outsider: Essays and Speeches* (Trumansburg, NY: Crossing Press, 1984), 99.

18. bell hooks, *Teaching to Transgress*, 7.

19. hooks, *Teaching to Transgress*, 10.

Contributors

Alisa Algava is a doctoral student at CUNY in the Urban Education Program. She serves as a preschool coach for the New York City Department of Education's Division of Early Childhood. She is also an instructor at Bank Street College in the Leadership Department.

Kimberly Arriaga-Gonzalez is a community programs specialist for Newton Community Center in Salisbury, Maryland.

Cindy Ballenger holds a PhD in applied linguistics from Boston University. Retired from the Cambridge Public Schools (Massachusetts), where she was a reading teacher for many years, she now teaches children with special needs part-time in a variety of settings. She has published many articles on her practice and a number of books, including *Teaching Other People's Children*. She is a founding member of the Brookline Teacher Researcher Seminar, an influential group of teachers whose work focuses on classroom discourse across cultural and social-class differences.

Meghan A. Brindley is a doctoral student in both cultural foundations and curriculum and instruction at Kent State University. She is a lecturer and program coordinator of Early Years Education and Care at Kent State University at Tuscarawas, as well as a speech language pathologist and licensed massage therapist with specialization in pediatrics. Her current research explores the idea of the rediscovery of teaching conceptually, as well as phenomenologically, through a qualitative study of an undergraduate social foundations course.

Stephanie A. Burdick-Shepherd holds a PhD in philosophy and education. She is an associate professor in the Department of Education at Lawrence

University and is director of Lawrence's Center for Teaching Excellence. She directs an innovative approach to elementary teacher certification in cooperation with local schools. Her current research interests include the ethics of working and teaching with young children, the philosophy of reading, and the philosophy of friendship.

Cristina Cammarano emigrated from Italy to the United States, where she is an associate professor of philosophy at Salisbury University. She has a PhD in philosophy and education from Teachers College, Columbia University, and is a Whiting Foundation Public Engagement Fellow. She leads a program of Philosophy in Schools in collaboration with the county public schools, and likes to think of philosophy as an education for anyone and everyone.

Joy Dangora Erickson, PhD, is an assistant professor of education at Endicott College, where she teaches courses in early childhood education, literacy and language development, and culturally sustaining pedagogies. Her research interests include early reading motivation and education for citizenship. Her scholarship has been featured in a variety of respected journals including the *Reading Teacher* and the *Journal of Early Childhood Literacy*. She recently published a book titled *Reading Motivation: A Guide to Understanding and Supporting Children's Willingness to Read*.

Sarah Freye is the associate director of Early College Programs at Western Michigan University. She is a former high school English teacher and is pursuing her MA in English and educational and instructional technologies. Her research interests include cultural and digital media, professional writing, gamification, and student success.

William Fulbrecht is a retired elementary school teacher with over twenty-five years of experience in the New York City public school system, and is a recipient of the Bank Street Early Childhood Educator of the Year Award (2003). He is currently coordinator of the Forest and Shore School Early Childhood Outdoor Programs at the Brooklyn New School, P.S. 146. He holds an MA from Teachers College, Columbia University and an MFA from the San Francisco Art Institute.

Cara E. Furman, PhD, is an associate professor of early childhood at Hunter College and a former teacher at an urban public school. She has a master's in education and a doctorate in philosophy and education, bringing together her two abiding commitments. She is the author of *Teaching from an Ethical Center: Practical Wisdom for Daily Instruction* and coauthored *Descriptive Inquiry in Teacher Practice: Cultivating Practical Wisdom to Create Democratic Schools*. She is the host of the podcast *Teaching from an Ethical Center: An Inquiry Among Friends* and cohost of *Thinking in the Midst*.

Jesse Haber, RCC, is a doctoral student in the Philosophy of Educational Practice and Theory Program at Simon Fraser University. He is a psychology lecturer at the College of New Caledonia in British Columbia, Canada, and maintains a private practice as a Registered Clinical Counsellor.

Glenn M. Hudak is a professor at University of North Carolina at Greensboro in philosophy of education. His research interests revolve around the ontological architecture of education, especially integrating the work of autistic studies scholars into our thinking about the origins and purposes of education. His latest work was published in *Ethics and Education* (2023) and is titled, "Putting the Pandemic on the Table: What This Crisis Says about the Essence of Education."

Kanako W. Ide is associate professor of Soka University in Japan, and adjunct professor at the University of Maryland Global Campus in Asia. She received her PhD from the University of Illinois at Urbana–Champaign. Her main research interests are democratic education, peace education, feminism, and aesthetic education from a philosophical perspective.

Michelle Johnson is currently a fifth-grade teacher and master of education student. She holds a BA in religious studies and a license in early childhood education.

Vikramaditya (Vik) Joshi is a doctoral student in philosophy and education at Teachers College, Columbia University. He has served as faculty within the Bard Prison Initiative (College-in-Prison Program) and the Philosophy Department at Fordham University; held fellowships at Columbia University's Center for Justice and Harry Belafonte's the Gathering for Justice; and serves as a special adviser to the executive director, Dr. Amra Sabic-El-Rayess, at the International Interfaith Research Lab at Teachers College, Columbia University.

Holly A. F. Lash is an elementary school teacher in Los Angeles, California. She has been a lead teacher at the same school for the past fifteen years. She received her MA in education with a concentration in leadership and social change from Antioch University. Her teaching passions include human development for k–6, social justice curricula, outdoor education, descriptive inquiry, and reading *Harriet the Spy* aloud to children.

Dini Metro-Roland is professor of educational foundations at Western Michigan University.

Chris Moffett, PhD, is a scholar working across philosophy, education, art, and technology. His current research centers on embodied practices in education, play, and diagramming. He is a research scholar at the Digital Futures Institute, Teachers College, Columbia University.

Jessica D. Murray is the director of Social Emotional Learning and Wellness for the Montpelier Roxbury Public Schools in Montpelier, Vermont. She is a doctoral student working toward a PhD in educational leadership and policy studies.

Kevin Murray, PhD, is director of Student Access and Disability Services at Colby College. He earned a doctorate in educational foundations, policy, and practice from the University of Colorado–Boulder.

Hillary Post is an elementary school teacher in Los Angeles, California. She holds an MA in education from Teachers College, Columbia University, with dual certifications in general and special education. Her professional interests include literacy instruction, storytelling practices, and Descriptive Inquiry.

Mary Louise Pratt is Silver Professor emerita of Spanish and Portuguese and Social and Cultural Analysis at New York University and Olive H. Palmer Professor in the Humanities emerita at Stanford University. Her recent publications include *Planetary Longings*, and she is coeditor of *Trumpism, Mexican America, and the Struggle for Latinx Citizenship* and author of *Imperial Eyes: Travel Writing and Transculturation*.

Tomas de Rezende Rocha, PhD, is an assistant professor in the Social and Cultural Foundations program at the University of Washington, College of Education. He received his doctorate in philosophy and education from

Teachers College, Columbia University. He has served on the editorial and coordinating collectives of the Latin American Philosophy of Education Society since 2015.

Melissa Rosenthal is a high school educator in New York, where she teaches global history and geography to grades nine and ten. She has a BA in political science and philosophy, as well as an MAT from Bard College with a concentration in history. Her pedagogy celebrates student voices and storytelling with an emphasis on the development of their character.

Kyleigh P. Rousseau is a kindergarten teacher in New Hampshire. She earned a BS in family studies and child development, as well as an MEd in early childhood special education at the University of New Hampshire. She has experience teaching in public and international schools. She is passionate about play-based learning and culturally responsive teaching practices.

Rachel Seher proudly serves as the principal of a public alternative high school in New York City. Rachel collaborates with young people, educators, and families to create a vibrant and personalized learning environment in which each young person can thrive.

Jamila H. Silver, PhD, graduated from New York University with a doctorate in educational leadership. She is currently partnership director at Equal Opportunity Schools and consults with the New York City Department of Education. In 2016, she interned with the Obama administration in the Office of the First Lady. In 2012, she was a Fulbright Scholar in Brazil. Her work has been featured on *NBC News*, *The Daily News*, the National Association of Independent Schools' *Independent School*, and NYU's *ArtsPraxis*.

Emily S. L. Silver, MA, is director of Social Emotional Learning at University Prep in Seattle, Washington. She cocreated *How We GLOW*, a piece of interview theater exploring LGBTQ+ youth identity that has been performed at over thirty schools and community spaces. She serves on the Educator Advisory Committee for GLSEN. Her work has been featured in the *New Yorker* and at the Apollo Theater in New York City. She lives and works with her partner, Dr. Jamila H. Silver, on Duwamish Land.

Elisabeth Tam holds a master's degree in early childhood education from Antioch University New England. Passionate about self-determined play, she believes all children deserve access to the outdoors and a variety of materials that deepen learning and provide connections to the natural world. Her stance on ECE and the rights of children was greatly influenced by the educational approach and philosophy created by Cheng Xueqin in Anji, China. She has taught in the US, Vietnam, Thailand, and now Singapore.

Lindsey Young is the director of Teaching and Learning at an elementary school in Los Angeles, California. She works closely with teachers, parents, and students to support mission-aligned pedagogy and practice. She was a classroom teacher at the school for ten years before moving into a leadership role.

Steven Zhao is currently a doctoral student studying philosophy of education at Simon Fraser University. His research revolves around questions regarding educational practice and theory in relation to political polarization and radicalization. Central to his inquiry is the examination of "meaning making" through an interdisciplinarity of phenomenology, systems theory, cognitive anthropology, and political philosophy. Outside of research, Steven collaborates with local summer schools to design and lead classes on philosophy and contemplative practices for transitioning high school students.

Index

Abowitz, Kathleen Knight, 5, 254
activism, 137
ADHD, 201, 211n12
Adorno, Rolena, 34n1
adult learning, 38–39, 43
"Adventures in Wuzzyville" (Bradbury), 130n19
AFL-CIO (labor union), xii
Allen, Danielle, 13, 215–21
The Ambiguity of Play (Sutton-Smith), 150
American military stations, 239–46, 249
Anderson, Benedict, 29, 32
anger. *See* rage
Anger and Forgiveness (Nussbaum), 87
"Anger Is Not a Bad Word" (Cherry—TEDx talk), 99
Anji Play, 151–52. *See also* play
antibias programs, 133–44, 146, 265
antidivisive concepts law, 10
antiracism, 45–51, 53, 133–34, 136–44. *See also* racism
Archbald, Jo-ann, 164, 166, 169n6
Arendt, Hannah, 254
Arizona, 110
artifacts, 101
artistic creation (discussion of), 61–67, 140–41. *See also* authenticity; creativity
authenticity, 40, 65–67, 89–90, 103–4, 107, 183–84, 188, 192–95. *See also* artistic creation (discussion of); originality
autism, 72–83, 226–32
autoethnographic texts, 22–24, 26–28, 101–2, 114n2
autonomy, 135–36, 144, 218
autos, 13, 223–24, 227, 231–36

Bank Street College of Education, 44
Barad, Karen, 120
baseball, 19–20
Bennett, William, xii
Bentley, Dana Frantz, 65
Berila, Beth, 189
Between the World and Me (Coates), 107–8
Bogost, Ian, 154
Bradbury, Joan, 130n19
Braiding Sweetgrass (Kimmerer), 165
Brighouse, Harry, 133, 135–36, 144
Brookline Teacher Researcher Seminar (BTRS), 72
Buen gobierno y justicia (Good Government and Justice) (Guaman Poma de Ayala), 23–27. See also *The First New Chronicle and Good Government* (Guaman Poma de Ayala); *Nueva corónica (New*

284 | Index

Buen gobierno y justicia (continued)
  Chronicle) (Guaman Poma de
  Ayala)
Burbules, Nicholas, 5, 254

career and technical education (CTE),
  216–17
Carini, Patricia, 38, 42, 71–73, 77
Carse, James P., 149, 154
The Case for Rage (Cherry), 85–91
Center for Racial Justice in Education,
  50, 53
change, 88–89, 91–95, 97, 263
Cheltenham Elementary
  Kindergarteners, 141–43
Cherry, Myisha, 85–91, 95, 98–99
citizenship, 32, 203
civic programs, 133–34, 136–44, 218,
  222
civic republicanism, 199, 202–8
Clarke, Matthew, 172–73, 176, 178
classroom environment, 58–61, 66
Coalition of Essential Schools, 44
Coates, Ta-Nehisi, 107–8, 111
Coetzee, J. M., 62
Colgan, Andrew, 2–3
Common Core Teaching Standards, 120
concepts, xiii–xiv
conscientização, 39, 42–43
Consortium for Performance-Based
  Assessment, 44
contactless zones, 10, 103–9, 112
contact zone pedagogy, 102–3,
  109–10, 112
contact zones (discussion of), 6–10,
  14, 21–29, 33–34, 101–6, 241,
  253–54, 262–63. *See also* artifacts;
  civic republicanism; Descriptive
  Inquiry; interests; nature-based
  education; Okinawa International
  Women's Club (OIWC); play;
  portal (classroom as); Pratt, Mary

Louise; rage; Social Foundations of
  Education (SFE)
coordinating committees, 45–53
Council on Diversity (New
  Hampshire), 139. *See also* diversity
COVID-19, xiii, 8–9, 85–86, 93,
  96–97, 107, 120–27, 161, 219,
  257–62. *See also* social distancing;
  virtual school
creativity, 93–94, 96, 126–28, 219. *See
  also* artistic creation (discussion
  of); play
critical race theory (CRT), 91–92, 107
critical social theory (CST), 115n3
cultural mediation, 34
culture circle, 42–43. *See also* Freire,
  Paulo
Curriculum and Instruction (C&I),
  172, 174

Deligny, Fernand, 226, 228–34
Delpit, Lisa D., 115n6
DeNicola, Daniel, 135
Derman-Sparks, Louise, 137–38
DeSantis, Ron, 107, 116n16
Descriptive Inquiry, 8–9, 37–54, 73,
  127–29. *See also* contact zones;
  Summer Institute on Descriptive
  Inquiry (IDI)
Dewey, John, 42, 59, 73
dialogue (discussion of), xii–xiii,
  41–42, 103, 106–7
Diamond, Julie, 57, 59–60
diffraction, 120
diminished self, 191
disability, 199–202, 205–10, 211n3,
  211n12. *See also* special education
disciplinary policies, 206
DisCrit, 200–201, 211n7
diversity, 32–34, 109–10, 137–38, 162,
  220–21, 243. *See also* Council on
  Diversity (New Hampshire)

"Divisive Concepts Statute" (New Hampshire), 139–42, 144
do now activities, 61, 69n10
Du Bois, W. E. B., 67
Duncan-Andrade, Jeff, 110

"Earth Action" (Envirokids Literacy Festival 2021 presentation), 160
Eccleston, Kathryn, 183, 191
economic justice, 37–38
educational philosophy. *See* theory (discussion of)
Edwards, Julie, 137–38
emergent curriculum, 65–66
Emilia, Reggio, 11, 151, 153
emotions (discussion of), 189–92, 195. *See also* therapeutic support
entanglement, 121–22
Envirokids Literacy Festival 2021, 160
environment. *See* classroom environment
equality, 136, 138–40, 241
ESL, 221
ethical tension, 61–62
ethics, 3, 86–87, 175, 186, 191, 246–49. *See also* morality
Ethics of Authenticity (Taylor), 192–94
ethnic studies, 110

failure (fear of), 103–4
fairness, 102, 134–44
Ferguson, Adam, 203
field notes, 72, 75–80
Finite and Infinite Games (Carse), 149, 154
The First New Chronicle and Good Government (Guaman Poma de Ayala), 21–28
Florida, 106–7, 109, 116n16
flourishing, 133–35, 144, 216, 220, 222

freedom (discussion of), 12, 89–90, 154–55, 188, 200, 203–8, 212n24, 260
Freire, Paulo, 40–43, 52, 89, 106. *See also* culture circle
friendship, 13, 66, 80, 240–45, 249, 258, 261–62
frivolity, 150, 194
Furedi, Frank, 191
Furman, Cara, 130n19

gag orders, 134
Garcilaso de la Vega, Inca, 28
Geertz, Clifford, 73–74
gender, 143, 242–43. *See also* women
generative themes, 41–42
"The Gift of Strawberries" (Kimmerer), 165
gifts, 165
Glass, Ronald, 6
Greeley, Kathy, 104
Grosz, Elizabeth, xiii–xiv
Guaman Poma de Ayala, Felipe, 21–28, 101

Habermas, Jürgen, 115n3
habits, 71
Hansen, David, 6, 61, 258–59
Haraway, Donna, 10, 120–28
Hayes, Dennis, 183, 191
healing, 125–26, 229
"Healing through Culture" (Waterfall), 163–64
Higa, Hideko, 241
hooks, bell, 1, 63–64, 89, 109–11, 263–64
Howes, Deb, 139–40
humanistic baseline, 215–20, 222–23

ideal speech situation, 115n3
identity, 137
imagined communities, 29–33

The Importance of Philosophy in Teacher Education (Colgan and Maxwell), 2–3
Inca people, 21–28
The Inconvenient Indian (King), 162
indigenous people, 159–69, 239–40, 247, 251n20
"Individual Freedom" bill, 106
Ineese-Nash, Nicole, 167
Institute for Descriptive Inquiry. *See* Descriptive Inquiry
interests, 9, 73–83
internships, 44

Japan. *See* Okinawa Islands
journaling, 50–51

Kaplan, Andrew, 83
Katzi Txumu'n, 160–62, 164–66
Kerr, George H., 246
Kimmerer, Robin Wall, 165, 167
Kindergarten (Diamond), 57, 60
King, Martin Luther Jr., 87
King, Thomas, 162
King Philip III, 21–22
Koikari, Mire, 241, 244, 246, 248
Kostecki-Shaw, Jenny Sue, 141–43

Laverty, Megan, 62
legislation, 106–7, 109, 116n16, 134–35, 139–42, 144
LiberatED, 104–5
literacy, 19–21, 28, 30, 34, 39
literature, 141–43
Lopez-Baralt, Mercedes, 34n1
Lorde, Audre, 87–89, 91, 95, 97
love, 87, 106
Love, Bettina, 58, 104–5, 111
Lucius Tarquinius Superbus, 202

"Making and Doing Philosophy in a School" (Carini), 42

mandates, 184–85, 191
Masschelein, Jan, 223, 233–34
mattering, 105–6
maturity, 227
Maxwell, Bruce, 2–3
McDermott, Ray, 200–201
meaningful themes, 42
Megumi, Ryunosuke, 244
Menchú Tum, Rigoberta, 116n34, 167
mental health, 184, 186–88, 190–91, 194, 196. *See also* therapeutic support
mentor texts, 141
Mesoamericans, 159–69
method (discussion of), 67
Miyagi, Etsujiro, 243, 246, 248
Miyanishi, Kaori, 244
MLA (Modern Language Association), xii
Molasky, Michael S., 243–44
morality, 87–88, 165, 192–93, 239–40, 247–49. *See also* ethics
mujinkoh, 247
multiculturalism. *See* diversity
mutual aid, 239–40, 247–48

Najita, Tetsuo, 247–48
"Naming, Normalizing, and Neuroscience," 124
National Rural Education Association, 222
nature-based education, 223–24, 227–35
negative education, 173, 176–78
neoliberalism, 2, 5, 216
neo-Roman tradition. *See* civic republicanism
New Hampshire, 134, 139–42, 144
Nieto, Sonia, 5
Nodding, Nel, 267
Nueva corónica (New Chronicle) (Guaman Poma de Ayala), 22–23.

See also *Buen gobierno y justicia (Good Government and Justice)* (Guaman Poma de Ayala); *The First New Chronicle and Good Government* (Guaman Poma de Ayala)
Nussbaum, Martha, 87

observation, 72–83, 138, 231
Ohio, 172, 174
Ohshiro, Tatsuhiro, 244
Okinawa International Women's Club (OIWC), 240–46, 248–49, 250nn10–11, 251n12
Okinawa Islands, 239–40, 246–47
On Beauty and Being Just (Scarry), 65
originality, 192–93. *See also* authenticity
Ortiz, Fernando, 24
overlapping consensus, 211n6

Paley, Vivian, 72
the pandemic. *See* COVID-19
"Parental Rights in Education" bill, 116n16
parenting, 124
Pay It Forward (movie), 249–50
Percy Jackson and the Olympians (Riordan), 162
Performance-Based Assessment Tasks (PBATs), 44
Pettit, Philip, 202–4
Phelan, Anne, 172–73, 176, 178
Philip III. *See* King Philip III
Philosophy of Education (PES) (conference), 6–8, 14n1, 254–58
Pietschmann, Richard, 20–21, 26
Pinar, William, 175
Planetary Longings (Pratt), 8
play, 11, 94, 142–43, 149–56, 227. *See also* Anji Play; creativity
policy directives, 2, 205

political economy, 104–5
political geography, 110
Political Liberalism (Rawls), 211n6
portal (classroom as), 9, 58–69
power dynamics, 6, 13, 21, 31, 85–86, 101, 107, 115n6, 226, 230, 253, 255–56
Pratt, Mary Louise, xi–xiv, 6, 8, 39–40, 61, 66–67, 71–73, 102, 107, 109, 150, 199, 253. *See also* contact zones (discussion of); *testimonios*
problem-posing education, 40–41
Prohibition on Teaching Discrimination Statute (New Hampshire), 139–42, 144
Prospect's Descriptive Processes, 38. *See also* Descriptive Inquiry

Q'um Q'um Xiiem, 164, 166, 169n6

race, 4–5, 38, 45–53, 67, 104–10, 136
Race Talk and the Conspiracy of Silence (Sue), 107
Racial Affinity Groups, 49–51
racial injustice, 87–88, 90–91, 96, 98, 111–12, 137
racism, 20, 37–39, 90–92, 108, 220. *See also* antiracism
rage, 9, 33, 85–99
Raleigh, Walter, 34n2
Ramsey, Patricia, 138
Rawls, John, 211n6
recollection, 129
Reflection of the Word, 123
reflexivity, 12, 184, 187–88, 192, 194–95
religion, 136
remote learning. *See* virtual school
renewal (process of), 67
research funding, 2
Riordan, Rick, 162
Roosevelt, Dirck, 77

Rosenthal, Melissa, 58–64
Royal Commentaries of the Incas (Garcilaso de la Vega), 28, 34n2
rural schools, 13, 215–22

safety, 33–34, 66, 105, 112–13
Same, Same, but Different (Kostecki-Shaw), 141–43
Santoro, Doris, 6
Sarmiento, Tony, 20
Sauvagnargues, Anne, 233–34
SB 148 (Florida), 106–7, 109, 116n16
Scapp, Ron, 263–64
Scarry, Elaine, 65
schole, 223, 232–33
school counselors, 185–86. See also therapeutic support
School without Walls (SWW), 37, 44–52
self-regulation, 226–27, 231–32
sexual exploitation, 244
"The Silenced Dialogue" (Delpit), 115n6
Simmons, Dena, 104–5, 107, 111
Simons, Maarten, 223, 233–34
Skinner, Quentin, 202–4
social distancing, 59–60. See also COVID-19
Social Emotional Learning (SEL), 98
Social Foundations of Education (SFE), 11–12, 171–78
social justice, 116n35. See also antiracism; economic justice; racial injustice
social memory, 66
Socrates, 108
Souto-Manning, Mariana, 42–43, 65
space (discussion of), 171–78, 223
Spanish conquest, 23–28
special education, 98, 207. See also disability
speech communities, 29–31

Spivak, Gayarti, 111
standardized curriculums, 216–18, 222
Staying with the Trouble (Haraway), 10, 120–28
stereotyping, 162
storytelling, 11, 34, 62–63, 69, 160–69
subaltern, 111
Sue, Derald Wing, 107, 109
Summer Institute on Descriptive Inquiry (IDI), 120–21, 123. See also Descriptive Inquiry
Sununu, Chris, 139
Sutton-Smith, Brian, 150
sympoiesis, 122

Taylor, Charles, 183–84, 192–94
teacher education, xii–xiv, 171–79
teacher-pupil language, 30–31
"Teaching for Human Dignity" (Furman), 130n19
Teaching to Transgress (hooks), 1
testimonios, 101–2, 110–12, 114n2, 116n34
theory (discussion of), 1–8, 42, 109, 199, 229, 253–54
therapeutic support, 12, 183–97. See also emotions (discussion of); mental health; school counselors
Tintiangco-Cubales, Allyson, 110
transculturation, 24, 28, 102, 106
Traugh, Cecelia, 37–38, 43

virtual school, 89–96, 107, 119, 259–60. See also COVID-19

Waterfall, Hilistis Pauline, 163–64, 167
We Are All Alike…We Are All Different (Cheltenham Elementary Kindergarteners), 141–43

Winnicott, D. W., 226–27
witnessing, 258–61
women, 87–88, 240–46, 248. *See also* gender
working partnerships, 263–67
world making, 219

Writing within the Contact Zone (conference), 1
Wuzzies, 130n19

yuimahru, 13–14, 239–40, 246–49, 251n20

www.ingramcontent.com/pod-product-compliance
Lightning Source LLC
LaVergne TN
LVHW041258080425
807816LV00002B/8